"This book is a much-needed resource for scholars and practitioners alike. As institutions look to scale up their support for first-generation college students, texts like this one will be required reading. Kudos to the authors for bringing this collection together."

La'Tonya Rease Miles, Scale & Support, Career Launch, USA

Developing and Implementing Promising Practices and Programs for First-Generation College Students

As first-generation students gain greater access to higher education, faculty, and staff at colleges and universities must provide intentional engagement that supports their persistence and graduation. This book serves as a guidebook for higher education practitioners seeking to implement or enhance first-generation programming at their institutions.

The chapters provide detailed descriptions of the development, implementation, and assessment of programs and practices intended to support the success of first-generation college students. Authors share insights on building allies, identifying and working through challenges, and applicable takeaways for implementing similar practices and programs at the reader's own institutions. Programming discussed in the book ranges in funding levels and includes activities such as faculty dinners, study abroad, bridge programs, living learning communities, peer mentoring, intrusive advising, and holistic well-being. This valuable resource helps higher education practitioners better support and position first-generation students for success.

Charmaine Troy is the inaugural First-Generation Program and Operations Manager at Georgia Tech, USA.

Karen Jackson is an Assistant Professor of Education and Associate Dean for Advising Programs at Georgia Gwinnett College, USA.

Ben Pearce is a Program Coordinator at Emory University, USA.

Diana Rowe is a Senior Student Success Advisor at Georgia Gwinnet College, USA.

Developing and Implementing Promising Practices and Programs for First-Generation College Students

Edited by Charmaine Troy, Karen Jackson, Ben Pearce, and Diana Rowe

Routledge
Taylor & Francis Group
NEW YORK AND LONDON

First published 2023
by Routledge
605 Third Avenue, New York, NY 10158

and by Routledge
4 Park Square, Milton Park, Abingdon, Oxon, OX14 4RN

Routledge is an imprint of the Taylor & Francis Group, an informa business

© 2023 selection and editorial matter, Charmaine Troy, Karen Jackson, Ben Pearce, and Diana Rowe; individual chapters, the contributors

The right of Charmaine Troy, Karen Jackson, Ben Pearce, and Diana Rowe to be identified as the authors of the editorial material, and of the authors for their individual chapters, has been asserted in accordance with sections 77 and 78 of the Copyright, Designs and Patents Act 1988.

All rights reserved. No part of this book may be reprinted or reproduced or utilised in any form or by any electronic, mechanical, or other means, now known or hereafter invented, including photocopying and recording, or in any information storage or retrieval system, without permission in writing from the publishers.

Trademark notice: Product or corporate names may be trademarks or registered trademarks, and are used only for identification and explanation without intent to infringe.

Library of Congress Cataloging-in-Publication Data
Names: Troy, Charmaine, editor.
Title: Developing and implementing promising practices and programs for first-generation college students / edited by Charmaine Troy, Karen Jackson, Ben Pearce, and Diana Rowe.
Description: New York, NY: Routledge, 2023. | Includes bibliographical references and index. | Identifiers: LCCN 2022014319 (print) | LCCN 2022014320 (ebook) | ISBN 9781032128092 (hardback) | ISBN 9781032128085 (paperback) | ISBN 9781003226321 (ebook)
Subjects: LCSH: First-generation college students Services for United States. | Counseling in higher education United States. | College environment United States.
Classification: LCC LC4069.6 .D48 2023 (print) | LCC LC4069.6 (ebook) | DDC 378.1/982 dc23/eng/20220617
LC record available at https://lccn.loc.gov/2022014319
LC ebook record available at https://lccn.loc.gov/2022014320

ISBN: 9781032128092 (hbk)
ISBN: 9781032128085 (pbk)
ISBN: 9781003226321 (ebk)

DOI: 10.4324/9781003226321

Typeset in Perpetua and Bell Gothic
by Deanta Global Publishing Services, Chennai, India

Contents

Preface ix

1 Laying the Foundation for Creating First-Generation Student Programming 1
Charmaine Troy, Karen Jackson, Ben Pearce, and Diana Rowe

PART I
First Year Experiences 11

2 Utilizing Intrusive Advising to Support First-Generation College Students at the University of South Carolina Upstate 13
Kimberly Walker, Tiffany N. Hughes, and Kadaisha Miller

3 University of Portland's Summer Launch Initiative 28
Matt Daily

4 From Denied to the Dean's List: Program Design that Makes a Difference 43
Erin L. Kline and Jefferson Lee IV

5 Developing First-Year Programming for First-Generation Students without A Budget: No Money, No Problem 57
Charmaine Troy, Ben Pearce, and Diana Rowe

PART II
Mentorship 71

6 Belonging and Well-being as Key Measures of Student Success: Promising Practices at University of Southern California's Topping Scholars Program 73
Trista Beard and Carina Gonzalez

CONTENTS

7 Capitalizing on Networks of Support: A Review of the Georgetown Scholars Program's Peer Mentor, Alumni Mentor, and Regional Network Programs — 98
   Yasamin "Yasi" Mahallaty and Albert Ramirez

8 Faculty Mentoring Dinners: Facilitating High-Impact Practices — 113
   Malaphone Phommasa, Yasmine Dominguez-Whitehead, Angelica Caudillo and Kari Weber

PART III
Learning Communities — 127

9 1st Gen Theme Community: Developing a Living-Learning Program for First-Year First-Generation College Students — 129
   Trebby L. Ellington

10 Living Learning Communities for First-Year First-Generation Students — 145
   Kiley Moody, Gregory Eiselein, Rebeca Paz, Tamara Bauer, and Kevin Cook

PART IV
Exploration and Transition — 165

11 Global Leadership for First-Generation Students: Implementing Custom Study Abroad Programs — 167
   Michelle L. Ashcraft and Lisa Lambert Snodgrass

12 Getting Career Ready at UC Riverside: The ORBITS Program — 184
   Thomas Dickson, Charlie Rodnuson, and Elizabeth Montgomery

13 First-Generation Transfer Students in an Honors College — 203
   Martha Enciso

14 What We Learned from the Pandemic: Using Digital and Virtual Spaces to Support First-Generation College Students — 217
   Karen Jackson and Charmaine Troy

About the Editors — 227
About the Contributors — 229
Index — 234

Preface

The purpose of the book is to provide meaningful context on developing and implementing promising practices and programs for first-generation students. This book aims to be a resource for higher education practitioners looking to develop and implement or enhance targeted programming for first-generation college students. This book does not attempt to identify a list of "best practices" for first-generation student support but identifies promising programs and practices that can be adapted at different types of institutions. Additionally, the lessons learned helps readers understand the things they need to consider and necessary steps when adapting or creating first-generation student programs for their unique campuses.

Each chapter provides detailed descriptions of the steps practitioners took to develop and implement promising programs and practices intended to support the success of first-generation college students. Authors share insights on building allies, identifying and working through challenges, and applicable takeaways that should be considered as readers look to implement similar practices and programs at their own institutions. Authors also share how they adapted their programs and activities to serve first-generation students during the COVID-19 pandemic.

This book is organized based on how programs engage first-generation college students during their matriculation. Chapters 2–5 offer insight on programs that support students as they transition into college. Chapters 6–8 discuss programs that focus on student mentorship. Chapters 9 and 10 discuss the development of learning communities that support first-generation college students. Chapters 11, 12, and 13 highlight programs that focus on study abroad, career development, and honors colleges, respectively. The final chapter discusses the impact of the COVID-19 pandemic on first-generation students and highlights ways to offer support in virtual spaces. The specific programs highlighted in this book are listed below.

- Chapter 2 focuses on an intrusive advising model used in the TRIO Support Services grant program at the University South Carolina. The program is intended to provide eligible students with academic development services such as tutoring, mentoring, and educational counseling services.
- Chapter 3 illustrates University of Portland's Summer Launch program. The program combines first-generation student research, best practices, rich campus collaboration, forward thinking, and unique local culture to develop an innovative pre-orientation experience for first-generation students.
- Chapter 4 is an overview of the development and implementation of a pilot program designed to address the educational equity gaps that exist at Southwest Minnesota State University (SMSU). SMSU's Mustang Pathway Program is an adaptive entry program designed to help students achieve growth, success, perseverance, and resilience to matriculate to graduation.
- Chapter 5 focuses on the development and implementation of first-generation programming at Georgia Gwinnett College without a dedicated budget. This chapter looks at how the Grizzly First Scholars first-generation learning community was able to implement programming through the forging of collaborative campus and community-based relationships.
- Chapter 6 highlights a nationally recognized program at the University of Southern California that has been in existence for over 50 years. The program integrates three levels of student support including financial assistance, academic and social programs, as well as community-building activities.
- Chapter 7 discusses the mentor programs of the Georgetown Scholars Program which serves 600+ first-generation and/or low-income undergraduates of Georgetown University. Through peer, alumni, and local regional mentors, the Georgetown Scholars Program supports students from the moment they enroll at Georgetown and evolves throughout the student experience.
- Chapter 8 showcases a faculty mentoring dinner initiative at the University of California, Santa Barbara, which has successfully implemented two unique mentoring programs: Dining with Faculty and Table Talk. These programs promote high-impact practices, particularly for first-generation college students and transfer students.
- Chapter 9 highlights the 1st Gen Theme Community at the University of Michigan, a residential living learning program of first-generation students. This chapter presents the design, administration, and implementation of the nationally recognized, cohort-based living-learning program.
- Chapter 10 focuses on the creation of a first-generation themed living-learning community at Kansas State. This chapter examines how living-learning communities impact first-generation student success, social integration, and sense of belonging.

- Chapter 11 focuses on a successful study abroad program at Purdue University and supplies information on how study abroad opportunities for first-generation students provide access while preparing students for life after college.
- Chapter 12 examines the development and exploration of career and life skills for first-generation students. The ORBITS program at the University of California, Riverside focuses on providing first-generation students with the necessary campus and career resources for continued career exploration.
- Chapter 13 examines the theme of first-generation transfer student support in an honors college. The chapter highlights the Weber Honors College at San Diego State University and discusses strategies for the recruitment, engagement, retention, and graduation of first-generation transfer students in an honors program.
- The final chapter discusses challenges that first-generation college students experienced during the COVID-19 pandemic and how digital and virtual spaces were created by the First Generation Student Support Office at Virginia Polytechnic and State University to support students during the pandemic. The chapter also discusses the successes and applicable takeaways of digital support efforts and how these practices can be utilized as students attempt to get back on track in a post-pandemic era.

Chapter 1

Laying the Foundation for Creating First-Generation Student Programming

Charmaine Troy, Karen Jackson, Ben Pearce, and Diana Rowe

Colleges and universities have seen a significant increase in the enrollment of first-generation college students; however, the retention and graduation rates of this student population continue to fall behind the rates of their continuing education peers. To increase the graduation rates of this student population, institutions must provide support that fosters students' sense of belonging and provide equitable college experiences. Supporting the success of first-generation students should be the responsibility of faculty and staff at their respective institutions. To achieve this goal, institutions must provide intentional engagement opportunities and resources for first-generation students. To enact intentional engagement opportunities, institutions that serve first-generation students should seek to understand the first-generation identity (Baldwin, 2018). The first-generation identity represents diverse identities that can serve as a powerful incentive for institutional change.

ADVANCING UNDERSTANDING OF THE FIRST-GENERATION IDENTITY

To advance understanding of the first-generation identity, the following core recommendations are suggested for connecting and catalyzing efforts across campus for greater institutional impact and engagement (Baldwin, 2018):

- Create a first-generation student definition that can be used across campus departments. For example, the following first-generation student definition has been used across some campuses: *A student is identified as a first-generation college student if neither parent or guardian has earned a bachelor's degree at a four-year college or university in the US.*
- Seek to understand the lived experiences of first-generation students. Understanding first-generation students' perspectives and journeys can

lead to serving the first-generation population at your institution better. Also, lived experiences are important in shaping who students become. Examples of lived experiences include:
- They owe it to their families to finish college since they are the first to attend. This perspective can put a lot of pressure on the student to excel resulting in possible mental health concerns.
- Missing home and family to the point that they want to go home every weekend. This limits engagement in campus life, activities, and student organizations, decreasing the student's sense of belonging.
- Lack of family support during their transition to college and during their time in college. While their families are excited for them to attend, they are unsure of how to support them or must focus on supporting other family members and siblings at home.
- Consider the intersectionality of first-generation students. In addition to holding the first-generation identity, students also hold other intersecting identities. Other identities that may intersect include those involving race, gender, class, and other individual characteristics. For example, first-generation students may be first-generation and minority, low-income, and/or LGBTQ.
- Use celebrated diverse identities to shift to an asset-based mindset. Practitioners should help first-generation students understand the assets they bring to the institution and help encourage them not to focus on their shortcomings.

Practitioners should avoid making assumptions about the intersecting identities of students that could create gaps in programming. Their assumptions may lead to misconceptions about first-generation students. Therefore, it is important to consider the intersecting identities of first-generation students on your respective campuses. Institutions that highlight and celebrate the diverse identities of their first-generation students will help contribute to a feeling of belonging and inclusion. Faculty and staff who are first-generation are also encouraged to self-identify to first-generation students on campus, invite them to engage and discuss their journeys, and join them in celebrating their diverse intersecting identities.

INTERSECTIONALITY

Intersectionality is a framework that addresses how people with multiple marginalized identities experience disadvantages and barriers resulting from multiple layers of discrimination and oppression (Crenshaw, 1989; Strayhorn, 2018). Marginalized groups experience systemic disenfranchisement by those who hold power and authority. This subjugation and discrimination is compounded at the intersection of one's multiple identities. Although intersectionality was originally used to discuss race and gender pertaining to social power and the marginalization of African-American women (Crenshaw, 1989), this lens can be used to understand how students construct meaning based on their multiple identities and how their social identities influence their higher education experiences.

In the 2015–2016 academic year, 56% of all undergraduates enrolled in college in the US were first-generation college students, based on the definition of neither parent having a bachelor's degree. Of those students, 60% were female, 46% were white, 18% were African-American, 25% were Hispanic, 8% were Asian-American, and 1% were Native American or Alaska Native, and 0.05% were Native Hawaiian or other Pacific Islander. First-generation students had a lower median household income and more unmet financial need than students whose parents attended college and had a median family income of $41,000 (compared to $90,000 for their continuing-generation peers) (RTI, 2021). Sexual orientation, physical ability, language, and various other identities contribute to the diversity of first-generation college students.

These intersecting identities have different levels of salience depending on the environment or situation. Consider the college experiences of two first-generation students, one with a higher socio-economic background and another with a low socio-economic background. While they both might have challenges understanding the hidden curriculum of college, the student from the higher socio-economic background might have an easier time adjusting to campus life because of the social capital (Bourdieu, 1986) gained through experiences and relationships associated with income level. While coming to campus with other forms of cultural wealth (Yosso, 2005), the student from the lower socio-economic background will not have the types of experiences and relationships that support navigating higher education. Additionally, this student has a greater chance of having financial concerns which could also affect campus engagement leading to a decreased sense of belonging. For example, students from lower socio-economic backgrounds tend to work more in college to alleviate financial shortfalls. More time spent working leaves less time for students to learn about and engage in extracurricular and cocurricular activities and high-impact practices. Soria and Stebleton (2013) found a statistically significant difference between the social capital and sense of belonging between middle-/upper-class students and working-class students with working-class students reporting lower social capital and sense of belonging. Social capital (Joanis et al., 2020) and sense of belonging (Strayhorn, 2018) have been identified as important influences of college completion. As such, institutions should address challenges and barriers that interfere with students feeling like they are a welcomed part of the campus community. Engagement opportunities that value strengths, knowledge, skills, and abilities students bring to campus also contribute to their sense of belonging and encourage students to utilize these attributes as they navigate the college landscape.

Racial and ethnic identities further nuance the college experiences of first-generation students. Classroom pedagogy and curricula content that are not culturally relevant and inclusive can decrease the level of engagement and sense of belonging for students of color. Furthermore, structural racism exists in the form of policies and practices that negatively affect particular racial groups (Arday et. al., 2021; Figuroa and García, 2006). In addition to culturally exclusive pedagogy and curricula, research has described how standard practices in higher education like hiring practices, culturally biased standardized testing, and remediation also contribute to structural racism, exacerbating feelings of hopelessness and disengagement (Ponterotto, et al., 2006).

First-generation college students have to negotiate multiple identities on and off college campuses. The intersectionality of their multiple identities influences their strengths, needs, challenges, perceptions, and experiences. Recognizing how students' first-generation identity intersects with their racial, ethnic, cultural, gender, class, ability, and other identities will help practitioners strengthen support for these students. This work cannot be done in isolation. The complexities associated with the multiple intersecting identities of first-generation students must be addressed by institutional efforts that cross divisional and departmental lines and support students inside and outside the classroom.

INSTITUTIONAL SUPPORT

Institutions can increase retention and bolster the academic performance of first-generation students by providing targeted opportunities and programming (Tinto, 2004). These opportunities often require an institutional shift with support beyond standard academic development programming. While the importance of academic support should not be downplayed, there are other key areas that can push the institutional shift just as far. Support for first-generation students can be realized through social, career development, and financial support.

Belonging on campus is a vital component of a college student's success (Strayhorn, 2018). This sense of belonging can often determine if a student will remain at a given institution (Thomas, 2012). Utilizing multiple departments/offices (financial aid, counseling, housing, student life, etc.) across campus to welcome and provide a variety of targeted programs is an excellent step to making first-generation students feel comfortable. A student's sense of belonging often comes from a physical space and this multifaceted approach gives students options to find a place that is meaningful to them.

Institutions should also look for ways to prioritize personal connections for first-generation students. Small-scale programming can help students feel comfortable asking questions and provide opportunities to connect with other first-generation students, faculty, and staff. The recognition of first-generation peers creates a bond within the group and across the institution. Finally, institutions need to communicate with and engage first-generation students' families, making sure they are a part of the orientation process and then continuing the connection as the student moves through their college career.

Institutional support for first-generation students also comes in the form of post-graduation services. Transitioning from the undergraduate experience to the workforce or graduate school is often an overlooked aspect of first-generation student support. Research shows that first-generation students can struggle with understanding of the career development process (Tate et al., 2015). Providing targeted resources and support can begin to break down those barriers. First-generation students believe that the lack of a professional network diminishes their chances of a successful career (Tate et al., 2015). Institutions can connect senior and graduating students with local alumni and professional organizations so that these students can begin to make these important professional connections. Once first-generation students understand that the career development process begins well before graduation, they can start to make connections earlier.

Finally, institutions should also consider expanded financial support for first-generation students. These students generally receive less financial support from their parents than continuing education students (Mehta et al., 2011). From an institutional perspective, going beyond traditional financial support can be instrumental in supporting first-generation students. Stipends or grants can be used for expected expenses such as textbooks, but for first-generation scholars may be needed for meals for family members or even a winter coat. These types of purchases can help reduce the outside the classroom stress that many first-generation students deal with.

ACADEMIC AND SOCIAL SUPPORT

Laura Rendón's Validation Theory highlights how faculty and staff at institutions of higher education can support first-generation students. Validation Theory essentially refers to positive affirmation of students both in- and out-of-class to recognize students as valuable members of their college community and to foster their personal and social development (Hickman, 2016). Validation is not about pampering students or making them weaker, rather, students are empowered to believe in their ability to learn, acquire self-worth, and increase motivation to succeed (Linares and Muñoz, 2011).

Studies have shown that students from disadvantaged backgrounds or were first-generation college students found success with applied learning and the guidance of a faculty or staff member who took the time to help them (Wickman, 2016). Research from Linares and Muñoz (2011) illustrate the following ways faculty and staff can engage and validate student experiences:

- Learn students' names and refer to them by their preferred name
- Ensure curricula reflect student backgrounds
- Encourage students and partner in the learning process
- Help students with course and future planning
- Encourage students to support each other (i.e., form friendships, develop peer networks, share assignments, provide positive reinforcement)
- Serve as mentors and try to meet with students outside of class in areas such as the cafeteria, library, or patio areas

The undeniable equity gaps in higher education should further implore faculty and staff to engage with students in meaningful and impactful ways that will effectuate pedagogical reform, yielding student success. The supportive relationships between students, faculty, and staff help support a healthy transition to adulthood (Raposa et al., 2021). Students can be validated academically and interpersonally, as noted in the aforementioned bullet points regarding ways to validate students' experiences. In a validating classroom, faculty actively reach out to students to offer assistance, encouragement, and support and provide opportunities for students to validate each other through encouraging comments that validate the work of peers (Linares and Muñoz, 2011). The validation is critical as first-generation students often experience invalidating actions from some faculty, believing faculty are unapproachable, inaccessible, and often dehumanizing toward students (Linares and Muñoz, 2011).

On-campus mentors can serve as institutional agents who provide guidance through the challenges of adjusting to college life by helping students understand and adapt to the academic rigors of college, while also translating cultural values and social rules (Raposa et al., 2021). Students enter college not having been told that in academe, there are unwritten and unspoken expectations (Chatelain, 2018). Addressing the hidden curriculum early in students' academic tenure is another way faculty and staff can support first-generation students. To fully transition to college and overcome freshmen year challenges, students need to possess an understanding of the institution's cultural context and social structures, or rather, the hidden curriculum (Minicozzi and Roda, 2020). According to Yosso (2005) culture influences how society is organized, how school curriculum is developed, and how pedagogy and policy are implemented. The cultural mismatch theory suggests that first-generation college students are often raised in a culture that values interdependent norms that conflict with the independent norms that are prevalent at American universities (Stephens et al., 2012). Due to the cultural mismatch that often occurs when first-generation students enter college, students need to be explicitly taught the hidden curriculum of college life, such as cultural differences between high school and college, learning how to manage their time and prioritize, communicating effectively with faculty, and seeking help when needed instead of struggling in silence (Minicozzi and Roda, 2020).

STRENGTHS AND CHALLENGES OF FIRST-GENERATION STUDENTS

Higher education in recent years has placed heightened emphasis on increasing access to historically underrepresented groups including first-generation college students (Schwartz et al., 2018). Although first-generation college students have often overcome the odds to attend college, they have dramatically higher college attrition rates than their continuing-generation peers, with data indicating that they are approximately twice as likely to leave college without a degree (Schwartz et al., 2018). The relationships, experiences, and knowledge that students gain during the college years can fundamentally shape their lifetime personal and career outcomes (Ramirez et al., 2021).

First-generation students experience many challenges as they transition in to college. Their lack of exposure to academic rigor puts them at a disadvantage when engaging in collegiate work. Many experience crippling self-doubt as a result of imposter syndrome (Clance and Imes, 1978). First-generation college students were likely to experience social and financial barriers that affected their academic success and well-being, such as food insecurity, educational expenses, and poverty at drastically higher rates than their peers (Vielma, 2021). Although first-generation students come to college with an array of challenges, they also possess the resilience needed to achieve success given the appropriate level of support.

Community Cultural Wealth acknowledges strengths and can be used to reframe deficit perspectives regarding communities of color in educational research (Juarez, 2020). Yosso's Community Cultural Wealth model categorizes six forms of capital: (1) aspirational, the ability to create and sustain goals for the future, even when faced with adversity; (2) linguistic, the ability to speak in multiple languages or styles and the ability to switch between them depending on the audience; (3) familial, the cultural knowledge and history a student carries from their family and community; (4) social, the social networks a student possesses and can create to lean on for support; (5) navigational. the skills amassed while maneuvering through social institutions that were not designed for them; (6) resistance, knowledge and skills developed while they identify, challenge, and seek to reform oppressive structures in society (Yosso, 2005). The Community Cultural Wealth model Yosso (2005) acknowledges the strengths of underserved populations and encourages them to identify experiences, skills, and knowledge as positive contributions. First-generation college students can use these assets versus focusing on their deficits.

REFERENCES

Arday, J., Zoe Belluigi, D., & Thomas, D. (2021). Attempting to break the chain: Reimaging inclusive pedagogy and decolonising the curriculum within the academy. *Educational Philosophy and Theory*, 53(3), 298 313.

Baldwin, Amy (2018, July). Defining the first-generation college student. Presentation presented at the Institute on First-Generation College Students, Columbia, SC.

Bourdieu, P. (1986). The forms of capital. In J. Richardson (Ed.) *Handbook of theory and research for the sociology of education*. Greenwood.

Chatelain, M. (2018). We must help first-generation students master academe's 'hidden curriculum'. *The Chronicle of Higher Education, 65*(8), 1 3.

Clance, P. R., & Imes, S. A. (1978). The imposter phenomenon in high achieving women: Dynamics and therapeutic intervention. *Psychotherapy: Theory, research & practice, 15*(3), 241.

Crenshaw, K. (1989). Demarginalizing the intersection of race and sex: A black feminist critique of antidiscrimination doctrine, feminist theory and antiracist politics. *University of Chicago Legal Forum, 1989*, Article 8.

Figueroa, J. L., & García, E. E. (2006). Tracing Institutional racism in higher education: Academic practices of latino male undergraduates. In M. G. Constantine & D. W. Sue (Eds.), *Addressing racism: Facilitating cultural competence in mental health and educational settings* (pp. 195 211). John Wiley & Sons, Inc.

Hickman, C. (2016, October 7). Laura Rendón shares ways validation pedagogy promotes student success. *Worcester State University News*. Retrieved March 16, 2022, from https://news.worcester.edu/laura-rendon-shares-ways-validation-pedagogy-promotes-student-success/

Joanis, S., Burnley, J., & Mohundro, J. D. (2020). Social capital's impact on college graduation rates, debt, and student loan defaults. *Journal of College Student Retention: Research, Theory & Practice, 0*(0), 1-20. Available online: 15 April, 2020, https://doi.org/10.1177/1521025120918879

Juarez, M. C. (2020). *And still we rise: Examining the strengths of first-generation college students* (Doctoral dissertation, University of Southern California).

Linares, L. I. R., & Muñoz, S. M. (2011). Revisiting validation theory: Theoretical foundations, applications, and extensions. *Enrollment Management Journal, 2*(1), 12 33.

Mehta, S. S., Newbold, J. J., & O'Rourke, M. A. (2011). Why do first-generation students fail?. *College Student Journal, 45*(1), 20 36.

Minicozzi, L., & Roda, A. (2020). Unveiling the hidden assets that first-generation students bring to college. *Journal for Leadership and Instruction, 19*(1), 43 46.

Ponterotto, J. G., Utsey, S. O., & Pedersen, P. B. (2006). *Preventing prejudice: A guide for counselors, educators, and parents* (2nd ed.). Sage.

Ramirez, G., Covarrubias, R., Jackson, M., & Son, J. Y. (2021). Making hidden resources visible in a minority serving college context. *Cultural Diversity and Ethnic Minority Psychology, 27*(2), 256.

Raposa, E. B., Hagler, M., Liu, D., & Rhodes, J. E. (2021). Predictors of close faculty–student relationships and mentorship in higher education: Findings from the Gallup–Purdue Index. *Annals of the New York Academy of Sciences, 1483*(1), 36 49.

RTI International. (2021). *First-generation college graduates: Race/ethnicity, age, and use of career planning services*. Washington, DC: NASPA. Retrieved from https://firstgen.naspa.org/files/dmfile/FactSheet-011.pdf

Schwartz, S. E., Kanchewa, S. S., Rhodes, J. E., Gowdy, G., Stark, A. M., Horn, J. P.,... & Spencer, R. (2018). "I'm having a little struggle with this, can you help me out?": Examining impacts and processes of a social capital intervention for first-generation college students. *American Journal of Community Psychology*, 61(1 2), 166 178.

Soria, K. M. & Stebleton, M. J. (2013). Social capital academic engagement, and sense of belonging. *College Student Affairs Journal*, 21(2), 139 153.

Stephens, N. M., Fryberg, S. A., Markus, H. R., Johnson, C. S., & Covarrubias, R. (2012). Unseen disadvantage: How American Universities' focus on independence undermines the academic performance of first-generation college students. *Journal of Personality and Social Psychology*, 102(6), 1178 1197. https://doi.org/10.1037/a0027143

Strayhorn, T. L. (2018). *College students' sense of belonging: A key to educational success for all students* (2nd ed.). Routledge. https://doi.org/10.4324/9781315297293

Tate, K. A., Caperton, W., Kaiser, D., Pruitt, N. T., White, H., & Hall, E. (2015). An exploration of first-generation college students' career development beliefs and experiences. *Journal of Career Development*, 42(4), 294 310. https://doi.org/10.1177/0894845314565025

Thomas, L. (2012). *What works? Student retention & success* (p. 6). Paul Hamlyn Foundation.

Tinto, V. (2004). *Student retention and graduation: Facing the truth, living with the consequences. Occasional paper 1*. Pell Institute for the Study of Opportunity in Higher Education.

Vielma, A. G. (2021, September 9). *The struggles (and strengths) of first-generation college students during the pandemic* (Stephanie W. Cawthon, PhD). Retrieved March 17, 2022, from https://www.stephaniecawthon.com/blog/first-gen-struggles-strengths

Yosso, T. J. (2005). Whose culture has capital? A critical race theory discussion of community cultural wealth. *Race Ethnicity and Education*, 8(1), 69 91.

Part I
First Year Experiences

Chapter 2

Utilizing Intrusive Advising to Support First-Generation College Students at the University of South Carolina Upstate

Kimberly Walker, Tiffany N. Hughes, and Kadaisha Miller

PROGRAM DESCRIPTION

The TRIO program at the University of South Carolina Upstate (USC Upstate) is funded through the Federal TRIO Student Support Services (SSS) grant program. The TRIO program refers to the original three (now eight) programs that were Upward Bound, Talent Search, and Student Support Services. The aforementioned programs are intended to provide eligible students with academic development services such as tutoring, mentoring, and educational counseling services. These services are designed to help students begin, persist, and complete higher educational training (US Department of Education, 2020). Any student receiving Federal Pell Grant funds is eligible to participate in the TRIO SSS program.

At USC Upstate, the impact of TRIO SSS is important given the role of the institution as a regional comprehensive within a larger state system and the diverse population of the students that are served by the university. As of the Fall 2019 data, USC Upstate has approximately 6,300 enrolled students, 5,853 of which are undergraduates. The institution is diverse with 61% of students being Pell-eligible and 52% of students identifying as White, 30% identifying as Black or African American, and 6% identifying as Hispanic or Latino. The Federal TRIO SSS grant funds 160 students at USC Upstate each academic year. The funding supports TRIO SSS students by providing (1) one-on-one tutoring for necessary subjects that supplements the tutoring services offered by the university at large; (2) in-depth assistance with course scheduling including advising on long-term educational goals such as graduate school; (3) individual counseling that addresses the personal, psychological, financial, academic, and career needs of each student;

(4) support regarding financial and economic literacy that addresses student loans and budgeting; (5) FAFSA assistance; (6) specialized course sections that include enrollment caps lower than those of the university at large and enrol. TRIO SSS students exclusively; and (7) social and cultural events that expose students to the arts as well as other non-academic enriching activities.

The USC Upstate TRIO SSS intrusive advising process is based upon Walter Earl's 1987 seminal work "Intrusive Advising for Freshmen." Earl's work focuses on helping students learn when and how to seek out assistance when needed. This is a core feature of the TRIO SSS advising process and is intended to help foster relationships between TRIO SSS staff, build student confidence, and ensure productive advisement meetings that contribute to student success educationally and personally. The individual counseling that addresses the personal, psychological, financial, academic, and career needs of the TRIO SSS students at USC Upstate is the program's implementation of intrusive advising. These services are intended to address the whole student by offering intentional contact with students that motivates them to persist and, ultimately, complete their degree (Varney, 2007). The culmination of structured and unstructured interactions constitutes the intentional communications between students and TRIO SSS staff that create a university environment where students feel seen, heard, and cared for by the university. The set of activities that determine each student's personal, psychological, financial, and academic well-being are the foundation of the intrusive advising process within the TRIO SSS program.

MISSION, GOALS, AND OBJECTIVES

The mission of the USC Upstate TRIO SSS program is *to provide educational resources and be a support system for underrepresented students as they complete their baccalaureate degree programs*. The program's mission is executed by using the following goals:

- To promote academic achievement
- To identify immediate and long-term career, academic, and personal goals
- To encourage career exploration
- To encourage greater self-awareness through personality and career assessment
- To promote positive self-image in students
- To provide activities and sessions which will promote academic, personal, and social development

The aforementioned goals are determined to be successful if the number of students who persist, retain, graduate, and attend graduate school increases to the goal set by the department. The mission and its goals are required to align with the overarching mission of the Federal TRIO grant as defined by the

Education Opportunity Act of 1964 (US Department of Education, 2020). The achievement of the goals of the USC Upstate TRIO SSS program would not be possible without the intrusive advising model. This is due to the relationship development necessary to understand the students' needs whether that be academic, financial, or psychological.

IMPLEMENTATION

To best utilize intrusive advising, students need to have a relationship built upon trust with their advisor (Fowler and Boylan, 2010). In TRIO SSS, the relationship building with students starts during the application process before the review committee decides if a student will be admitted to the program. As a part of the application process, the students are required to meet with TRIO staff for an interview. Each introduction includes the staff's personal experiences as a first-generation/low-income (FGLI) student, being TRIO Alums, and/or their history of working with FGLI students. The remainder of the interview is spent getting to know the students, who they are, where they are from, what fears or apprehensions they have about attending college, and what they hope to gain from being a participant of the program.

After students are accepted into the program, they participate in an on-campus orientation. Important components of the orientation process include course selection and a recommitment to the students' academic, personal, and professional success. In addition to providing guidance regarding course selection, TRIO advisors dedicate considerable time to learning about the students including: (a) what subject areas they do well in and the subjects that require additional study time, (b) their preferred time of day for academic work, (c) whether they will be living on or off campus, and (d) potential financial needs related to their selected courses. As the semester begins, students will have had substantial involvement with TRIO advisors to begin building the necessary authentic relationship that makes intrusive advising possible.

Students spend their first three days with TRIO program participants and staff. During this initial period, students are engaging with one another by participating in bonding activities with upperclassmen, staff, and their cohort peers. To further help build the relationship between the student and the TRIO staff, new students are enrolled in the first-year seminar course that is taught by their assigned academic counselor. This ensures that students are interacting with their counselors regularly without requiring an exorbitant number of meetings. In addition to enrollment in the first-year seminar course with their assigned academic advisor, students are required to meet with their academic counselor twice each semester. The initial appointment ensures that the students have everything they need to begin the semester and to set goals for academic and personal development. Through guided conversations and intentional questions, the TRIO staff can ascertain whether students have all the resources necessary to be successful. The second appointment is used as a mid-semester check-in. During this appointment, TRIO staff can address any concerns or issues the student may have, in addition to providing academic advising. By the time TRIO staff conducts the mid-semester check-in (the academic advising appointment), students will have had several formal and informal opportunities to communicate with their assigned advisor; which allows for the intrusive advising technique to be more effective.

The most extensive formalized intrusive advising practices take place during the first year for TRIO students; however, this process leads to ongoing networks, relationships, and friendships that the students depend on throughout their undergraduate career. These networks assist students with finding employment, pursuing graduate school opportunities, and provide a core group of peers with whom they have shared experiences. The formalized process exists as part of two mandatory advising sessions per semester for each student enrolled in the program. While these sessions are referred to using the general terms of "advising meeting," students are asked questions regarding their financial situation (because many of the TRIO SSS participants work at least part-time), their academic successes and struggles, their personal relationships (friendships, dating partners, roommates, etc.), and their current mental state. Centering ongoing mental health has always been a key component of the USC Upstate TRIO SSS advising process; however, it became even more central to retaining students during the Covid-19 pandemic. What was once merely an aspect of the mandatory advising sessions became central to these meetings as students went home to largely rural areas with limited broadband internet access and limited resources for maintaining mental well-being. Moreover, many of these students were experiencing online classes for the first time in their academic lives, which brought on new challenges for the TRIO advisors to help them work through.

As advisors worked to provide the students with the resources and tools to successfully complete the spring semester of 2020, it became apparent that the intrusive advising process provided a necessary and unexpected benefit. Students were willing to readily reveal their issues and concerns regarding internet access as well as fears regarding moving back home where they might be expected to help younger siblings, contribute to household finances, or be pressured to leave school altogether. While faculty and advisors within the university shared frustrations regarding students providing this information *after* failing a test or even the entire course, USC Upstate TRIO students would share this information forthright with their advisors, allowing for more immediate remediation of any issues and concerns. The remediation included issuing hotspots from the campus IT, specialized sessions from the library regarding the use of online resources, as well as small group online tutoring sessions for TRIO students in traditionally difficult classes.

STAKEHOLDERS

The TRIO SSS program at USC Upstate has several stakeholders and partners that range from the local high school Upward Bound Programs to State and Federal Representatives who help to determine the program's federal budget and funding models. Each type of stakeholder has varying degrees of involvement when it comes to servicing TRIO students.

Students

The TRIO SSS students of USC Upstate are its most important stakeholders. Without student interest, application, and enrollment, the program would cease to exist in its current form as supported by the Federal TRIO grant program. More important than student participation is their willingness to share their successes with their colleagues, friends, and family members who then encourage other prospective students to apply to the TRIO SSS program.

High Schools

The students who enroll in USC Upstate are largely from a ten-county area of the state that surrounds the university. Given this enrollment trend, it is imperative that the TRIO SSS staff maintain relationships with not only the Upward Bound counselors, but also the high schools' guidance counselors, administrators, and influential classroom teachers. The nurturing of these relationships includes attending college fairs at the high schools in support of enrollment services staff, hosting fairs at the home collegiate institution, and encouraging current students to volunteer as mentors with various community groups and organizations. These are important, due in part to the large number of students who are first-generation in the ten-county area. They are not always aware of TRIO SSS, the services that are offered, or how to access the services upon college enrollment. Thus, when TRIO SSS staff maintain good relations with local high schools, they are afforded more opportunities to expose high school students to the benefits of participating in TRIO programs.

University Administrators

As part of the USC Upstate strategic plan, the university has an ongoing focus on increasing student enrollment, retention, and graduation rates. These data are scaled and weighted based upon the university leadership's determination regarding the importance of these data to the continued success of the university. As detailed in the forthcoming *Assessment* section, these data are currently collected as part of the Annual Performance Report for the Federal TRIO SSS grant and contribute to the institution's success.

Faculty

Faculty who instruct TRIO SSS courses are provided additional training and support from the Executive Director of Student Support Services (the office that supervises TRIO programs) and the Director of TRIO SSS. This additional training and support helps to educate the faculty regarding the student population, how best to support the students, and what services are available should student needs exceed what the faculty members are able to offer. Moreover, faculty who instruct within the TRIO program are informed of the ways in which higher education can unintentionally create barriers to student success. For example, insisting that students have cameras on during synchronous online courses. This can be a barrier because broadband internet access is not readily available across all areas of South Carolina. Having the camera active during a class may interrupt the internet connection, slow down the connection, or cause the internet to disconnect entirely. TRIO SSS staff help to reduce the occurrence of barriers by informing faculty of the unintentional impact that certain rules or guidelines can have for students.

Legislators

As TRIO SSS is a federally funded program, it is entirely dependent upon the federal budget for funding. While the state leaders maintain positive relationships with state level representatives, the largest and most widely attended Federal TRIO event is the annual Policy Seminar (Council for Opportunity of Education, n.c.). This seminar allows for TRIO staff, alumni, politicians, US Department of Education representatives and educational officials from across the country to gather and discuss the successes of TRIO programs as well as the resources, policies, and regulations necessary to ensure its sustained success. Historically, TRIO SSS has received sustained funding levels with appropriate increases over the years. Unfortunately, this funding cannot be taken for granted by the staff and alumni who are invested in the program's success. In recent years, the TRIO programs have encountered delays in application and questions of whether the funding levels would continue. It is imperative that legislators understand, appreciate, and support the services offered by the TRIO programs to ensure funding stability.

ASSESSMENT PLAN

The USC Upstate TRIO SSS program's assessment efforts are multipronged in that the scheme requires accountability to the university's strategic planning process as well as the Federal TRIO grant program. The university's assessment process is referred to as a "Continuous Improvement Blueprint." This process requires an annual plan that addresses the TRIO SSS office's (a) outcomes, (b) alignment with the university's divisional "scorecards," (c) an action plan for achieving the outcomes, (d) the necessary resources to achieve outcomes, (e) the methods and criteria that will demonstrate achievement. In addition to the plan, the office submits a report that details the results that align with the methods and criteria and the outcomes. The Continuous Improvement Blueprints are reviewed annually by the Office of Institutional Effectiveness, a taskforce of trained staff who review the documents for process feedback, and the Vice Provost and Associate Vice Chancellor for Academic Affairs who led all campus efforts related to assessment and accreditation. The feedback provided addresses the process as well as the data contained within to ensure that improvement efforts are data-driven, student-focused, and implemented in a manner that does not lend itself to punitive actions by individuals nor human resources.

In addition to the university requirements, the Federal TRIO grant process is substantially more involved and requires the submission of an Annual Performance Report (APR) (US Department of Education, n.d.). The APR requires a detailed accounting of the students that are served. This accounting includes: (a) demographic information of the University of South Carolina Upstate TRIO SSS student population, (b) information regarding the types of services that students access during the academic year, (c) student academic performance (example: grade point average), (d) financial aid award packages, (e) matriculation status, (f) degree progression, (g) retention, and (h) graduation. These data are delivered to the US Department of Education and determine whether the TRIO SSS program, as administered, meets the stated goals and objectives of the program.

OUTCOMES

The University's TRIO SSS program measures its overall success in a multitude of ways that include both direct and indirect measures that are quantitative and qualitative. Moreover, students' thought processes and ability to initiate dialogue when they experience issues are considered a successful byproduct of intrusive advising. For example, when a student is unable to register for a class that they have been advised to enroll in for that semester, the TRIO advisor would expect for the student to contact them to discuss other options as opposed to the student randomly registering for a different class. Another example of this type of success is the student maintaining ongoing contact with their TRIO advisor once they have been assigned a faculty advisor. This ongoing contact with TRIO advisors helps the student as well as the faculty advisors. Anecdotally, faculty advisors have shared that TRIO students tend to arrive much more prepared for their advisement appointments compared to non-TRIO students. The students will have reviewed their curriculum, understood their course prerequisites, and will have a general idea of what courses they need in the subsequent semester and academic year.

In terms of direct measure quantitative data, TRIO student success is measured by the number of students that are retained from semester to semester and those who persist from year to year in addition to the graduation rates. These data are sent to the US Department of Education with the Annual Performance Report (APR). The USC Upstate TRIO program's outcomes exceed that of the university for persistence, retention, and six-year graduation rates (Table 2.1).

These data represent the outcomes for the comparable university cohort for which the most up-to-date data is available in terms of persistence, retention, and graduation rates. The Fall 2013 cohort of university students had a six-year graduation rate of 48.1%. By comparison, the Fall 2013 cohort TRIO participants had a graduation rate of 62%. Additionally, this TRIO participant cohort experienced a 95% persistence. The University of South Carolina Upstate TRIO SSS program exceeded each of the stated objectives for its APR

By meeting or exceeding the goals it sets for itself along with outperforming the university at large, the TRIO SSS program continues to demonstrate that its processes – particularly, the intrusive advising process – yield results that contribute to continued student success (Table 2.2). Additionally, the USC Upstate TRIO SSS program is most successful in the areas in which the university's current strategic plan is focused including persistence, retention, and graduation rates.

Table 2.1 Fall 2013 Cohort Demographic Information for All University of South Carolina Upstate Students

Fall 2013 Cohort[a] Race/Ethnicity	Total	Persisted-SP14 (%)	Retained-FA14 (%)
American Indian or Alaska Native	56	95	70
Asian	16	94	88
Black or African American	280	96	78
Hispanic Latino	27	96	67
Non-resident Alien	3	33	33
Unknown	17	82	71
White	355	93	71
Grand total	754	94	74

[a]First-time, full-time degree-seeking students.

Table 2.2 Fall 2013 Cohort Graduation Rates Disaggregated by Race for All USC Upstate Students

Fall 2013 Cohort[a]	Grand Total	Graduated (%)
American Indian or Alaska Native	56	41.1
Asian	16	62.5
Black or African American	280	47.1
Hispanic Latino	27	48.1
Non-resident Alien	3	33.3
Unknown	17	41.2
White	355	49.9
Grand total	754	48.1

[a]First-time, full-time degree-seeking students.

LESSONS LEARNED

Despite the students in the program embodying the many labels of higher education marginalization which include low-income, first-generation, and students of color (Eitzen et al., 2016), the USC Upstate TRIO SSS program produces retention and graduation rates that exceed that of the general university (Table 2.1 & Table 2.2). Based on the 2018–2019 APR (the latest data available), 94% of students persisted from Fall to Fall, 94% of students were in good academic standing, and 62% of participants completed their degree program within six years or less. In contrast, the numbers for the university at large are not as promising. This success can be attributed to the intrusive advising processes that align with Rowh's five Traits of Successful Proactive-Advising Programs.

With intrusive advising, potential problems that students may experience are identified before they become major barriers (Rowh, 2018). According to Rowh, there are five traits that signify a proactive intrusive advising program. The first trait is *robust technology*, such as data analytics. Having robust technology is key to the success of an intrusive advising program because it allows for tracking first-generation students' progress, as well as generating early alerts for when students miss classes (Rowh, 2018). The next trait is *early intervention* which encourages interactions with students as early as the summer before the first semester starts. This allows for advisors to build personal relationships with the student, which in turn make it easier to be intrusive. *More than academics* is the third trait which conveys that there are multiple areas that students may need advising in that are not academic concerns which could range from financial to mental issues.

Discussing these more personal matters calls for *careful communication*, which is the fourth trait in Rowh's Successful Advising Program. When participating in intrusive advising, it is imperative that advisors are careful in what they consider to be the types of behaviors that warrant outreach, and how to best communicate concerns with students (Rowh, 2018). Lastly, *campus buy-in* is the fifth trait, which is when support for the intrusive advising is gathered from administration throughout the campus.

Robust Technology

Robust technology ensures that advisors have a top-tier connection with their prospective students. The difference between robust technology and other manual processes is that not only does it track a student's success, but also it helps identify students who are at risk of academic failure. This technology is especially needed for students at risk because it makes it easier for advisors to guide them to the services that they need before it is too late (Rowh, 2018). Robust technology can do this via the utilization of advanced data analytics.

As the University of South Carolina Upstate grew at an unprecedented rate, it became exceedingly clear that the manual processes that had previously been sufficient to track student progress and success were no longer effective. To help assist academic advisors, faculty, and administrators, the university invested in an academic progress and early alert system called *Starfish*. Starfish allows faculty, academic advisors, and administrators to provide immediate feedback, concerns, or kudos to students and campus partners. The system connects faculty to professional advisors, advisors to students, and everyone to administrative leadership.

Early Intervention

Early intervention is a key trait to intrusive advising because it allows for advisors to connect with students well before the start of the semester. The earlier that an advisor reaches out to the student, the more time they have to form connections and foster a positive advising relationship. It is important to create a relationship of trust with the student due to the intrusive nature of the advising approach. Early intervention will also allow for advisors to learn a student's behavior and the signs they exhibit that warrant outreach. This also helps with determining the best communication style for the advisor and the student.

Due, in part, to acquiring Starfish, faculty are able to quickly and efficiently communicate with academic advisors regarding student progress or concerns. Conversely, the Starfish system allows a faculty member to send an alert with preselected concerns (for example: attendance, grades, counseling center recommendation, etc.) to the student's advisors with just a few clicks within the automated system. Moreover, the faculty member can do so for the entire class without having to find individual advisors for each student separately. The Starfish system helps to facilitate early intervention by reducing the barriers of communication between faculty, academic advisors, administrators, and campus support offices.

More Than Academics

Many at-risk students have trouble with navigating college whether it is pertaining to their academic, personal, or social life. This means that it is crucial for advisors to form a relationship with students that is comforting enough for the student to share other aspects of their life that they may need assistance with navigating. This connection is a benefit for the advisors because this allows them to see why a student may have troubles in certain areas. For the students, it lets them know that they have someone in their corner who is truly rooting for their success in all aspects in life.

TRIO advisors and staff spend a considerable amount of time building a rapport with their students when they initially enter the university. This relationship building allows advisors to ask honest, and sometimes difficult, questions while facilitating open and honest dialogue with students.

Careful Communication

Careful communication is vital for intrusive advising. To form a trusting relationship with their students, advisors use careful communication with them. This means that the student and advisor should come to an agreement about how often they communicate and the preferred communication methods that work best for them. Communications can range from the formal to informal including email, text, and even social media messaging. Using their preferred communication methods will add to the student's comfort and trust allowing the advising relationship to flourish.

The TRIO SSS program communication and rapport building begins before students enroll in classes or come to campus. It is important that ongoing formal and informal communication is established as an expectation for students who are in the program.

Campus Buy-In

Campus buy-in is an important step to intrusive advising. Without the support from university leaders and administration, the materials needed for intrusive advising would be difficult to achieve. University administration and other campus leaders aid with the implementation of intrusive advising. They help not only by training faculty and other administration on how to use the data analytics and applicable software services, but also, they help conceive of an effective plan of communication to bring faculty on board. This facilitates an organized and smooth transition of the campus from a traditional advising model to an intrusive advising approach.

Campus leaders and administrators are aware of the ways in which TRIO SSS supports student success and they continue to try to scale up these procedures and processes across the broader campus community. This includes hiring dedicated professional advisors, utilizing smaller class sizes, and making systems like Starfish available to the entire campus community. In turn, administrators help to ensure that TRIO staff can attend conferences, have time to write the Annual Performance Report and apply for continued access to the federal grant, and provide consistent, public recognition of the work that takes place within the program.

Recommendations

The structure of a successful intrusive advising program can be difficult given the necessary staffing, dedication, and expectation of ongoing and frequent communication (Cannon, 2013; Schwebel et al., 2008). This was an even greater task at USC Upstate as the University enrollment increased by almost 20% during a ten-year period from the 2007–2008 academic year through the 2017–2018 academic year. Since that time, USC Upstate has continued to grow to its current size of almost 6,300 students. During that same time, staffing has remained roughly the same. This means that during a time of tremendous growth for the university, diversification of the student body, and greater brand recognition, the number of individuals completing the day-to-day work has remained the same. The levels of staffing remained consistent in the TRIO SSS program as well.

Given the ongoing success of the USC Upstate TRIO SSS program during a time of university growth, increasing institutional diversity, and an international health crisis, there are several overarching recommendations to consider should an institution endeavor to incorporate intrusive advising into its co-curricular institutional efforts: (a) build rapport with the students from the very first interaction (Cannon, 2013), (b) use institutional data to identify opportunities within the program and to demonstrate effectiveness (beyond the federally required APR) (Smith, 2007), and (c) ensure consistent, frequent, and high-expectation advising because students find the interactions to be valuable and helpful (Donaldson et al., 2016).

The USC Upstate TRIO SSS students represent a highly diverse and traditionally marginalized student population. They are often high-achieving students in some of the lowest performing schools in the state. The students are normally very self-motivated and accustomed to figuring out issues on their own. This, coupled with their first-generation status, often translates to the students possessing less knowledge regarding who to contact when problems arise. If rapport is intentionally developed from the advisor's initial interactions or communications, whether in-person or virtual, students will feel more comfortable asking the necessary questions that will help them with their ongoing success. The intrusive advising relationship between a staff member and student is based upon trust that can only be reinforced through the rapport building process.

Although TRIO SSS is a federally funded initiative, the university's support is also important. The support can come in many forms including financial support for resources; classroom space and equipment; freedom to construct, promote, and operate the program as one sees fit; and opportunities for the students and staff to be featured in marketing communications. These types of university-based support can be difficult to accumulate due to competing priorities and limited institutional capacity. However, data-informed decisions are highly valued at USC Upstate. The university is making a concerted effort to encourage, support, and grow impactful programs on campus through $1,000 "mini-grants" and opportunities to share successful ideas with the Chancellor and the relevant institutional cabinet members. The ability to demonstrate effectiveness with the use of consistent university data could translate to ongoing support from the leadership and should be used from the outset when attempting to replicate the USC Upstate intrusive advising success.

Intrusive advising is labor-intensive and requires a considerable amount of staff resources to implement successfully. These resources may extend beyond those that are offered within the confines of the federal grant; thus, requiring university intervention and support. This support can be secured most readily by utilizing data that demonstrate the effectiveness and overall success of the program and its processes. The time commitment to continually contact and advise 160 students (the USC Upstate TRIO SSS enrollment for the Fall 2020 academic year) on their academic, personal, and professional endeavors strains the current team of three staff persons. However, with additional university resources for first-year seminar courses, the Starfish alert system, and specialized supplemental instructional services, the staff is able to meet their intrusive advising obligations.

REFERENCES

Cannon, J. (2013). Intrusive advising 101: How to be intrusive without intruding. *Academic Advising Today*, 36(1)

Council for Opportunity in Education. (n.d.). Policy seminar. Retrieved January 14, 2021, from https://coenet.org/policy_seminar.shtml

Dix, N., Lail, A., Birnbaum, M., & Paris, J. (2020). Exploring the "at-risk" student label through the perspectives of higher education professionals. *Qualitative Report*, 25(11), 3830–3846.

Donaldson, P., McKinney, L., Lee, M., & Pino, D. (2016). First-year community college students' perceptions of and attitudes toward intrusive academic advising. *NACADA Journal*, *36*(1), 30–42.

Earl, W. R. (1987). Intrusive advising for freshmen. Retrieved from http://www.nacada.ksu.edu/Resources/Clearinghouse/View-Articles/Intrusive-Advising-for-Freshmen.aspx

Eitzen, A. M., Kinney, M. A., & Grillo, K. J. (2016). Changing the praxis of retention in higher education: A plan to TEACH all learners. *Change*, *48*(6), 58–66. https://doi-org.uscupstate.idm.oclc.org/10.1080/00091383.2016.1247584

Fowler, P. R., & Boylan, H. R. (2010). Increasing student success and retention: A multidimensional approach. *Journal of Developmental Education*, *34*(2), 2–10.

Graham, L. (2011). Learning a new world: Reflections on being a first-generation college student and the influence of TRIO programs. *New Directions for Teaching and Learning*, *127*, 33–38. https://doi.org/10.1002/tl.455

Helm, J., Coronella, T. & Rooney, T. (2018, June 24–27). *Identifying at-risk freshmen and providing enhanced advising support through intrusive academic advising interventions [Presented at first-year programs division postcard session 1: Retention and student success strategies]*. Salt Lake City, UT: American Society for Engineering Education. https://www.asee.org/public/conferences/106/papers/22545/view

Miars, L. (2019, December 19). What is proactive caseload management and what does it mean for students? Retrieved January 13, 2021, from https://eab.com/insights/blogs/student-success/proactive-caseload-academic-advising/

Patel, V. (2014, December 5). To improve graduation rates, advising gets intrusive by design. *Chronicle of Higher Education*, *61*(14), A6.

Rowh, M. (2018). Intrusive advising: 5 Traits of successful proactive-advising programs. *University Business*, *21*(9), 31–34.

Sanacore, J., & Palumbo, A. (2015, May 22). Let's help first-generation students succeed. *Chronicle of Higher Education*, *61*(36), 1–5.

Schwebel, D. C., Walburn, N. C., Jacobsen, S. H., Jerrolds, K. L., & Klyce, K. (2008). Efficacy of intrusively advising first-year students via frequent reminders for advising appointments. *NACADA Journal*, *28*(2), 28–32.

Smith, J. S. (2007). Using data to inform decisions: intrusive faculty advising at a community college. *Community College Journal of Research and Practice*, *31*(10), 813–831. https://doi.org/10.1080/10668920701375918

The Glossary of Education Reform. (2013, August 29). At-risk definition. Retrieved January 14, 2021, from https://www.edglossary.org/at-risk/

U.S. Department of Education. (2020, September 25). Student support services program. https://www2.ed.gov/programs/triostudsupp/index.html

U.S. Department of Education. (2020, December 08). TRIO home page. https://www2.ed.gov/about/offices/list/ope/trio/index.html

U.S. Department of Education. (n.d.). Student support services program. *Instructions on completing 2019 20 Annual Performance Report*. https://www2.ed.gov/programs/triostudsupp/sssaprinstructions1920.pdf

Varney, J. (2007, September). Intrusive advising. *Nacada*. https://nacada.ksu.edu/Resources/Academic-Advising-Today/View-Articles/Intrusive-Advising.aspx#:~:text=Intrusive%20Advising%20involves%20intentional%20contact,increased%20academic%20motivation%20and%20persistence

Chapter 3

University of Portland's Summer Launch Initiative

Matt Daily

This chapter discusses the launching of the University of Portland's (UP's) First-Generation (FGEN) program and, specifically, our Summer Launch Pre-Orientation initiative that has aided in the transition of first-generation students. The Summer Launch initiative also offers a practical example of how our FGEN program identified incoming student needs, designed and executed a pre-orientation program, and made critical adjustments to both program format and structure every year. The lessons we have learned are important considerations for all seeking to support first-generation college students.

UP's FGEN program has grown over the past six years out of a necessity to support its first-generation student population. UP utilizes the U.S. Department of Education is a definition of "first-generation college student." First-generation college students are defined as students within the higher education environment whose parents or guardians have not earned a four-year bachelor's degree but may have some postsecondary college experience (Redford & Hoyer, 2017, p. 3). Currently, 20–25% of the UP undergraduate population identifies as first-generation.

UP's FGEN program has swiftly transitioned from infancy to a national model of excellence since its inception in 2015. In 2017, the National Center for First-Generation Student Success, the nation's first recognition program acknowledging higher education institutions for their commitment to first-generation student success, named UP an inaugural First-Gen Forward institution (Center for First-Gen Student Success, n.d.). In 2021, UP was named an Advisory Member of the First-Gen Forward initiative, formalizing a leadership role among its higher education peers. The success of UP's FGEN program recognition and success is attributed to institutional collaboration, innovative practices, and a drive to continue to evolve and grow with its students.

LISTENING TO THE VOICES OF STUDENTS

The Office of Development highlighted then senior UP FGEN student Mellonie Mwawai in its "25 Days of Christmas" campaign (Lamb, 2020). The narrative described that while UP had been Mellonie's "dream school," she faced several hurdles during her first year and nearly transferred to another school. These barriers included the need to connect socially within the greater school community, financial challenges, and, most importantly, an overall lack of understanding of the hidden curriculum on campus (Collier & Morgan, 2008). Finding support within UP's FGEN program was one of the factors in Mellonie's decision to stay at UP. Her involvement in the program also connected her with a faculty member who also identified as a first-generation college graduate. Over time, Mellonie became immersed in biochemistry research with her professor, and they bonded over their shared first-generation college student identities, as well as their love for science. Before graduating, she also worked with peers to create and produce "The FGEN Experience" podcast.

OUR MISSION

As the mission of UP's FGEN program has solidified, stories like Mellonie's have become increasingly common. Students at UP come from diverse geographical and cultural situations. Having a fundamental understanding of our program's existence while being sensitive to the various backgrounds of the students we serve allows our program to be successful. The mission of UP's FGEN program is "to provide guidance and support to first-generation students during transitional periods at UP." Additionally, the FGEN program helps students meet their academic and personal goals through student-centered programs and events intentionally designed with the first-generation experience in mind. Finally, first-generation students can express their worries, challenges, and needs to FGEN student peer leaders through open, personalized peer-to-peer mentorship, thus forging authentic bonds.

Foundations of the FGEN Program at UP

UP's FGEN program is built upon the framework that the community is stronger as a collective body (Bandura, 1977; Donohoo et al., 2018). The program highlights the natural gifts and strengths of our domestic students and international students. The program also establishes an integrated and efficient system of relationships that allows first-generation students to navigate their college experience. Finally, the FGEN program draws strength from collaborations, listening to varying personal voices, and accommodating the perspectives of all individuals.

Much of UP's FGEN program is based on the research and work of others. As an example, Pike and Kuh (2005) suggested that as first-generation students encounter unique challenges, it is important to consider innovative solutions that inform any program's mission, goals, and objectives. Colleges and universities must put their efforts into targeted interventions specific to the first-generation population. In our own program, we realized the program's foundation, development, and execution must be unique and varied to fit the needs of the UP first-generation student population.

Where We Needed to Go

As we initially designed and established the FGEN program, we placed the emphasis on its mission, goals, and objectives for success.

Current Goals and Outcomes for FGEN Program

- Before and during arrival to the UP campus, FGEN program administration will *develop* interventions for FGEN students by *instilling an awareness of UP's resources and culture* unique to the UP-college experience.
- Stressing peer-to-peer connections and interactions: UP's FGEN program will *foster student engagement and belonging* for its students through the four-year college experience. Programming and events designed for each year of study are student-conceived and student-run.
- By designing a peer-to-peer mentor program available to all new FGEN students, new stakeholders to the UP FGEN community *will gain a better understanding of UP processes* by demystifying the "hidden curriculum" within UP and accessing the higher education system. Participants will draw upon this foundational knowledge as they continue with their UP experience. The mentor program has a curriculum specifically designed and implemented by UP first-generation students for their peers new to the university.
- Targeted FGEN *students will learn and build upon success skills vital for their own academic success* before, during, and after their first year of study. Events and workshops, specifically designed for each class year of study, will focus on the academic and learning skills necessary to be successful at the university. The workshops are executed to create additional buy-in for all.

SUMMER LAUNCH

Summer Launch was one of the first initiatives of the FGEN program. In addition to what was offered during the school year, FGEN's Summer Launch was the only program designed and offered by FGEN when school was not in session. Summer Launch, a pre-orientation program, gained energy and momentum due to the efforts of a committee composed of representatives from the offices of Undergraduate Scholarly Engagement, Student Activities, Residence Life, and the Shepard Freshmen Resource Center, along with additional faculty, staff, and current students.

FGEN and Its Partners

As the Committee imagined Summer Launch as an experience for first-generation students prior to their arrival to campus, collaboration and partnerships were always going to be a critical aspect of the pre-orientation program's success. In the summer of 2015, when the Committee first conceived of a pre-orientation opportunity for first-generation students, they leveraged their professional capital and connections on campus to gain support for the initiative. Collectively, this well-balanced team emerged as important stakeholders for the growth of the FGEN program.

As Summer Launch continued its growth and expansion, organizers reached out to additional campus partners, including Admissions, Student Accounts, the Learning Commons (peer-to-peer academic tutoring), and Outdoor Pursuits (recreation) to participate. Each entity was eager and willing to support this pledge to support UP's first-generation students.

The Committee made concentrated efforts to recruit and engage current UP first-generation students, hoping that they may be motivated to assist. In its early stages, initially, the Committee designed, planned, and executed Summer Launch whereas, at a later stage, the Program Manager for Special Populations fulfilled these responsibilities. Initially, Committee members would reach out to all returning first-generation students on campus and simply ask if each would like to volunteer to help with the event. Eventually, the Committee established a Summer Launch coordinator position and paid student positions to support Summer Launch and its participants.

Summer Launch in Its Infancy

UP currently defines a first-generation student whose parents or guardians do not have a four-year college degree; however, this has not always been the case. Prior to January 2018, UP focused most of its efforts on those students whose parents or guardians had not attended any type of college. This more targeted subset of first-generation students typically formed approximately 7% of the student population. The first-ever Summer Launch was small and involved a diverse set of on-campus experiences for those incoming first-generation students that opted to participate. Events began at 9 AM and concluded at 3 PM. This event focused on students within this targeted 7% student population.

A ROBUST SCHEDULE AND FEEDBACK FROM PARTICIPANTS

Once the participants arrived and checked in, they were taken to Campus Safety to get their University ID card. Additional activities for participants included student-led mixers and an insider tour of campus. Academic Affairs staff offered a presentation entitled "How to Survive and Thrive your Freshman Year" followed by a Q&A panel with returning students. Before departure, participants completed a survey about the efficacy of the Summer Launch program and were invited to the next scheduled event for first-generation students at UP. Common themes from survey results were as follows: the most valuable aspects of Summer Launch 2015 involved meeting other first-year peers before the start of school, hearing stories and advice from current UP first-generation students, and understanding how college life works compared to high school. Suggestions included a hands-on activity with professors, inviting more people, considering shortening the event, and giving out free swag to all those that participated.

LESSON LEARNED: ADJUSTMENTS IN STRUCTURE FROM FIRST TO THE SECOND EVENT

The planning of the second Summer Launch during Summer 2016 began to take shape based on feedback from Summer Launch participants and the student volunteers. The new program manager helped coordinate the efforts for the second Summer Launch effort. While the single-day format remained the same, different themes were considered. The participants were responsible for daily outcomes: themes to consider in the experiences included the lenses of personal health, financial literacy, academic skills, and social connection. Session topics included:

- The invisible language you need to succeed as a first-generation student
- Getting involved and connecting right away
- Common stresses and anxieties for students
- The professor/student relationship
- The pilot academic road map

Prior participant feedback formed part of this program. Additional campus partners participated, and smaller group interaction allowed incoming students to connect with one another. Students found the information that they received as informative and useful. Participants wanted more time to engage with returning FGEN students to help ease their anxieties about the upcoming transition to college.

Places for Improvement

While students entering UP valued the Summer Launch experience, something seemed amiss with the structure of the event. While receiving information, students wanted to meet more returning students and have time to make friends before the start of school. The objectives of the Summer Launch initiative became clear at this moment. It seemed as if the focus on the previous years' programs had been heavy in offering information to students. However, the program was unable to create the coveted sense of belonging that we understood all students craved before arriving on campus.

LESSON LEARNED: COURSE CORRECTIONS

By 2018, we had considered many of the previous ideas and redesigned Summer Launch. As mentioned before, new stakeholders emerged, thus paving the way for the development of a brand-new, paid Summer Launch Student Ambassador position like the FGEN Ambassador position already created for use during the school year. The Summer Launch Ambassador position was official, which entailed making payments to Ambassadors due to an additional private donation secured with help from UP's Development staff. The endeavor was to enhance Summer Launch's objective, allow for greater success with its established program goals, and deepen the impact of the experiences. Finally, one of the current FGEN Student Ambassadors served as the first-ever Student Summer Launch Coordinator. Once hired, she spent countless hours with the Program Manager designing training for her Summer Launch Ambassador staff, finalizing the schedule, and contacting all necessary stakeholders.

Participant and Program Expansion

UP had recently expanded its definition of the first-generation student to include students where neither parent nor guardian had earned a four-year college degree. More students were contacted to ask if they might be interested in attending the Summer Launch event. Ambassadors came to campus to reach out via phone to personally invite students to attend the event. Also, all participants were asked to apply to participate in the event and if selected, provide a $75 deposit, which helped to offset expenses related to food and housing. The rationale was to increase participant buy-in for the event and to gauge interest in attendance. Fee remission was offered for participants through an additional application process.

In the second iteration of Summer Launch, we addressed gaps perceived by students due to the hidden curriculum in the classroom. While students would be going through the orientation process a few days before school, there would be no formal classroom interaction with professors prior to class. Several national summer bridge programs offered course classes for credit, but what if we did something different and unique? According to past participants, students wanted to encounter and interact with professors during Summer Launch.

FACULTY STAKEHOLDERS CREATED A MOCK CLASS EXPERIENCE

We approached two professors with the idea of creating a "mock class" during Summer Launch. While the experience would not be for credit, it would function as a model for what students would encounter in the coming weeks as first-year, first-generation students. Could the professors create a "mock syllabus," go through the syllabus, and explain its significance in general terms? For instance, the professor could offer due dates included on a calendar/tracking system. Office hours could be discussed by the professor. Our classroom management system, Moodle, could be used, so students can begin to understand how UP faculty use this to enhance the classroom experience. Finally, the professor could offer qualitative feedback to participants. As students enter the mock class, the faculty member could take a few moments and talk about the importance of seat selection on the first day of class. Why is class participation important early in the semester, even if one feels a bit nervous? The possibilities were endless, and staff got to work collaborating with faculty stakeholders. We ultimately decided to offer participants a "mock writing assignment." The FGEN Ambassadors would help with the writing prompt that evening, participants would turn the assignment in, and faculty would return the writing assignment with feedback about how the participant would have done had it been a genuine college assignment. Finally, participants would leave with feedback from a professor. This experience sought to address the concern that participants were still not feeling confident about the nuances of the college transition, and feedback might help to build confidence as research had demonstrated that it was critical for first-time FGEN students' success.

LEVERAGING PORTLAND'S NATURAL BEAUTY FOR GROUP SUCCESS

We implemented another experience unique to UP and the Portland area. Two faculty members lived locally at Sauvie Island, a 15-minute drive from campus. Sauvie Island is known as an area rich with hiking trails, crops, agriculture, and natural beauty. During spring 2019, we asked the faculty if they would collaborate for Summer Launch. We discovered that one faculty member owned a berry farm adjacent to their home. What if participants could pick berries at this faculty member's home and after, ask some of the professors' questions about what to expect in the upcoming college experiences in a casual farm environment? The faculty members readily agreed, and we had had an additional experience unique to Summer Launch.

Last, we engaged with Outdoor Pursuits, the office on the UP campus that leads outdoor excursions for students, as well as offering free equipment to check out. The staff agreed to lead students on a low-stakes hike on Sauvie Island. The hike also gave students an opportunity for connecting with one another while exploring the local Portland area. Each student checked out a bicycle and we rode bicycles together down to a local park. Our excursion included lunch and interaction with one another. We felt confident that this newly designed Summer Launch accounted not just for the academic information, but also created a sense of belonging for all participants.

LESSON LEARNED: VALUE OF PROGRAM ASSESSMENT

Summer Launch has continued to grow and progress, mostly due to its focus on the assessment of established goals and outcomes for the FGEN program. It was clear that Summer Launch needed to be fine-tuned as it continued to grow, but adjustments needed to be strategic and based on current best practices. In addition, it was important to consider student opinions. These were the considerations while re-examining Summer Launch. The Committee designed both a qualitative and quantitative survey for both student participants and volunteers when Summer Launch was first designed. This data helped to gain a short-term and long-term assessment of the first Summer Launch iteration to inform revisions.

As Summer Launch continued to evolve, these assessments also shifted gradually to fit the structure of the program. We realized that if we truly wanted to design a comprehensive and successful summer bridge/pre-orientation program, we needed to be clear that the program was accomplishing its intended goals and objectives. Thus, assessment became a critical component of Summer Launch's informed structural changes. During the most recent Summer Launch, with the assistance of UP's Office of Institutional Research, we asked quantitative and qualitative survey questions anonymously of all Summer Launch participants. For this purpose, we used a Likert scale comprising the following: strongly agree, agree, neutral, disagree, strongly disagree.

Twenty participants opted in to respond, and the results helped to assess if the event met desired goals and outcomes. Figure 3.1 offers the detailed responses from the 20 participant responses.

As evidenced from Figure 3.1, 90% of the participants strongly agreed that the program was informative, thus meeting the outcomes of *instilling an awareness of UP's resources and culture* unique to the UP-college experience. Similarly, 80% strongly agreed that they would build positive relationships with other students while also networking with other students, thus fostering *student engagement and*

Assessment Question	Likert Scale Response	Percentage
Summer Launch was informative	Strongly Agree	90%
I had an opportunity to network with other first-generation students	Strongly Agree	80%
I was able to build positive relationships with other students	Strongly Agree	80%
Because of Summer Launch, I am aware of the support system UP provides	Strongly Agree	75%

Figure 3.1 2019 Summer Launch Participant Survey Responses

belonging. Also, the fact that 75% of participants strongly agreed that they became aware of the support system UP provides met the outcome of gaining a *better understanding of UP processes*.

When asked in an open-ended portion about the best part of Summer Launch, one participant shared the following:

> Meeting the other first-generation freshmen, who I had the privilege to meet. I say this because not only are they reflective of me, but we also formed a bond we can carry into our fall semester. This is important for the sole reason that we need a support group; and we now have the UP FGEN family to be there for us. That, I believe, is something that is irreplaceable, especially at a special point in life where we are, for the first time, able to be independent and learn more about ourselves.

FIRST-GEN ONWARD – WHAT HAVE WE ACCOMPLISHED?

Goals and outcomes for the Summer Launch initiative mirrored those that were identified for the overarching FGEN program's development. These included developing a specific awareness of UP's culture and awareness, fostering student engagement and belonging, gaining an understanding of UP processes to demystify the hidden curriculum, and learning and building upon success skills for academic achievement.

First, upon considering facilitating awareness of UP's culture for first-generation students, we analyzed systems already in place by UP. Currently, UP has a single orientation format that runs before the start of school, typically taking three to four days. We looked at experiences, information, or systems that were not a part of the general orientation process but could be vital to our goals and outcomes. This informed, for example, Summer Launch's mock class experience, and the emphasis placed upon facilitating meaningful (formal and informal) interactions with faculty and staff. This also informed having a mock assignment and feedback from a faculty member, as students would become embedded into the student-professor relationship prior to class. This experience involved an emphasis on success skills, further layering for participants what to expect as a college student in the coming weeks.

Next, when seeking to foster student engagement and belonging, we looked at creative ways that participants and stakeholders could come together in a neutral environment for honest conversation. The idea of having informal conversations with two faculty members on their local farm creatively addressed this outcome. Students could have their first connection with a UP faculty member to be an informal one that modeled the family spirit of UP. We provided participants with the bonus of an outdoor experience together, which modeled that outdoor recreation was a mere ten minutes away.

Summer Launch assessment data connects back to our established outcomes for the FGEN program. As an example, between 75 to 80% of Summer Launch participants suggest that their experience allowed them to build positive relationships with others while creating awareness for UP support systems. This data reinforces our greater FGEN outcomes of a) the FGEN program fostering student engagement and belonging for its students and b) FGEN students developing a specific awareness of UP resources and culture. This informal assessment data confirms that Summer Launch participants are experiencing the intended outcomes for the greater FGEN program.

What We Didn't Expect

Unlike before, Summer Launch Ambassadors served as connectors between faculty/staff and participants, which allowed for a better understanding of UP processes. It was common for us to observe incoming participants pull aside Ambassadors and ask for clarification after a session. In one instance, a participant asked an Ambassador if they could learn more about the degree auditing software mentioned in one of the day's sessions by a staff member. During the evening, we observed as the Ambassador promptly opened her laptop on cue and offered a training session on how to use the software while additional FGEN participants gathered around enthusiastically. Participants' access to trained peer leaders removed barriers, encouraged them to ask questions, and gave students the necessary insights into building self-confidence.

The participant/Student Ambassador connection was meaningful for both parties throughout Summer Launch, which surpassed our expectations. While participants were in the middle of their orientation, several stopped our Ambassador leaders and asked how they could serve in a similar role next summer for the next group of incoming students. This was surprising as this gave us informal feedback that positive connections, and a sense of belonging, were taking place. Within one to two days, participants already felt a sense of ownership that this was *their* community, even though classes had yet to commence. Ambassadors, in turn, took their leadership seriously and had no hesitation in offering layered advice or support, even if it was by doing a quick lesson, as mentioned, on a laptop.

LESSONS LEARNED

In reflecting upon Summer Launch's evolution over time, impactful lessons learned along the way have been most important. As the program shifted from one year to the next, important themes of note began to emerge.

Lesson #1: Invest Personal Time in People and Relationships Right Away

Summer Launch has evolved into its current state due to the many lessons that have been learned throughout its development process. One thing that cannot be stressed enough is the importance of finding the FGEN student champions on campus. As Summer Launch required additional structure, this required additional stakeholders as well. For example, additional funds became necessary to assist with the marketing and costs of the event. When considering the new formats and structures, we shared these with the UP Office of Development. They welcomed this feedback, as it allowed their major gifts officers to articulate the vision for FGEN and find ways of serving the students. Faculty and staff are also critical first-generation champions. Even if funds are limited, it is important to invest time in getting to know people on campus that have an interest in first-generation or identify as first-generation graduates themselves. Ask these stakeholders to share their thoughts and reflections throughout the school year and connect them with students in a fun and informal way as we did. As big ideas emerge when working with stakeholders, resist the urge to build and create something vast right away. Instead, find value in taking the time to learn the culture of the campus community, make mistakes, and create time to tell the Summer Launch narrative with enthusiasm to potential partners.

Lesson #2: Emphasis on the Experience Itself, Less on Educating and Transferring Information

During the first few iterations of Summer Launch, we placed the emphasis on having participants learn information before matriculating to campus in the early fall. We wanted incoming first-generation students to feel there weren't any gaps or lack of knowledge. While this is a critical outcome to present information to incoming freshmen, we saw that the information was better received when participants underwent experiential learning opportunities. For example, in Summer Launch 1–3, we emphasized participants' involvement. We suggested that Outdoor Pursuits was a great way for students to meet one another and diversify their UP campus experience by renting recreational equipment or going on a hiking trip. However, engaging with Outdoor Pursuits was emphasized via a PowerPoint lesson, and students had met their capacity for retaining new information. This was a mistake we made in our curriculum design. Therefore, we shifted from sharing useful information and opportunities, to modeling or immersing students within them. With Outdoor Pursuits, we changed our design. The format went from a PowerPoint presentation to a field trip format, where we took participants to the building, showed them how to check out equipment, and led them on a neighborhood bike ride to the park where we had a picnic. This way, participants had the chance to meet one another, and get a better understanding of how this process worked. We built on this experience to include the aforementioned low-stakes hiking trip to nearby Sauvie Island. Our desired outcome was for participants to recognize that there were vast outdoor experiences just a few minutes away. This allowed Summer Launch to plant seeds of knowledge with participants.

Lesson #3: Peer-to-Peer Exchanges Are Valued above All Else

One of the most important adjustments for Summer Launch was deepening and formalizing UP first-generation current student involvement. Information is valuable, but even more valuable when it comes from peers. Throughout Summer Launch, we encouraged leaders to be truthful when responding to questions. This way, we could start building a bridge of trust between our FGEN program, returning FGEN students, and the participants that would be coming to campus shortly.

Lesson #4: Designing the Paid Summer Launch Ambassador Position Was Critical

In previous iterations of Summer Launch, we had asked students if they would be interested in helping as volunteers for the event. From a financial standpoint, this was terrific, but it did not facilitate accountability for those assisting. Moreover, officially establishing the Ambassador positions, coupled with the fact that UP was investing resources for success, implied added significance of the event. After establishing the position, we interviewed, hired, and trained the students who had applied for the openings. This process made the event leap to a higher level. One outcome that was not anticipated was the impact this would have on the Ambassadors. For many, serving as Ambassadors empowered them as well, and changed their experience for the remainder of their time at UP. One Ambassador shared, "I really enjoyed getting the opportunity to be able to help these incoming first-generation students and give them the advice that I wish I could have received when I was in their position." Added another, "I enjoyed the outdoor activities, getting to know not only the participants, but the fellow ambassadors as well. It felt good to have participants ask me questions."

Lesson #5: Importance of Relationships

UP is an extremely relational and collaborative campus. Our mission as a Catholic, Liberal Arts, Congregation of Holy Cross institution is deeply rooted in community. Faculty and staff are eager to increase their involvement, especially if it will contribute to student success. We learned that establishing relationships is key, but also using them is critical. This enhanced participant buy-in and created a greater sense of belonging for all. In addition, many members of the Committee shared that they became drawn into supporting first-generation students. Students and their voices are important. It is important to create time and space for first-generation students.

DEMYSTIFYING POWER RELATIONSHIPS

Upon establishing Summer Launch, much of our assessment revealed that students appreciated our efforts to demystify the faculty/student relationship, but it still seemed both foreign and intimidating. For example, it is quite possible in high school, many first-generation students may only have had to speak to a teacher when they found something wrong or challenging, and this might have shaped their understanding of building relationships in colleges as well. We learned how important it was to take nothing for granted and assume that students may have no understanding of what the relationship should be. We wanted to attack this notion of the "hidden curriculum." As a result, we challenged this perception early on and found that Summer Launch was as good a place to do so. Creating an inviting space, such as the faculty member's farm, and building relationship with faculty, was both memorable and invaluable. Participants walked away with a positive experience engaging with faculty that built up their confidence.

"YOU ANSWERED QUESTIONS THAT I DIDN'T KNOW I EVEN HAD"

This was a comment shared by a participant, not on a questionnaire, but overheard in conversation while casually strolling on campus. According to our observations, FGEN students don't know what questions to ask, given they have not been previously immersed in the college setting. Once information and experiences intersect, and peers are accessible, questions begin to emerge. Moreover, we have seen that the assessment process takes on many forms, and informal assessment is just as important as a formal assessment. As a program leader, being mindful and present to all that is taking place, and being a good listener and observer is an incredible form of program leadership. Written surveys are good, but keep in mind feelings and observations are best at the moment.

Lesson #6: Take the Pressure off Participants to "Remember Everything"

We learned a great theme from one of the Committee members from Academic Affairs. In her work with UP students, she often shares:

> I just shared a lot of info with you; I don't expect you to remember it all. I've been taking notes for us. If you drop by later, even tomorrow, and ask me to repeat everything, I am happy to do so.

We found that offering this layer to participants on the first day of Summer Launch proved invaluable. Coach them to relax, soak in information, and not to capture it all by taking copious notes. According to our observation, this strategy creates a happier and more authentic Summer Launch experience for all.

CONCLUSION

The growth model of UP's Summer Launch has been substantial to over 100 first-generation students at the university. It has offered each participant the chance to build confidence, create friendships with peers, and have a much better grasp of the foreign land of college that they are about to enter. While our context at the University of Portland is unique, we believe there are many similarities between our conceptual framework and that of other institutions looking to build or improve their FGEN program. In the end, we hope that future students welcome the opportunity to participate so that each can be genuinely welcomed. The students must feel as if they belong and have something to offer the college community. As student practitioners, our constant challenge is to hold up individual mirrors to students, confirming the gifts and talents they possess that we see every day, and to create spaces and opportunities where individuals can continue to explore their passions and work hard to actualize their dreams.

REFERENCES

Bandura, A. (1977). Self-efficacy: Toward a unifying theory of behavioral change. *Psychological Review, 84*(2), 191 215.

Center for First-Generation Student Success (n.d.). About the center and first-gen forward. https://firstgen.naspa.org/about-the-center

Collier, P., & Morgan, D. (2008). Is that paper really due today? Differences in First Generation and traditional college students' understandings of faculty expectations. *Higher Education, 55*, 425 446.

Donohoo, J., Hattie, J. & Eells, R. (2018). The power of collective efficacy. *Educational Leadership*, 75(6), 40 44.

Lamb, J. (2020, December 16). The power of scholarships and mentorship. *Giving at UP*. https://www.giving.up.edu/s/1797/doc.aspx?sid=1797&gid=2&pgid=964

Pike, G., & Kuh, G. (2005). First-and second-generation college students: A comparison of their engagement and intellectual development. *Journal of Higher Education*, 76(3), 276 300.

Redford, J., & Hoyer, K. (2017). First-generation and continuing-generation college students: A comparison of high school and postsecondary experiences (NCES 2018-009). U.S. Department of Education. National Center for Education Statistics. Retrieved from: https://nces.ed.gov/pubsearch/pubsinfo.asp?pubid=2018009

Chapter 4

From Denied to the Dean's List

Program Design that Makes a Difference

Erin L. Kline and Jefferson Lee IV

This chapter is an overview of the development and implementation of a pilot program designed to address the educational equity gaps that exist at Southwest Minnesota State University (SMSU). Similarly, as seen across the state and other institutions of higher education, SMSU is working to implement programs, culturally responsive pedagogy, and other intentional equity-based practices and policies to address the disparities seen in graduation rates among first-generation students of color. Minnesota has one of the highest equity gaps for students of color in the nation, which is reflective of the impact of institutional racism and a history of inequitable policies, practices, and procedures (Minnesota State, n.d.). The university's focus on diversity, equity, and inclusion helped to launch the Mustang Pathway Program (MPP) in the summer of 2020 where it hosted 17 first-generation students. Placing equity at the center of program design, implementation, and student experience is at the heart of what drives programming that makes a difference in the lives of the students who are served. Equity by design must have commitment and support from leadership in order for institutions to be student-ready spaces (Landrieu and Shah, 2020; Whitford, 2018). The Mustang Pathway Program is designed based on these principles and is the result of identifying the equity gaps that exist on the SMSU campus.

OVERVIEW

SMSU is a liberal arts university tucked in the agricultural corner of the state sharing borders with South Dakota and Iowa. SMSU is known for its affordable, high-quality liberal arts education with degree programs that range from accounting to the culinary arts, and is known for educating Minnesota's K-12 teachers, farmers, entrepreneurs, historians, social workers, and medical professionals. Southwest Minnesota State University follows the Minnesota State system guidelines for identifying first-generation status, which outlines this status based on the education level of the parent(s) who the student regularly lives with.

These guidelines also state that the parent can have a post-high school degree other than a four-year bachelor's degree, and reflects the guidelines established by the Higher Education Act (Sharpe, 2017). As of 2018, the SMSU campus is comprised of 50.4% first-generation students, a status that is not new to the campus. That percentage has remained relatively unchanged, however; 25–30% of students categorized as first-generation are also members of the Black, Indigenous, People of Color (BIPOC) subset of the population, a group increasing in number on campus. The Mustang Pathway Program largely developed in response to a desire to improve access for first-generation and BIPOC populations, specifically among those in the population who were denied admission to the university. Therefore, this program serves both BIPOC individuals and white or European American students who qualify as first-generation students. The program works as a bridge for students to have an opportunity to demonstrate what they are capable of when they would have otherwise been denied admission due to the circumstances surrounding their academic performance in high school.

A fundamentally important element of this type of program is the collaboration between the faculty, staff, and personnel who support students admitted to MPP. Literature on college and university program development clearly outlines the value and importance of feeling a sense of belonging on the college campus (Means and Pyne, 2017). These practices must extend to the entire campus to truly impact the ability of the institution to retain first-generation students and students of color (Means and Pyne, 2017). This sense of belonging is clearly an extension of the role that faculty and staff play in supporting the work of the program and the students who benefit from it.

Fostering a sense of belonging also includes the ability of the program to help students cultivate their own cultural capital and recognize it as an asset in the collegiate environment. It is important to note that many of our students came to us already with high levels of emotional intelligence and resiliency as well as an awareness of their cultural assets. However, it was in many cases, the first time in their academic careers where these skills were identified and named as valuable contributors to their education, defined as a source of cultural capital (Gary and Swinton, 2017; O'Shea, 2016; Stephens et al., 2014; Yosso, 2005).

Research continues to provide supportive evidence for program design that emphasizes individual agency, enhancement of cultural assets, influential peer mentors, and the opportunity to access "difference-education" interventions (Gray and Swinton, 2017; Kiyama and Luca, 2014; O'Shea, 2016; Stephens et al., 2014; Yosso, 2005). Fostering a sense of belonging focuses on creating an environment that is student-ready, where students interact with support personnel, but also see themselves represented in the curriculum, their peer mentors, and participate in programming that normalizes their experience within higher education (Stephens et al., 2014). We see this represented in Stephens et al.'s (2014) work where the focus is on the use of difference-education interventions that bring first-year, first-generation students into contact with upper-level first-generation students through panel discussions that emphasize the value of difference and educational success. This level of agency building begins with the creation of a framework that is affirmed by other students who have come from or represent similar educational backgrounds.

Ultimately, through this process, programming can be developed that includes elements of difference-education (Stephens et al., 2014), Community Cultural Wealth Walk (Fujimoto et al., 2016), and an awareness of Community Cultural Wealth (O'Shea, 2016). All of which can be woven together to inform programming, equitable design, curriculum, and support pillars required to propel students toward their academic goals. In addition, this type of programming and knowledge strives to eliminate racial, ethnic, gender, and class bias that traditionally has been used as the measure of academic achievement and success (Gary and Swinton, 2017; Kendi, 2019; Kiyama and Luca Guillen, 2014; O'Shea, 2016; Stephens et al., 2014; Yosso, 2005). The steps taken to develop a program where equity is the guiding principle, and where multiculturalism is emphasized and valued require intentional practices that equity by design helps to outline.

Equity by design provides a lens through which one can view how a program is constructed, for example, who is invited to speak, what the focus of the topic includes, where the program is held, etc. (McNair et al., 2020). An element of equity by design is offering a tool that is accessible to students, while also working to change practices involved in program and policy development. One such tool is the use of peer mentors as a part of student support infrastructure (Beltman et al., 2019; Kiyama and Luca Guillen, 2014; McNair et al., 2020). The role of peer mentors can be a valuable source of decoding the hidden curriculum that exists within higher education, and can provide helpful insights and support for students as they proceed through academia (Beltman et al., 2019; Downing and Brennan, 2019; Gabriel, 2008; Kiyama, 2018; Kiyama and Luca Guillen, 2014; Yosso, 2005). Peer mentors provide an excellent opportunity for difference-education interventions (Stephens et al., 2014), and can also be a valuable source of recruitment and retention. Furthermore, the use of peer mentors paired with equity by design, which emphasize enhanced access, student academic success, and student engagement and support (Beltman et al., 2019; Landrieu and Shah, 2020; Means and Pyne, 2017), is a powerful intersection of connection, belonging, and evidence-based practices.

PROGRAM DESCRIPTION

The Mustang Pathway Program is an adaptive entry program with transition points that meet students where they are. The program is designed to help students develop perseverance and resilience, experience academic and personal success, and matriculate to graduation. Students in the MPP begin their work at Southwest Minnesota State University in a free five-week summer experience that aims to strengthen English, reading, and math skills in a highly interactive, student-centered environment. The Mustang Pathway Program provides students with access to opportunities they would traditionally be denied due to their academic history. Students who have a high school GPA of a 1.7–2.5 or an ACT score of 14–20 are invited to take part in the five-week residential summer program that prepares them for admission to the university.

Another important aspect of programming is the development of influential and positive academic and social relationships. The program supports peer-to-peer mentoring and relationship building, and provides opportunities to do so throughout the five-week summer program and during the academic year. Furthermore, the program focuses on the importance of mentorships with university staff and faculty through the process of career exploration. At the root of the peer mentoring and career exploration is the outgrowth of collaborative relationships and experiences that "enhances the quality of life for students" (Magolda 2005 as quoted in Marquez Kiyama 2018, p.36).

The next phase of the Mustang Pathway Program is students' participation in a first-year cohort. Successful Pathway students are required to enroll in the Pathway Scholars cohort for the fall and spring of the academic year that follows the summer program. Pathway Scholars is comprised of MPP students who earned a minimum of a C in the summer program courses. Their participation in the Pathways Scholars cohort further establishes their connection and commitment to success. Students are exposed to a variety of programming as Pathway collaborates with the Office of Diversity and Inclusion, Access Opportunity Success, and the Student Success and Advising Center among other offices. Additional support services include programming that emphasizes developing leadership skills, effective study strategies developed in nearly 200 hours of guided study tables, and residing in a Living and Learning Community where characteristics of student success are demonstrated and celebrated.

RECRUITMENT ACTIVITIES

Recruitment activities were a challenging aspect of program implementation, but campus visits and virtual campus tours helped with these efforts. Recruitment involves sharing the culture of your campus with prospective students and helping them to imagine themselves as students at the university. Part of this process is helping students understand the journey they are about to begin. It was important to work directly with admission counselors to ensure they had an understanding of how to present an alternate admission program. This required discussing the objectives of the program and who the program serves, and when possible, participating in organized and scheduled recruitment events.

Other forms of recruitment relied on connections with statewide programs, local and regional high schools, and their student support staff. It is through these relationships that opportunities were created to inform counselors, teachers, and administrators about the benefits of the program and the program-targeted audience. Students who have underperformed in high school are often automatically excluded from pursuing a four-year college or university. We recognize these students as untapped potential. We have found that counselors and other administrators are simultaneously confused and delighted when we share with them the fact that we are looking to recruit students with GPAs below a 2.5.

One way we helped counselors and administrators better understand the program was by offering short online informational sessions. We provided informational sessions for high school counselors, teachers, and other school administrators to learn about the program. We sent a survey link that allowed them to select a date for one of the sessions. We also provided the option for them to request an individual Zoom session with the program directors. In addition, virtual tours that highlighted specific offices and services that intersect with the program were scheduled throughout the year. Current MPP students also participated in the virtual visits and discussed their experience in the program.

One especially effective recruitment strategy was utilizing current students to call prospective students. Current students shared information about the program, answered questions, and directed prospective students to apply to the program using an online application. These recruitment calls were guided by the director of the program; however, students were encouraged to develop their own scripts for the calls. In addition, emphasizing the importance of discussing this opportunity as a *referral* as opposed to being *denied* admission to the university, was a key part of this recruitment call. Traditional recruitment efforts included traveling to area high schools to meet with high school counselors, students, and staff in after-school programs. We also worked to build trust with parents and family members as they made decisions that impact their child's educational future.

Finally, applicants who did not meet university admission standards were referred to the MPP. The language used in admissions denial letters was changed to state students are *referred* to SMSU's Mustang Pathway Program for an alternate admission opportunity. Changing the language from *denied* to *referred* is an important part of changing how we think of and respond to students involved in the program.

FUNDING AND MARKETING STRATEGIES

A grant from the system office was used to support the launch of the pilot program. An additional source of funding was a Foundation Grant awarded by the university's Foundation Office. The university is supportive of developing a long-term strategy that includes allocation of funding sources for the program; however, at the time of writing, these sources of funding have not been determined. Potential funding sources include the statewide system office, the university's Foundation Office, private donors, and grants. The University Foundation Office has secured a $50,000 anonymous donation to support future students in the program.

The marketing plan for the Mustang Pathway Program emphasized meeting students where they are along their academic journey. It included language, as mentioned earlier, that emphasized a referral process as opposed to a denial strategy. Additionally, in our brochure and public presentations we indicate we are seeking *students of promise* where life circumstances may have gotten in the way of academic success. Marketing strategies also included the use of digital marketing platforms, a free online application, and text messaging campaigns that included links to the webpage and contact information for the program director.

IMPLEMENTATION

SMSU welcomed 18 Mustang Pathway students to campus for the July 2020 pilot program. Move-in day was organized by the MPP peer mentors as they guided and helped move students' personal items into their individual rooms. The MPP partnered with Chartwells, the residential dining services, to provide a welcome picnic for students and their families. The goal of the day was to provide an exciting and welcoming atmosphere as students and their families settled into their new environment.

A series of informational and orientation sessions started the first evening on campus. Sessions included a brief overview of university and program policies and provided fun interactive programming. Students were introduced to their peer mentors and peer groups and reviewed the schedule for the coming weeks. They began to connect with other students in the program through several Kahoot! quizzes and interactive discussions. The days that followed included a series of brief orientation sessions, a campus scavenger hunt, building trust and bonding as a group.

Students also completed the ACCUPLACER reading and English tests to assess their prior learning. As part of our partnership with the local Adult Basic Education program, also housed on our campus, students agreed to a pre- and post-test in reading. This form of summative assessment helped us understand students' strengths and weaknesses, and was used in conjunction with other formative assessment measures.

The intentional design of the summer program included multiple interventions and touch points with students that began with our Launch Sessions. Launch Sessions focused on time management, navigating Desire 2 Learn Brightspace, communicating with faculty, online learning strategies, and a variety of motivational topic areas. Launch sessions provided meaningful and practical information that students used to assist them with transitioning to college.

On the second day of the program, students began courses in English, reading, and Global Experience. The Global Experience course included instruction in student success and connected current events to the learning process and the course content. This can be a powerful way of utilizing culturally relevant pedagogy that brings students to the center of the learning process. This course was also used to facilitate mandatory study tables and student success programming focused on helping students find personal motivation and success in higher education.

Other campus offices or departments that we partnered with included Counseling and Testing and Health Services. Students sometimes experience a high level of stress and anxiety as they participate in an intensive five-week summer program, and having the necessary health services available is an important part of supporting student success. Furthermore, it allowed for students to become familiar with these services and recognize that utilizing mental health support is part of academic and personal progress. Peer mentors played an important role in supporting students academically, but also offered even greater social and emotional support.

The implementation of the peer mentoring component began with the hiring and training of a group of current students who are primarily self-identified as first-generation students able to provide "difference-education" interventions (Stephens et al., 2014). For example, skilled peer mentors should be individuals with a high level of emotional intelligence who are able to share their personal experiences with students and are able to gauge the needs of a student. As the program progressed, each mentor found their strengths and demonstrated the importance of collaboration to reach individual and group success. In this process, students began to see that they too have the skills and intellectual abilities to become leaders as they witnessed this among their peers. We have seen these experiences and relationships continue into the academic year and act as sources of support and encouragement for both the mentor and mentee.

Faculty selection involved meeting with departmental chairs or department heads to discuss programmatic needs. Faculty who demonstrated excellence in culturally responsive pedagogy or worked with designing developmental courses were highly sought after. The ability of the faculty to establish trust and build relationships has tremendous value in furthering academic achievement for student groups. Such relationships were fostered in the classroom through the presentation of course content, but also through the assessment process. For example, formative assessment involves a high level of detailed feedback in order to establish a feedback loop. This feedback loop was part of the assessment process that continued outside of classroom instruction in the form of individual conferences with course instructors. Students were expected to be prepared to engage and participate in the assessment process, thereby creating a higher level of investment by the student in the learning process. The feedback loop was established at the start of the program; however, it became more elemental in the third week of the program in the form of individual conferences. The timing of these conferences aligned with when students completed the ACCUPLACER post-test and the Adult Basic Education reading test known as the College and Career Readiness Standards for Adult Education (CCRS). This pivot point is where decisions were made about remaining in the program. Student progress was assessed based on classroom performance, assessment tests, individual conferences with instructors, and contributions from peer mentors on social and behavioral issues. Assessing student progress at this point in the program was critical as it offered unsuccessful students an opportunity to pursue other alternatives prior to the start of most academic years. This feature of the program reflects equity by design and our commitment to student success on a variety of levels.

STAKEHOLDERS

In addition to the campus stakeholders previously mentioned, the SMSU Foundation office has provided program support. The Foundation has been an avenue for connecting and informing alumni of the efforts of the Mustang Pathway Program. The Foundation has helped us share how we are supporting first-generation college students. The $50,000 anonymous donation was a result of a feature story about the university's efforts to support first-generation students, students of color, and PELL Grant-eligible students.

Other important stakeholders include the admission office counselors and staff that identify potential students and develop recruitment strategies. Additional stakeholders can include partners like Financial Aid, Residence Life, the Office of Diversity and Inclusion, Access Opportunity Success, Counseling and Testing, Disability Services, Career Services, Health Services, Institutional Research and Reporting, and the Student Success and Advising Center. We utilize campus-wide professional development days to build relationships with these partners and to share best practices that might be beneficial to program participants.

As mentioned earlier in the chapter, equity by design is data-driven programmatic change that moves the institution toward being a student-ready institution, which requires understanding the institution's blind spots and equity gaps. Such an endeavor requires direct and consistent communication with the institution's Research and Reporting Office. From this perspective the programming should reflect the institutional gaps and allow for programming to fill those gaps or at least begin to address them. It is through this process where data-driven decision-making reflective of the institution's understanding of equity can assist in the process of creating a space that fosters growth and belonging and is ready to meet the needs of different student groups.

ASSESSMENT PLAN

The Mustang Pathway Program utilized multiple measures to holistically evaluate student progress in the program. Students in the summer program took English, reading, and a math workshop taught by instructors skilled in developmental education techniques and strategies. Students also completed an ACCUPLACER pre-test and post-test for English and reading during the third week of the program. Students benefited from one-to-one student to faculty conferences where they discussed progress strategies for successfully completing the course content. A secondary evaluative measure was peer mentors' use of formative assessment strategies. Students were assigned a peer mentor to work with throughout the summer program and participated in a feedback loop focused on student progress. A program evaluation was administered in the final week that speaks directly to the experience of the students.

OUTCOMES

Most students entering the program were students who experienced social, emotional, and life situations that interrupted their high school academic experience, and impacted their ability to maintain a GPA required for admission to SMSU. Students accepted to the MPP had high school GPAs that ranged from 1.48 to 2.50 and reported ACT scores of 14 to 19. A total of 94% were PELL eligible, 62.5% were students of color, and 62.5% were first-generation students. By the end of the program 14 students (87.5%) earned at least a B or higher in all three courses (including developmental courses) (see Table 4.1). Program GPAs ranged from 2.40 to 4.0. The summer program was designed to utilize multiple interventions to foster a highly capable, resilient, and motivated group. Of the 18 who began the program, 16 (89%) were admitted to the university and enrolled in 15 course credits with Pathway Scholars.

Study tables were an important part of developing foundational study skills, time management, and collaboration with students and peer mentors. Students attended two mandatory study tables twice per day, often studying and working on class projects for upwards of six hours per day. In sum, students spent anywhere between 210 and 220 hours over the course of five weeks in study tables.

In the first week of the program, students took an ACCUPLACER test and a College and Career Readiness Standards for Adult Education (CCRS) pre-test in English and reading. An overview of test results revealed a marked increase in the English and reading scores in ACCUPLACER among the students who completed both the pre- and post-tests (see Figure 4.1). Four students tested directly into the college level English course (ENG 151) on the pre-test, thus were not asked to complete the post-test. While the average score increased ten points, one student's score increased 21 points.

Table 4.1 Grade Percentages by Course

	English (%)	Reading (%)	Global Experience (%)
Earned a B or Higher	93.75	93.75	100
Earned an A- or Higher	37.5	62.5	87.5

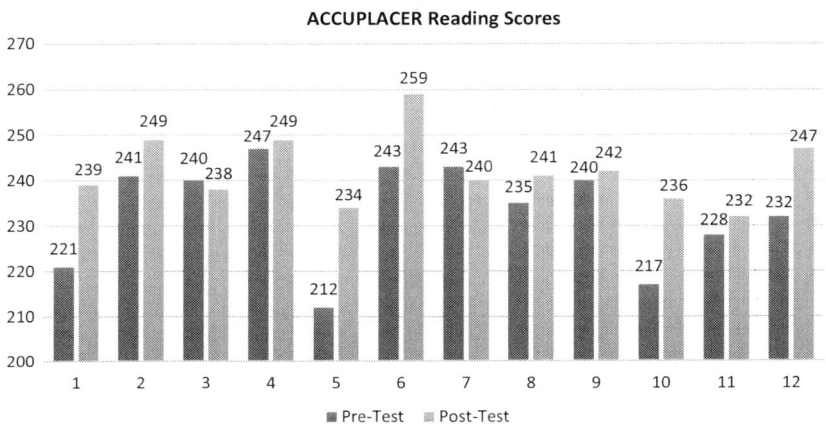

Figure 4.1 Accuplacer Reading Scores

MPP students engaged with the campus community through a variety of clubs and organizations. Three students were accepted to the new eSports team, one of whom was offered a scholarship to play for the team and is a team captain. Multiple students began working in a wide variety of positions across campus. Students became actively involved in campus clubs and organizations including student senate, the Black Student Union, campus ministry, Living and Learning Community "Achieve" meetings, and twice weekly study tables in the Academic Commons.

STUDENT EVALUATION OF THE PROGRAM

In the last week of the summer program, students completed an anonymous program evaluation available as a Forms Survey. Below is an excerpt from the qualitative section of the student evaluation.

> I believe this program made me feel more prepared for college which I was so overwhelmed about. I met amazing people and I learned how to be responsible and independent.
>
> (MPP Student Evaluation)

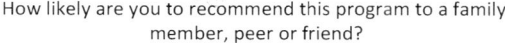

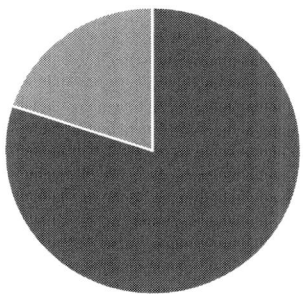

Figure 4.2 Students Who Recommend the Program

> The opportunity meant more than many will ever know. I walked in without knowing what to expect, but within five weeks, learned that no matter what, keep [sic] being UGLY, keep pushing because at the end it's you and your choices.
>
> (MPP Student Evaluation)

> The program has helped me a lot. I feel more confident when it comes to college and I learned how to construct an academic essay. I also learned patience!
>
> (MPP Student Evaluation)

Students were asked questions about their overall experience in the program, the difficulty level of courses, and the program impact on college preparation. One hundred percent of the respondents indicated that their experience in the MPP positively impacted how prepared they felt for college. A total of 80% of the students who took the survey indicated that they were "very likely" to recommend the program to family members and friends, while 20% said they were "somewhat likely" to recommend the program (see Figure 4.2).

LESSONS LEARNED

The outcomes and student feedback suggest the Mustang Pathway summer experience contributed to a positive college transition for the participants. However, it was not without its challenges. Limited staff and resources made it difficult to continuously communicate with applicants and support them through enrollment in the program. Text messaging, emails, and calling campaigns were used to mitigate this challenge. Another challenge was related to mental health services for program participants. There were several instances during the summer where a student demonstrated mental health concerns, but refused to obtain help. This was exacerbated by the fact that mental health and health services staff were accustomed to being off-campus during the summer. This breakdown in communication resulted in challenges connecting students with mental health professionals. Though mental health and health services staff were regularly on-call for students, we underestimated the need for continued mental health support for students in the summer program. As previously stated, most of the students experienced some form of disruption during their high school years that affected their academic performance. In some cases, different forms of trauma can impact an individual's willingness to seek help or support. This was especially evident among some students of color for whom the process of asking for help seemed to escalate concerns around vulnerability and shame (Burke and Brown, 2021). It is important to note that the trauma that some individuals carry with them to college can be especially acute in high stress situations as was experienced in the five-week program.

Another important takeaway from the summer program is the value of intentional, authentic, and supportive relationships developed between peer mentors, mentees, faculty, and staff. Students worked with the same mentor throughout the program allowing them to develop good working relationships, accountability, and trust in the work of the mentor. Some groups worked together better than others, and could have benefited from a more organic organization of mentors and mentees as opposed to assigning mentors a group of students to work with. Mentors and mentees had the opportunity to develop relationships both during their classes and outside of class time. These relationships are crucial to the success of any intensive summer bridge program, but it is important to also ensure the peer mentors are also receiving the support they need from professional staff (Beltman et al. 2019). The role peer mentors play in supporting the continued needs of students cannot be understated, and likely carry over into the academic year. We have addressed this need with the implementation of Pathway Scholars, which operates as the next phase of the program and offers continued advising, tutoring, social and emotional support. Furthermore, the Living and Learning Community, monthly meetings, study tables, work with mental health services, and academic progress meetings continue to meet student needs throughout the academic year.

In summary, communication and active involvement with a variety of offices on campus are key to offering a holistic and supportive program for first-generation students. Interdepartmental collaboration allows campuses to maximize resources including funding and the expertise of faculty and staff to create change. This mirrors the message we share with our students. We stress the importance of building relationships and seeking support and guidance from others on their quest for academic success.

REFERENCES

Beltman, S., Helker, K., & Fischer, S. (2019). 'I really enjoy it': Emotional engagement of university peer mentors. *International Journal of Emotional Education, 11*(2), 50 70.

Burke, T. & Brown, B. Ed. (2021). *You are your best thing: Vulnerability, shame resilience, and the black experience, an anthology*. Penguin Random House UK.

Downing, S., & Brennan, J. (2019). *On Course: Strategies for Creating Success in College, Career, and Life*. Boston, MA: Cengage Learning.

Fujimoto, M. O., Fujimoto, E., & I-Chen, H. (2016). Community culture wealth walk. *Adventures in teaching*. https://profteacher.files.wordpress.com/2016/11/community-cultural-wealth-walk-revised-july-2016-by-oropeza-fujimoto-huangin-progress.pdf

Gabriel, K. (2008). *Teaching unprepared students: Strategies for promoting success and retention in higher education*. Stylus

Gray, J., & Swinton, O. H. (2017). Non-cognitive ability, college learning, and student retention. *The Journal of Negro Education, 86*(1), 65 76. http://www.jstor.org/stable/10.7709/jnegroeducation.86.1.0065?seq=1&cid=pdf-reference#references_tab_contents

Kendi, I. (2019). *How to be an antiracist*. One World, Penguin Random House

Kiyama, J. M. (2018). Relationship and trust-building between researchers and practitioners: Toward educational equity for underserved populations. *Reflections on Connecting Research and Practice in College Access and Success Programs*, 36 42. http://www.pellinstitute.org/downloads/publications-Reflections_06_Venegas.pdf

Kiyama, J. M., & Luca, S. G. (2014). Structured opportunities: Exploring the social and academic benefits for peer mentors in retention programs. *Journal of College Retention, 15*(4), 489 514. http://dx.doi.org/10.2190/CS.15.4.b

Landrieu, J., Shah, P. (2020, May 26). *Equity by design: Discussion with senior academic affairs officers* [Unpublished manuscript]. Office of Equity and Inclusion, Minnesota State.

McNair, T. B., Bensimon, E. M, & Malcom-Piqueux, L. 2020. *From equity talk to equity walk: Expanding practitioner knowledge for racial justice in higher education*. John Wiley & Sons.

Means, D. R. & Pyne, K. B. (2017). Finding my way: Perceptions of institutional support and belonging in low-income, first-Generation, first-year college students. *Journal of College Student Development, 58*(6), 907 924.

Minnesota State Equity 2030. (n.d.). *Minnesota state equity 2030*. Minnesota State. https://www.minnstate.edu/Equity2030/what.html

O'Shea, S. (2016). Avoiding the manufacture of 'sameness': First-in-family students, cultural capital and the higher education environment. *Higher Educ* 72, 59 78. https://doi.org/10.1007/s10734-015-9938-y

Sharpe, R. (2017, November 3). Are you first gen? Depends on who's asking. *The New York Times.* https://www.nytimes.com/2017/11/03/education/edlife/first-generation-college-admissions.html

Stephens, N. M., Hamedani, M. G., & Destin, M. (2014). Closing the social-class achievement gap: A difference-education intervention improves first-generation students' academic performance and all students' college transition. *Psychological Science 25*(4), 943 953.

Whitford, E. (2018, October 4). Maximizing success for first-gen students: More four-year colleges are working to help first-generation college students succeed. But a new report says real progress requires institutional shifts not just adding new programs. *Inside Higher Ed.* https://www.insidehighered.com/news/2018/10/04/institutional-change-required-better-serve-first-generation-students-report-finds

Yosso, T. J. (2005). Whose culture has capital? A critical race theory discussion of community cultural wealth. *Race Ethnicity and Education, 8*(1), 69 91. https://doi.org/10.1080/1361332052000341006

Chapter 5

Developing First-Year Programming for First-Generation Students without A Budget

No Money, No Problem

Charmaine Troy, Ben Pearce, and Diana Rowe

The first year of college is arguably one of the most difficult transitions for incoming students. The first six weeks of college marks a critical time period where many students may drop out due to academic rigor, social interaction and experiences, increased exposure to diversity, and lack of finances. When students experience disconnection from the campus community, the result is often poor academic performance and attrition (Tinto, 2001). As partners in education, faculty and administrators cannot assume that it is solely the responsibility of the student to navigate the campus and its culture on their own. As educators, we should create the best climates for learning and transition to campus life, especially for first-generation students.

INSTITUTIONAL CONTEXT

Opening its doors in 2006 as the first four-year college founded in Georgia in over 100 years, Georgia Gwinnett College provides access to students from underserved populations in the Greater Metropolitan area. With an enrollment of around 11,000 students, 40% of entering students at Georgia Gwinnett College are first-generation. At Georgia Gwinnett College, a first-generation college student is defined as a student whose parents did not earn a bachelor's degree at a four-year college or university.

IMPLEMENTATION

Funding

In order to serve the growing population of first-generation students attending Georgia Gwinnett College, the idea of creating a first-generation learning community was proposed to senior leadership. However, the program had to be proposed utilizing programming components that cost little to nothing for implementation or operation. There was no funding available to create a budget for the Grizzly First Scholars program. While the creation of a first-generation learning community would continue Georgia Gwinnett College's mission by empowering first-generation students with opportunities for holistic development, the learning community was unable to offer scholarships or other financial incentives to first-generation students due to limited availability of funding.

Strategic Programming Efforts

The Grizzly First Scholars learning community was launched in the fall of 2017 and spearheaded by the School of Transitional Studies. The learning community was designed to support first-generation students as they transition from high school to Georgia Gwinnett College. In addition to taking a developmental English (ENGL 0999) and English 1101 course, the scholars were enrolled in a first-year seminar course (GGC 1000) that aids in the development of skills that support academic achievement, including time management, study skills, major selection, research/writing, and information financial literacy. Grizzly First Scholars combined several high-impact practices, including service learning and collaborative learning, aimed at increasing student engagement and success. These skills are applied in a variety of ways across the semester and culminate in a service-learning project. The learning community also prepared first-generation students for their academic and social experience through their first year and beyond by connecting them with peers, faculty/staff, mentors, and campus resources.

GOALS AND OBJECTIVES

Research shows students who get involved in learning communities are more likely to stay in college, earn a higher-grade point average, and experience greater satisfaction during their years in college (Hill and Woodward, 2013). Grizzly First Scholars was built upon the mission of promoting the persistence and graduation rates of first-generation students by developing their academic success skills, providing academic support and connecting them to the larger campus community.

Grizzly First Scholars provides the following core programming components to meet the needs of first-generation students at Georgia Gwinnett College:

- **BEAM Peer Mentoring Program:** The Bears and Encouraging and Mentoring (BEAM) peer mentoring program was created to provide

incoming first-generation students with support from a first-generation upperclassman. The goal of the peer mentoring program was to create more student-to-student interaction among peers. Our initial pool of mentors was unpaid. BEAM peer mentor responsibilities were three-fold: facilitate discussion and community meetings; serve as an academic mentor (academic study skills, academic advising, midterm/finals programming); and event staffing (Fall Meet & Greet and Symposium).
- **Workshops**: A variety of workshops were offered throughout the school year to specifically meet the needs of first-generation students. Workshops included time management, note-taking, study skills, and writing labs.
- **Linked Courses**: The learning community was anchored by two courses: the GGC 1000 First Year Seminar course; a developmental English course (ENGL 0999) and a college-level composition course (ENGL 1101). The GGC 1000 course is a first-year seminar course designed to develop college-level skills for academic success by focusing on life skills, the purpose of higher education, the students' role in a college environment, strategies for academic success, connecting with the GGC campus and surrounding community, and foundations for global learning. Students are encouraged to use critical thinking skills to set goals and make responsible decisions regarding academics, major selection, career planning, and student engagement. The first-year seminar course was taught by academic advisors from the Advising Center.
- **Tutoring**: When the program first began, students received optional weekly math tutoring in the Advising Office from tutors with the Academic Enhancement Center. After two months, tutoring was suspended due to students not using the service.
- **Service Learning**: A service-learning project component was incorporated into the GGC 1000 first-year seminar course to give first-generation students the opportunity to engage with their peers, faculty, staff, and community partners.
- **Curricular Advising**: First-generation students in the learning community were assigned a dedicated student success advisor in the Office of Advising during their first year to ensure proper course selection and advising.

BUILDING A FIRST-GENERATION MENTORING PROGRAM

Unlike traditional mentoring, peer mentoring connects mentors and mentees who are roughly equal in age and status for academic and social support (Angelique et al., 2002; Terrion and Leonard, 2007). This equality can be helpful in building comfort and trust during the initial stages of the mentoring relationship. There are, however, some significant differences that must be taken into account when examining programs specifically targeted at first-generation students. Because of their first-generation status, a peer mentor in this program may not be equal in age and social support. First-generation students may also need different types of targeted support such as broader introduction to college resources. Finally, the differences in the level of college experience that often exist must be taken into account. This experience gap is the most important component of the first-generation peer mentoring relationship and one that Georgia Gwinnett College kept in focus when designing the peer mentoring program outlined below.

GGC's first-generation peer mentoring program was initially envisioned as part of the Grizzly First Scholar Learning Community, before pivoting to a stand-alone model. When building the Bears Engaging And Mentoring (BEAM) program, the team (composed of Student Success Advisors from the college's School of Transitional Studies) focused on two key elements: mentor recruitment and mentor training. Each one of these foundations were both an opportunity to shape the program, and without an operating budget, a hurdle to overcome.

Much like the other aspects of the GGC's first-generation programming, there was minimal budget available to start the first-generation peer mentoring program. The lack of funding influenced many of the decisions during the genesis of the program. The team working on the project knew they were going to have to be creative and lean on campus partners for support. For example, Student Life donated T-shirts and other promotional materials that remained from previous events. Giving these GGC-branded items (shirts, small book bags, pens, notebooks, etc.) to the incoming mentors was important, as the mentors reported that the gesture made the program feel more official while also providing an alternative to monetary compensation. The mentors were also provided four meal tickets to the dining hall to cover meals for the mentors and mentees. These tickets were left over from previous programs run by the School of Transitional Studies. The opportunity for mentors to "pay" for a lunch for their mentees was meaningful for both.

Mentor Recruitment

The initial goal of BEAM was to provide the first-generation students in the larger Grizzly First Scholar program with a peer mentor who could help them adjust to college life. The Grizzly First Scholar team hoped to add another resource for the first-year students while also providing some opportunities for upperclassmen to give back to the academic community and earn valuable leadership experience. Another original element of the program was to require the mentors to also be first-generation, but despite the large first-generation population at GGC, the mentor applicant pool did not allow the team to be restrictive in the hiring process. The program pivoted to a more inclusive model that allowed all students to apply to be peer mentors. This idea was an important lesson learned throughout the program building experience: flexibility is key. When elements do not meet initial expectations, the ability to pivot quickly to solve problems is vital. In the initial group of ten peer mentors there were five first-generation and five continuing generation students. As it turned out, student feedback indicated that traditional students serving as mentors were able to connect as well if not better with the first-generation mentees than the first-generation mentors.

The team approached mentor recruitment through several avenues. A digital flyer was displayed on screens around campus and contained a brief synopsis of the program and highlighted some of the benefits such as "making a difference" and "leadership skills." The team worked to push the desirable traits of the program because of the initial concerns that we would receive limited interest from a busy student body. More than half of GGC students have jobs outside of campus and many students seeking jobs on campus are looking for paid positions. The flyer also mentioned the full academic year commitment and stated that this was a volunteer position. We found it is important to establish the fact that this role was unpaid from the outset to avoid students seeking paid positions showing initial interest and then walking away when they find out more information. The promotional material also mentioned that this program was targeted to support first-generation students.

The student listserv is the most direct and convenient line of communication to students, and we did utilize it, but knew we needed to look beyond email. A total of 72% of college students say they treat student organization emails as spam and 54% do not always read emails from the university or academic departments (Ha et al., 2018). Understanding the challenges of finding enough applicants, the team needed to reach more students through multiple streams. A meeting with GGC'S Honors Program Director turned out to be a great resource. The Honors Program is an excellent source of high-achieving students, many of whom were interested in mentoring roles. Several of the mentors ended up coming from Honors. Other ways to reach a variety of majors and students from diverse backgrounds included connecting with student organizations. Quick presentations at club meetings (Biology Club and Women in Tech Club) and organizations (African American Student Organization and Organization of Latin American Students) turned out to be excellent sources of potential applicants as well. These brief visits during a club or organization's meeting to introduce/explain the program are a powerful recruiting tool to a captive audience.

After collecting the applications online, the team reviewed and narrowed the applicants and began to set up interviews. A standardized interview sheet for each applicant was completed by each interviewer. The interview sheet contains a list of questions as well as reminders that the interviewer would list to students. We found that program facts and expectations are important to cover not just during orientation but during interviews as well. Due to scheduling difficulties, we utilized a rotating team of interviewers from the advising and student-life offices. Whoever was available at the time of the interview would jump in. Again, because we did not have a dedicated coordinator or staff to run the program it was a group effort. The identical interview sheets allowed whoever was conducting the interview to feel comfortable and standardized the entire process. Perhaps the most interesting answers in the interviews came from the question that asks students about motives. This question brought out important stories from candidates about why they wanted to be mentors. For the first-generation students that applied, these stories would often coincide with students' own first-generation stories. There were also some traditional students who had first-year stories that mirrored those of first-generation students. We found the interviews to be much more revealing than the applications and that sometimes strong peer mentors can come from unexpected places. Past leadership or mentoring experience was not as important as current fit or passion for the role. Our best peer mentors were often brand-new to this type of work. After one round of interviews the team was able to narrow down the applicants and make offers to the candidates best suited to the role.

Another key consideration that emerges during the mentor selection process is the number of years/semesters the mentors would have remaining until graduation. There were times that it felt like after we got a student mentor trained and set up in the peer mentoring system it was time for them to graduate and leave the program. Also, seniors can have other priorities, such as job searches, which leaves them with even less time to devote to the program and a mentee. Second-year and third-year students can be ideal depending on your recruitment/training window.

Peer Mentor Training

After completing the interview process, offering the position, and hiring mentors, the next step was training. The BEAM peer mentor training session was a one-day, four-hour program held the second week of classes, after the add/drop/swap period had ended. This timing allowed for students to settle into their courses and schedules before adding on another responsibility. It is important to remind all student participants that their own academic responsibilities must remain a priority throughout the semester. The training format followed a loose structure of introductions, icebreaker games, guest speakers, and then program expectations. Our schedule of guest speakers covered several modules including training from college staff based in the offices of financial aid, CAPS (counseling), the Tutoring Center, and Student Success Advisors covering time management and cultural competency. These offices volunteered their time. Again, not having a budget prevented bringing in outside speakers. However, there are advantages to having campus partners deliver these speakers. It allows staff/faculty from other offices to be stakeholders in the program and meet our mentors while also ensuring the students hear from the experts in their respective fields.

The training session is also a time to adjust mentor expectations. We found many mentors to be high achievers who were not accustomed to struggle or failure. When mentees did not follow expectations or respond to mentors, the mentors struggled with the feeling that they were doing something wrong. It is vital to set expectations during the training and ensure that the mentors know that this experience is not going to be a perfect relationship where they are always in control.

Another primary goal of the training is to emphasize the mentor role. Reminding students that mentors are not advisors, tutors, or psychologists. Mentors later reported their mentees requesting tutoring and course selection/registration advice, among other requests that should be handled by college staff. It is vital at these points that the mentor understand the resources available on campus and point students in the right direction. Helping first-generation students feel comfortable asking questions and utilizing the proper campus resources is an excellent feature of a peer mentoring program like this.

This idea of helping mentees understand what is available to them on campus goes back to one of the core concepts that the team emphasizes throughout the training and during the semester as well. Mentors should think of themselves as tour guides. A guide who walks alongside the mentee for the whole semester. Again, first-generation students often do not know what they do not know. The peer mentor's job is to help fill in those gaps and the goal of the peer mentoring program is to put the mentors in the best position possible to succeed.

After training and the mentor-mentee assignments, the staff intervention decreases. There are required weekly electronic check-ins for mentors and three meetings spread throughout the semester that allow mentors to share progress and ideas with one another, but the lack of a budget severally limits opportunities for events during the semester.

COORDINATING A SERVICE-LEARNING PROJECT

Service-learning supports academic success in undergraduate pre-professional programs and communities, but can be challenging to plan and implement (York, 2019). When Georgia Gwinnett College implemented the Grizzly First Scholar first-generation learning community in Fall 2017, one of the research questions posed was: what are the experiences of first-generation college students in learning communities with a service-learning component? The School of Transitional Studies worked with campus and community partners to incorporate the high-impact practice (HIP) of service-learning into the Grizzly First Scholar first-generation learning community curriculum (GGC 1000 FYE course). Designing an effective service-learning course activity requires the collaboration of various stakeholders, inclusive of faculty, students, community-based agencies, and service recipients (Bringle et al., 1997). This is particularly important when an institution, office, or department is trying to leverage resources. When implementing a service-learning project as part of the Grizzly First Scholars first-generation learning community, assessing the communities and campus needs were key aspects of programming.

Service-learning affords students the opportunity to apply classroom learning to real-world situations (Brownwell and Swaner, 2009). Students that participate in service-learning generally demonstrate gains in moral reasoning, their sense of self and civic responsibility, and in the development of social justice orientation (Brownwell and Swaner, 2009). Research done by Conefrey (2021) outlines how incorporating various means of high-impact practices that addresses the academic and social engagement of the "whole student" is essential for first-generation student retention. Incorporating integrative assignments across courses in the Grizzly First Scholars learning community, in addition to shared grading rubrics for an end of term symposium, are examples of High Impact Practices (HIPS) used for engagement. The service-learning symposium was a platform for students to not only present their perspectives and experience with a service-learning project, but to reflect and illustrate many topics taught in the GGC 1000 course modules.

Researchers have documented the benefits of organizational collaboration including greater efficiency, effectiveness, and perhaps most important for higher education institutions, it can enhance student learning (Kezar, 2006). Careful and strategic thought was put into incorporating service-learning as part of the Grizzly First Scholars first-generation learning community. Having no budget allocated for first-generation initiatives presented many planning and programming dilemmas, however, being able to be creative and leverage campus and community resources filled that deficit. Food, space, transportation, T-shirts, giveaways, etc., are some of the items that were needed for successful programming. Not having a dedicated office for first-generation programming and working with a non-existent budget, such resources were able to be retrieved through allies on campus and the community. Forming allies is essential to access resources.

Campus and Community Allies

It is important to cultivate relationships and networks before trying to conduct collaborative work (Kezar, 2005). Campus partners tapped for programing assistance included the Assistant Director of Civic Engagement, the Office of Student Involvement, the Career Development and Advising Center (CDAC), the Office of Student Financial Services, and faculty from academic disciplines. Referrals from campus partners helped forge additional relationships with community partners.

The Office of Student Involvement has played such a pivotal role in supporting service-learning projects. The Assistant Director of Student Involvement hosted service-learning mini-institute workshops for faculty, staff, and students. These workshops highlighted the various types of service-learning and the benefits. The service-learning mini-institute workshops also facilitated a panel session composed of faculty, staff, and community liaisons hence it was a platform to make connections and network. The Office Student Involvement (OSI) was the primary supplier of T-shirts for service-learning events such as the Rainbow Village college symposium, sexual assault awareness town hall, and Junior Achievement volunteer events. The OSI had funds earmarked for students and student activities, so they were a great resource to offset the cost of T-shirts. The OSI was also tapped for giveaways for events. This enabled goody bags to be issued at the various aforementioned service-learning events. The Admissions Office was also another great resource for giveaways, as that office had items allocated for recruitment activities. Obtaining such items from the Admissions Office and the OSI afforded reciprocal benefits to all, as the institution was able to be advertised and marketed, while resources for giveaways were provided.

When coordinating a service-learning project it is hard to know where to begin and who are credible community entities to partner with. Networking with campus departments and disciplines can be done in meaningful ways yielding benefits to all parties. Campus departments benefited by program exposure and institutional marketing. Some of the Grizzly First Scholars learning communities had major or career-based focus areas (i.e. Business, STEM, non-STEM). The goal was to enrich a student's experience with a project that would reflect the learning communities focus area(s).

Departmental Deans or faculty are other resources for networking and collaboration. Through a meeting with a School of Business faculty member/administrator a partnership was forged with the Junior Achievement organization. The Junior Achievement organization serves to educate students in grades K-12 about entrepreneurship, work readiness, and financial literacy through experiential, hands-on programs JA of Georgia (2021, October 30). Junior Achievement thrives and functions through volunteers, so the relationship was mutually beneficial. Georgia Gwinnett College students in the Business focus area learning community and those from other focus areas were able to mentor middle school students through an interactive service-learning event at the Junior Achievement Discovery Center of Gwinnett County. Junior Achievement was just one of several community partners that was developed from a campus partner referral. Through the service-learning mini-institute event, a collaboration with a mentor program for young girls helped develop a partnership with a high school senior seeking to obtain her Girl Scouts Gold Award through a sexual assault awareness project. The student from the mentor program's project led to the creation of a service-learning town hall event revolving around the topic of sexual assault. Another partnership was forged with a homeless transitional living organization that created a student led and organized college symposium service-learning activity.

When transportation or off-campus event scheduling presented a challenge, Grizzly First Scholars GGC 1000 instructors collaborated with the Assistant Director for Civic Engagement. There are on campus service-learning programs that can be utilized such as the MicroFarm campus garden. Examples of other campus-based no-cost events include voter registration drives, mentoring and pen pal programs with local middle schools, etc. The Assistant Director of Civic Engagement works for the Office of Student Involvement, so monies and resources allotted for student programming could be accessed.

Service-Learning Symposium

As part of the Grizzly First Scholar learning community curriculum an end-of-semester symposium was also incorporated in the program. Unlike volunteering, service-learning has a reflective component (Reynolds, 2009). Students were required to present on their service-learning experience and the impact of the project on their lives and academic experience. The Service-Learning Symposium was an end of term event that replaced students in the Grizzly First Scholars learning community (GGC 1000 FYE course) final exam. Students were tasked with creating a PowerPoint or some type of electronic presentation that highlighted key points from a rubric and assignment guideline. Usually, a large room with standing mini tables was reserved for individual student setup with laptops. Students that did not have laptops had the option of borrowing a laptop from the Office of Information Technology. The event was marketed to faculty, staff, and administrators to attend with special invitations sent to faculty and staff that identified as first-generation. For many students this was their first time presenting on an individual basis to faculty and staff.

The symposium initially was an event coordinated by the Grizzly First Scholars GGC 1000 instructors. The symposium eventually branched off to a larger Learning Community Day event. Learning Community Day was an end of term event showcasing learning communities at Georgia Gwinnett College, and some of the activities and projects that were part of the curriculum for learning community courses. As the service-learning symposium evolved as part of the Learning Community Day event, light refreshments were funded through the support of the Office of Student Engagement and Success.

OUTCOMES

Leadership and department restructuring, staff changes, and the COVID-19 pandemic have impacted the assessment process and retention of data. Data previously collected at the initial Grizzly First Scholars focus groups highlighted impactful benefits to students, GGC 1000 instructors, and peer mentors. Feedback from students in focus groups regarding service-learning illustrated how students believed they built leadership skills, gained a sense of accomplishment, and were introduced to volunteering and service. BEAM mentors reported increased confidence in their leadership abilities, and mentees reported feeling more connected to the college. One specific statement from a BEAM mentor communicated a sense of accomplishment for helping others while recognizing their own continued struggles as a first-generation student. Working as a peer mentor led this student to realize that they didn't need to be perfect to be able to serve others.

Anecdotally, the consensus from instructors was that service-learning projects allowed them to step back and allow students to lead, and provide a platform for them to emphasize the skills of persistence, preparation, teamwork, confidence, and communication to students. Students commented that the service-learning symposium allowed them to have opportunities to be experts, shape their confidence, and build public speaking and research skills. For instructors the symposium provided an opportunity to assess learning and engagement, connect with the larger college community, and adhere to academic goals and objectives.

LESSONS LEARNED

There is vast room for improvement in the area of assessment for the Grizzly First Scholar Learning Community and associated programming. Several focus groups were conducted at the onset of the program, with the intent of collecting qualitative data to specifically explore the impact of learning communities, peer mentoring, and service-learning on first-generation students at Georgia Gwinnett College. Focus groups are a great way to assess the student narrative regarding students' overall experience with the learning community and associated programming (i.e. peer mentoring and service-learning projects). However, perhaps the breadth of the focus group studies could be expanded to include more groups, yielding more results and data. Expanding assessment for cross analysis to look at other first-generation student intersectionalities such non-traditional students, commuter and part-time students, etc., and how varied groups and their experiences compare. Beyond evaluating students' experience in the learning community, also assessing how students' progress in classes outside of the learning community, and looking at how students connect with varied types of service-learning, are other areas of assessment that can be implemented. Student voices play a critical role in programming. Recommendations for future programming should include expanded first-generation student input in the development stages.

Further ideas to consider for future first-generation programming are: standardizing focus group meetings at the end of each semester, use of pre- and post-surveys, and creating a central place where data can be accessed if staff or leadership changes. Another avenue to be explored for programs with limited financial resources is to consider recruiting students to establish a first-generation Registered Student Organization (RSO). Monies from the Office of Student Involvement are allocated for RSOs and more robust programming can occur.

Forging relationships with allies, collaborating, and networking are all key ways in which funding and resources can be accessed to support various program initiatives. While a limited budget can be a frustrating roadblock for faculty and staff looking to build first-generation programming, it does not have to limit the possibilities. Thinking creatively and utilizing all available avenues can still lead to real success.

REFERENCES

Angelique, H., Kyle, K., & Taylor, E. (2002). Mentors and muses: New strategies for academic success. *Innovative Higher Education*, 26(3), 195–209.

Bringle, R. G., Hatcher, J. A., & Games, R. (1997). Engaging and Supporting Faculty in Service Learning. *Journal of Public Service & Outreach*, 2(1), 43–51.

Brownell, J. E., & Swaner, L. E. (2009). High-impact practices: Applying the learning outcomes literature to the development of successful campus programs. *Peer Review*, 11(2), 26.

Conefrey, T. (2021). Supporting First-Generation Students' Adjustment to College With High-Impact Practices. *Journal of College Student Retention: Research, Theory & Practice*, 23(1), 139–160.

Ha, L., Joa, C.Y., Gabay, I., & Kim, K. (2018). Does college students' social media use affect school e-mail avoidance and campus involvement?. *Internet Research*, 28(1), 213–231. https://doi.org/10.1108/IntR-11-2016-0346

Hill, W., & Woodward, L. S. (2013). Examining the impact learning communities have on college of education students on an urban campus. *Journal of College Student Development*, 54(6), 643–648.

Kezar, A. (2005). Moving from I to We: Reorganizing for Collaboration in Higher Education. *Change*, 37(6), 50–57.

Kezar, A. (2006). Redesigning for Collaboration in Learning Initiatives: An Examination of Four Highly Collaborative Campuses. *The Journal of Higher Education*, 77(5), 804–838. http://www.jstor.org/stable/3838788

Kuh, G., O'Donnell, K., & Schneider, C. G. (2017). HIPs at ten. *Change: The Magazine of Higher Learning*, 49(5), 8–16.

Langhout, R. D., & Gordon, D. L. (2021). Outcomes for underrepresented and misrepresented college students in service-learning classes: Supporting agents of change. *Journal of Diversity in Higher Education*, 14(3), 408–417. https://doi.org/10.1037/dhe0000151

Mission. JA of Georgia. (n.d.). Retrieved October 30, 2021, from https://www.georgia.ja.org/mission

Reynolds P. (2009). Community engagement: What's the difference between service learning, community service, and community-based research? *Journal of Physical Therapy Education (American Physical Therapy Association, Education Section), 23*(2), 3–9. https://doi.org/10.1097/00001416-200907000-00001

Tinto, V. (2001). Rethinking the first year of college. *Higher Education Monograph Series*, Syracuse University, *9*(2), 1–8.

York, T. T. (2019). *Service-learning to advance access & success: Bridging institutional and community capacity*. Information Age Publishing.

Part II
Mentorship

Chapter 6

Belonging and Well-being as Key Measures of Student Success

Promising Practices at University of Southern California's Topping Scholars Program

Trista Beard and Carina Gonzalez

For 50 years, the Topping Scholars Program (Topping) has been meeting the academic, financial, and social needs of low-income and first-generation college students at the University of Southern California (USC), particularly students who have demonstrated extraordinary community awareness through a history of service. The USC Norman Topping Student Aid Fund (Topping Program) was created in 1970, when two African-American students from South Los Angeles, seeing very little representation of low-income students of color, lobbied the student government for a referendum vote, to earmark a portion of student fees to fund scholarships for low-income and first-generation students from the surrounding neighborhoods. The USC President (then, Dr. Norman Topping) worked with the Board of Trustees to establish an endowment that would grow over time, from providing 20 scholarships per year (in 1970) up to 170 scholarships annually (by 2022). Topping awards about 150 scholarships per year, supporting both undergraduates and graduate students, and has grown its advising and programming in intentional ways to support the health, academic progression, and goals of all our first-generation scholars. At USC, a first-generation college student is a student whose parent did not complete a four-year college degree. The undergraduate population at USC is approximately 20% first-generation students, 20% historically underrepresented, and 20% Pell-eligible.

Topping's mission is to "*empower* our Topping Scholars and Fellows to realize their full potential at USC, in their communities, and in life beyond the University. To achieve this mission, [Topping] provides support and guidance, community-building programs, and financial assistance." Topping realizes this mission by committing to students' academic support, well-being, belonging, and career exploration – building skills, and building community, for life beyond graduation. Practitioners align the learning goals of the support programming

DOI: 10.4324/9781003226321-8

to meet both the Topping mission and the USC student affairs mission: to empower students to transform the world, by cultivating a culture driven by student well-being.

The Topping Program is an award-winning, holistic, student services program, and serves as a model for how to build a community that supports first-generation college student development. All Topping Scholars attend a variety of programming, designed to bring students together. The time spent on authentic community-building yields incredible results. Students consistently report they feel a strong sense of community, feel less alone, know where to go for help, and know that they have the resources needed to achieve their goals. We also have a 100% six-year graduation rate, but that pales in comparison to the value that Topping adds to the student experience – belonging, community, and care for well-being.

A UNIQUE SET OF STAKEHOLDERS

To best serve the recipients of the Topping Scholarship, the program relies on a unique funding and shared governance model. All enrolled students pay a scholarship fee each semester to contribute specifically to the Topping Fund, making every enrolled student a donor. This is an exceptional institutional commitment to supporting first-generation and low-income students. USC students voted to add this tax to the fees in 1970 and since then, students still hold a majority of seats on the governing board of the Topping Fund. Sustainability of the Topping Program is built into the Topping Charter and our shared governance structure. The bylaws dictate that student leaders, who represent the student body and its commitment to first-generation student success, are always a central voice in decision-making. Although the bylaws saw major revision and revitalization in 2018–2019, after 30 years of stasis, the spirit of student leadership, advocacy, agency, and engagement remain as strong now as during the formative years. As long as students-at-large pay into the Fund, then students will control a majority vote on the policy-making board.

The governing board works to review and approve programming initiatives, keep an eye on finances, accept feedback from scholarship recipients on programming and support services, and create mission-centered accountability for the program staff. It is a complex chain of command, but one that subverts traditional academic hierarchies and places students in governance positions that are rare in higher education. The 20 voting members of the board also review and select the scholarship recipients each year. Student representatives apply for a two-year term each August, with staggered start dates (e.g. between seven and eight seats turn over each fall). Longer terms for student board members allow cohesive bonds to form among board members and contribute to the efficacy of the board (Rall & Maxey, 2020). Student representatives are selected by the executive committee of the board, comprised of students and staff, after reviewing personal statements and resumes, and interviewing finalists on their leadership and advocacy experiences. Along with 15 students, there are two alumni, one faculty member, and staff from Admissions and Financial Aid on the board, as well as ex officio Topping office staff. Board members select scholarship recipients, review policies and practices for improvement, and attend signature events with Topping Scholars to report back to the wider student body that their investment in first-generation student success initiatives is being well used to build community, foster belonging and well-being, and raise awareness of the experiences of First-Generation, Low-Income (FGLI) students at the university. Topping is committed to first-generation students' success, and the unique funding model and student-led board create a cycle of shared accountability that pushes the program to keep developing and succeeding, to meet complex student needs as they arise.

APPLICATION OF RESEARCH AND THEORY

The theoretical framework used most often in Topping's program development and assessment is Rendón's (1994) validation theory. Validating students as assets to the college community encourages their social and academic growth, and allows support services staff to develop coaching practices and programs that equally aim to improve academic outcomes and well-being. The Topping Program director developed a unique coaching protocol, called "L.I.V.E. Advising," to be used for individual meetings (T. Beard, personal communication, March 13, 2020). The core actions are to *listen, inquire, validate,* and *empower* students. Questions intertwine to get a full picture of how the student is doing: *How are your classes going? What are you doing for fun outside of class? How are your family/friends? Where is home for you? What are you doing to take care of yourself and stay well?* A holistic approach allows staff and students to build trust, which is the foundation of promoting help-seeking behaviors, and keeps Topping grounded as a culturally engaged environment (Museus et al., 2017).

The advisors also utilize tools from cognitive behavioral therapy (CBT) during student appointments to promote autonomy and growth. CBT focuses on challenging and changing behaviors that are not helpful to the client, while also helping them to develop coping strategies (Sharf, 2016). Often first-generation students experience imposter syndrome and feel they do not belong or are not good enough (Parkman, 2016). This can lead to negative self-talk and catastrophizing. Advisors ask probing questions to help students shift to a more asset-based mindset. Additionally, advisors assist students in developing coping strategies to overcome setbacks. Interventions include creating a motivation board, journaling about long-term goals, or articulating why the student is pursuing a college degree. Advisors then remind them to celebrate their

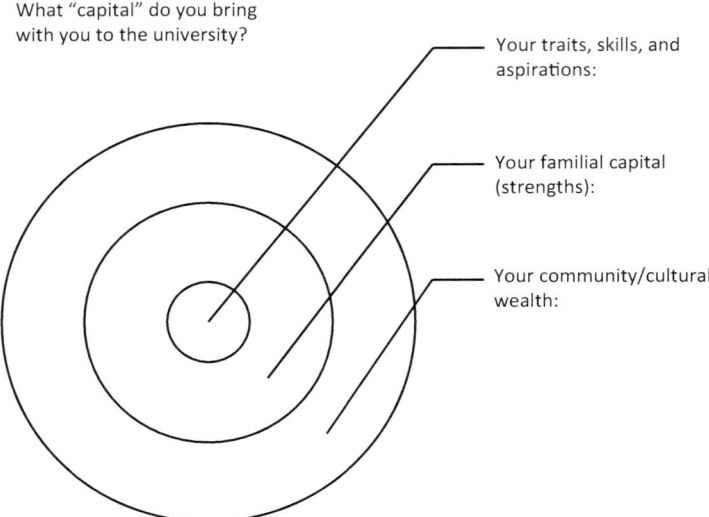

Figure 6.1 "Recognize Your Assets" Exercise

victories, both big and small. This technique from CBT of giving the students reflective homework aims to empower students to problem-solve on their own, building self-efficacy.

Because Topping serves exclusively FGLI students, we are sensitive to the complexity of their lives. The majority of them work as well as go to school; many help their families with finances or childcare or translating, or a dozen other chores and errands that are necessary to support the communities they care for deeply. We draw upon Yosso's (2005) concept of community cultural wealth to validate students' assets. Because Topping is committed to three interconnected levers of support (scholarship funding, holistic advising and success programs, and community-building), an asset-minded position is vital to cultivating trust in Topping. Reflective exercises for self-assessing community cultural wealth (Figure 6.1), demonstrate how Topping uses theory to inform educational activities to meet our mission and goals.

GOALS AND OBJECTIVES

The Topping Program mission builds upon a foundational understanding that the goal is not only to get *into* college, but also to get *through* college. We measure student success not by academic achievement alone, but also in the way students interact with the campus community and beyond, and their well-being throughout the student life cycle. Through a variety of activities and interventions, Topping supports networking, academic exploration, skill-building, and community-building. Even faced with increased distance learning, all events have transitioned online to meet our student learning outcomes. Topping actually expanded programming during the time of remote learning to include more virtual lounge sessions, socials, guest speakers, and collaborations with campus partners, offering additional social experiences and opportunities to engage with peers and resources.

Topping provides three integrated levers of support (Figure 6.2) to address the needs of FGLI scholarship students. First is financial help. Grants come from the scholarship endowment established in 1970 combining the student fees given over time and the matching gift President Topping coordinated with the USC Associates (Topping, 1990). Scholarships, like Topping's, are supplemental to need-based grants, often replace or reduce loans, and help students reduce work hours. Programs like Topping, that have degree progress and GPA requirements tied to funding, aim to keep students on track to graduate. These are levers of equity, increasing completion rates for low-income students. (Dynarski, 2003; Goldrick-Rab et al., 2016). The *honor* of winning a prestigious scholarship or grant also helps motivate students to shine. They are a part of something extraordinary and often rise to the expectation.

Beyond the financial help, the individualized, holistic, educational counseling provides an emotional home base at a PWI (predominantly white institution), where working-class students and underrepresented students often feel minoritized. The Topping office has professional advisors and a study lounge where students can rest from the stress of performing the as "average college

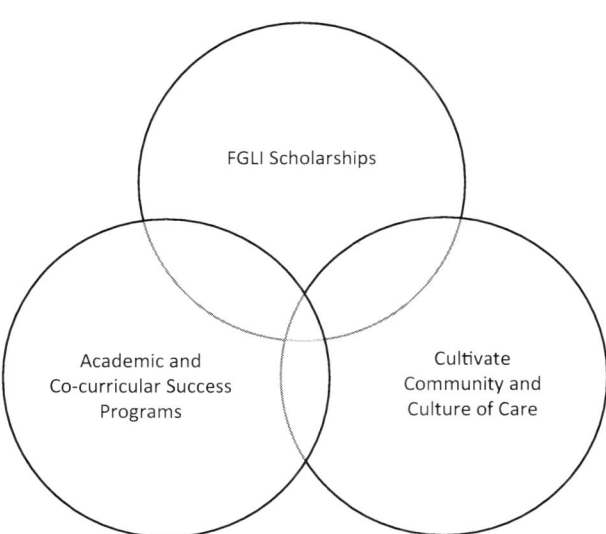

Figure 6.2 Three Types of Support Provided by Topping Program

student." The physical space for students to commune is a gift, and our students take advantage of it to build connection and community, just as many students use campus cultural centers for the same reason. The third and most important student need that Topping meets is fostering community. The power of peers, peer mentoring, and near-peer models cannot be overstated. Seeing another student who shares parts of your identity (multiple identity markers, intersectional identities) and is making academic progress, using campus and community resources, navigating the labyrinth of the institution, balancing school and home/work/family, considering the health and well-being of self and others, and shares their struggles is informal mentoring and modeling at its best. A community of students fighting together to reach their goals, instead of being in competition with one another, is the most significant outcome because the investment in a student's confidence and empowerment pays dividends well beyond the college years. Preparing students to seek out community, to invest in themselves and others, to be engaged in improving society, and to build as they grow, is the ideal of a college education. That is how we live up to our mission "*empower* our Topping Scholars and Fellows to realize their full potential at USC, in their communities, and in life beyond the University."

IMPLEMENTATION

Funding

Topping was fortunate to be founded as a scholarship fund, and therefore be able to offer need-based grants to FGLI students as a part of their financial aid packages, replacing loans for 60% of our undergrads, and helping graduate students reduce their loan burden. The Topping Fund has given out nearly $20 million in scholarships over 50 years, and a sustainable endowment should allow Topping to continue to give 160–170 awards each year for the near and long-term future. For students, the scholarship money is the only value they can see at the time of application to the university; and upon graduation, it is still rated as the most valued support of the Topping Program by about a quarter of the students (Figure 6.3).

The initial scholarship funding helps to address access to higher education for FGLI students, but access is not equal to opportunity. To assist students in realizing their full potential, they need to be able to participate in academic enrichment activities without constant concern for their tight budget. A second level of opportunity funding addresses this privilege – the privilege of having choices. Often FGLI students have to work one or more jobs to pay for the extra costs that even an excellent financial aid package does not cover: health insurance, co-pays, software or other tech needs (i.e. Wi-Fi, hotspots, newer laptop), an expensive textbook, and even basic needs, like enough food or clothing.

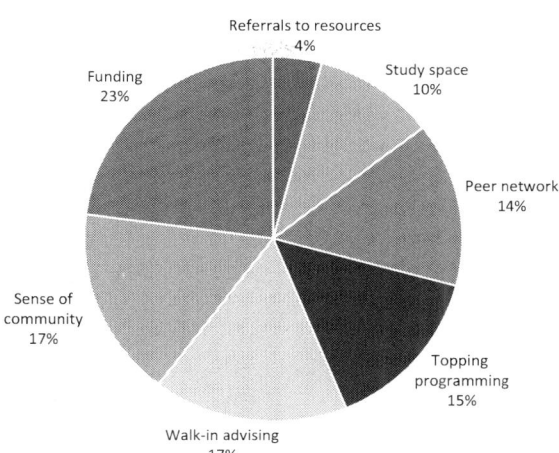

Figure 6.3 Ranking of the Most Critical Support Offered by the Topping Program. Note: Data Collected from Exit Surveys of Graduates in 2020

Many students work a campus job, but FGLI students are more likely to work more hours and work off-campus, to the detriment of their study schedules and campus engagement (Mehta et al., 2011). FGLI students are less likely to take advantage of a unique academic opportunity, like study abroad, or undergraduate research (RTI, 2021). For many FGLI students, the absolute *need* to make enough money to cover expenses removes the true choice of opportunities (Jack, 2019). Topping offers "exceptional funding" opportunity grants to meet the academic exploration goals of students with less financial resources. Students can apply for grants (with a statement of purpose) to cover graduate exam fees, exam preparation course, academic-related travel to a conference, study abroad program, or service-learning trip, and to cover fees for honor societies, professional associations (i.e. APA, NASPA, PRSA, SWE, etc.), or academic journals. Exceptional funding aims to level the playing field by assisting students who need the financial support to reach resources that will cultivate their learning and development. On average, 60% of Topping students take advantage of these micro-grants at some point during their time at the university, which also supports graduates' reasoning to cite funding as a critical support for their success in college.

Strategic Programming and Interventions

Topping coordinates a variety of intentional programs, events, workshops, and advising and coaching opportunities designed to challenge students to develop their navigational capital, knowing this will increase their access to resources and opportunities. Navigational capital is one lens from Yosso's (2005) community cultural wealth model that is particularly useful in exposing first-generation students to the hidden curriculum of higher education. This sociological model of six forms of cultural capital aims to reveal unrecognized wealth and knowledge that working-class students of color bring *into* college campuses (Yosso, 2005). The concepts give name to the assets historically marginalized students already possess, and the staff at Topping use the concepts as a philosophical underpinning to build upon, not to replace with dominant forms of cultural capital.

Higher education is ripe with unspoken rules and cultural norms, such as when and how to speak to professors, to promote one's achievements, or to work with others on projects. FGLI students need support as they navigate new college spaces, as well as have opportunities to practice the social skills needed to gain access to greater resources as they progress in school and in the working world beyond college. A strategic calendar of mandatory events provides skill-building scaffolding so students can engage in new experiences. All programs, events, and workshops have measurable goals and linked assessments. Samples include a conference-style student retreat, "Navigating College" seminars, community service hours and events, career exploration activities, graduation celebration, mandatory advising, and supplemental coaching sessions. Additional programmatic components include welcome events for new scholars, peer mentoring program, student-led study sessions and workshops, TED-style talks from upperclassmen, alumni mixers, and other leadership development opportunities.

The skills we seek to develop that make up the "hidden curriculum" are cultivating relationships, advocating for oneself, and seeking out opportunities. Mandatory programs like the Annual Scholar Retreat or faculty-student luncheons ensure that students have the chance, each year, to interact with new campus administrators, instructors, and other gatekeepers, to gain ease with asking questions, seeking help/advice, and letting people get to know them. Topping staff are explicit about the need to develop relationships; the benefits of getting to know instructors and program gatekeepers are access to new knowledge and opportunities. Many FGLI students arrive at campus unsure of their place, and grapple with imposter syndrome. Reassuring them that they *do* belong here, and that being a student means asking questions, absorbing information, and trying new things (all learning is uncomfortable), gives them permission to find their voice and share their stories.

In order to encourage self-advocacy and facilitate students' practice of taking initiative, we give students assignments to speak with a campus partner or instructor. Topping staff role-play with students, to outline a rough script or a few questions to ask – anything to ease the anxiety. Students who do not have a lot of practice with these types of interactions may feel vulnerable to feelings of rejection by someone they view as "important," and negative interactions can inhibit students from trying to build their support networks further. Topping offers networking workshops for new students (with a faculty member) and for continuing students (with career counseling staff) on ways to start conversations and share their achievements. Many FGLI students have expressed that they do not feel as accomplished as peers, or that it is not appropriate to "brag," but without sharing their wins, the advisors and mentors they want on their "team" will never know their interests or accolades. Once administrators and faculty know more about students' achievements, only then will they be able to suggest and share new opportunities. This is why planning and preparing *with* a student will build their confidence, ease their discomfort with help-seeking behaviors, and improve their ability to pursue opportunities for growth.

Seeking out new challenges is essential for first-generation students to get the most out of their college experiences. Cultural capital is a collection of experiences and translates into the ability to face new environments with more ease and less culture shock (Bourdieu, 1986). In order to assertively seek out new opportunities, students should have built up their self-advocacy and networking skills. Topping staff are well connected throughout the university; the staff purposefully build new bridges across campus systematically. Utilizing these contacts to further the reach of students to new people and new experiences is how we model network-building for students, and support their transition into the "new world" of college and beyond. Programs are designed to get students interacting and engaging with as many institutional agents as possible, to practice cultivating relationships, using their voice, and push themselves into new experiences.

Community awareness is a central tenet for selection as a Topping recipient. Successful applicants demonstrate community awareness through a history of service to a chosen community. Since the inception of the Topping Program, students have been required to complete service hours every semester, with organizations of their choice. Community service is a learning experience that pays dividends. Participating in volunteer activities increases awareness of community needs, but also provides first-generation students with the motivation to persist, inspiration to set long-term goals beyond college, and the opportunity to engage with different leaders and community members/networks, drawing new connections between one's field of study and real world applications (Beard, 2018). Volunteering builds up access to and experiences with institutional agents, aspirational capital, social capital, and resistance capital (Yosso, 2005) as students are exposed to other community models of persisting in the face of struggle, obstacles, and oppression. The navigational capital and social capital fostered through strategic programming and interventions is a unique asset that Topping leverages to increase first-generation success. Empowering FGLI students to build self-efficacy skills, cultivate a strong support network, and activate their voice is the core value we imbed into our learning objectives, implementation, and assessment.

Well-being as a Core Value

It takes a concerted effort to address whole student well-being in equal proportion to supporting academic progress. However, that is the only way to offer equitable support to our first-generation students: by creating a unique culture that *explicitly* communicates equal value to students' academic growth *and* their well-being. Topping utilizes the professional expertise of the program staff in parallel with the peer modeling and coaching that happens in our spaces on campus, and now across virtual platforms. The research on persistence to degree supports the power of community-building and cultural engagement to increase students' sense of belonging, which leads to more positive experiences and outcomes (Strayhorn, 2018). Topping is consistently using assessment and evaluation to improve the overall program, and innovating to meet the student development needs of FGLI students.

In implementing academic culture, skill-building, and community-building events, we begin each program design with a focus on the foundation: cultivating care for the whole student. This practice also builds upon the assumption that the hierarchy of needs (Maslow, 1943) must be met, for students to be able to engage in the creative and critical thinking expected of them in college. Students cannot be successful academically and reach their full potential without equal consideration for their well-being. That is our starting point at the Topping program. There is no separation of a student's academic life and their health. The student is both the instrument and the product of their learning, and their well-being cannot be separated or compartmentalized.

As mentioned earlier in this chapter, we use a partnership approach with students, explicitly expecting them to make decisions for themselves. We listen, we advise, we share resources, but the onus is always on the students to take the next step. In the on-boarding process, all students attend an annual retreat, with dozens of workshop options, and some mandatory sessions. One required session focuses on using the Six Dimensions of Wellness (NWI, n.d.) as a tool for students to self-assess and develop action plans to address areas that need more attention. Helping students understand the interconnectedness and interactions of their emotional, social, occupational, physical, intellectual, and spiritual health exposes them to systems thinking and negates deficit-mindedness.

Topping staff and campus partners work with students throughout the college life cycle to offer broad support for well-being in all aspects of their lives. Using the Six Dimensions of Wellness framework allows staff and students to discuss and assess areas of their lives that impact their academic progress. This is a powerful tool for working with FGLI students to build self-efficacy and motivation by helping students recognize their strengths, successes, and resilience. First, ask them to pause to celebrate areas in which they are thriving. Then, consider what dimensions need more attention to lift them closer to their goals. Finally, work with them to develop a plan of actions they can take to make improvements in the areas they choose.

Belonging and Community-building

Belonging is a by-product of community connection. Students feel part of something larger than themselves. The students feel understood, seen, and a full sense of inclusion in a community where they can be accepted for their intersecting identities. One of the outstanding benefits of peer support is collective care. Peer networks are often underestimated in their power to assist students in overcoming obstacles; mutual aid is given in many ways among peers, and the lateral connections are just as fruitful as hierarchical ones (Beard, 2021). Students coach each other through difficult situations, explain campus processes (often bureaucratic) to one another, and share hard-to-find resources. One of the most important aspects of collective care is the vetting process. Because the students get to know one another through Topping's required events, artificial boundaries come down, and they share an understanding of what it means to be an FGLI student. Slightly more experienced students share their stories about accessing resources on campus and tell peers who to see, when to go, what to ask. These are mentoring interactions, and even peers with similar experience levels are able to guide others through emotional difficulties and academic obstacles (Loots, 2009).

Topping's required events also give students the opportunity to take part in activities that they may not otherwise join. For example, Topping hosts a faculty-student luncheon every semester. This opportunity allows students to invite a faculty member they want to get to know better, and build a connection with, to a formal lunch, organized by Topping. Connecting with professors who can mentor students is key to getting the most out of college. However, it can be intimidating for students to approach faculty members and begin to make those connections. By making the Faculty-Student Luncheon a requirement, students are gently pushed to take a step forward in networking. Topping advisors coach students on how to approach faculty and invite them to the luncheon teaching useful skills for networking. During times of social distancing, Topping hosted a week of virtual meetings called the Faculty Lunch & Learn Series. Faculty from different fields (psychology, cinema, writing, engineering, medicine, communications, etc.) engaged in dialogue with a staff moderator and students, sharing personal stories about college and career experiences. Students noted that after attending Faculty Lunch & Learn talks they felt more comfortable approaching faculty members (85% agreed) because they saw them as relatable (96% of respondents agreed). Students reported viewing faculty as approachable and interested in getting to know students (96% agreed). The Faculty Lunch & Learn series also helped students to feel more connected to Topping and the overall campus community (87% agreed). These gatherings reinforce a positive

Topping Scholar identity and remind students there are others like them in the university, and they belong here. These gatherings also reduce the perceived power distance between students and professors.

Our approach to community-building, both for challenging students with new ideas and for supporting their growth and sense of belonging, relies on Stanton-Salazar's (2011) concept of bridging agents. The Topping Program offers access to professional staff and a wide network of colleagues that serve as bridges to all kinds of knowledge and resources across campus and beyond the university walls. Some of Topping's biggest student success stories are because of the bridges we maintain, creating a supportive web of interconnectivity. Our evaluations show that the supportive environment and sense of community contribute to a strong sense of belonging to a campus "family." Using Arslan and Duru's (2017) school belongingness scale, students reported gains after more exposure to peers and institutional agents (Figure 6.4). The scale used is a four-point Likert scale with five items related to social acceptance and five items (reverse-scored) related to social exclusion. In this evaluation, we compared the answers of students who had completed their first semester and those who had been at the university two years or longer. In the first semester of the program, new students must attend at least four required events, bringing them into close contact with advisors, peers, and campus partners for 10–12 hours of engagement activities. Compound that by each semester, and the trend supports the correlation between the amounts of time spent on intentionally designed group interventions and increased feelings of acceptance and belonging.

New students reported they *agreed* or *strongly agreed* with the statement "I can be myself in this program" with a mean of 3.25; while returning students' average rating was 3.55. The increased time spent interacting with Topping staff and peers influenced the response to having "close/sincere relationships with advisors and peers," where returning students' score was 32% higher. Nearly all items on the acceptance scale went up and most negative items in the exclusion scale went down. The most significant difference from new students to continuing students is the perception of close relationships (+.85; see Appendix). The effect was flat for "I feel I am accepted." One possibility is that early engagement activities intensely focus on fostering a culture of belonging, celebrating first-generation assets, and on-boarding new students to the Topping Family identity, that there may be no perception of change on that item. Time spent engaging in academic, co-curricular, and social activities increases the belonging and acceptance FGLI students perceive and decreases feelings of isolation and marginalization. Belonging has a clear effect on persistence, and interventions, like sustained contact with faculty and staff, peer support, early integration and engagement activities have been shown to increase sense of belonging (Hausmann et al., 2007), as well as mediate the anxiety of taking chances, exploring new opportunities, and overcoming challenges (Terenzini, 2020).

BELONGING AND WELL-BEING

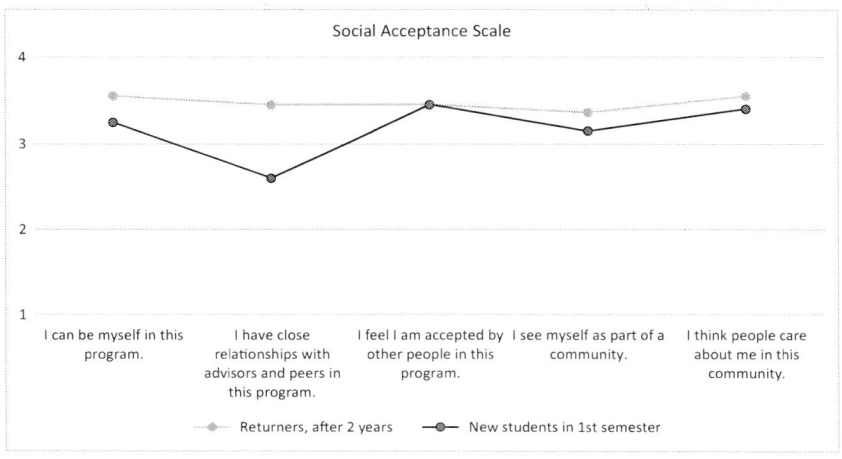

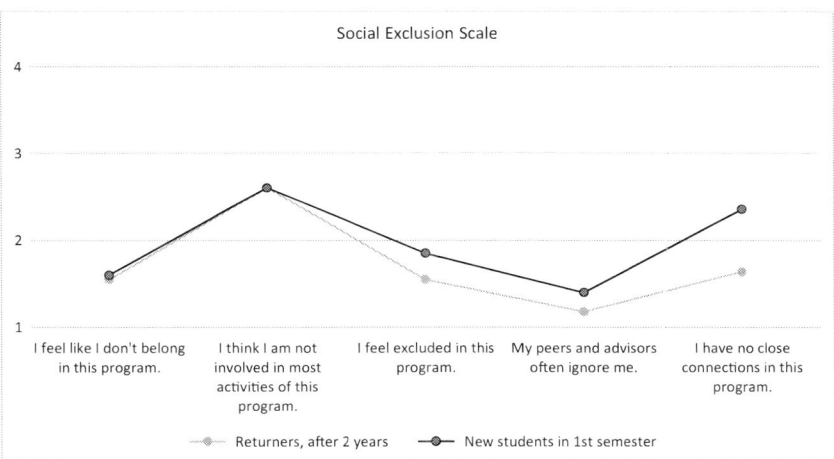

Figure 6.4 Comparison for Social Acceptance and Social Exclusion

Campus-wide Partnerships

The Topping Program relies on social capital theory to drive bridge-building activities, which creates a strong network of institutional agents to support students' learning and development. College is an inherently social experience and FGLI students need a network of support to thrive. Connecting students to campus partners also promotes their sense of belonging on campus and empowers students to self-advocate. Topping intentionally uses social media channels (e.g. Instagram, LinkedIn, etc.) to share campus/community resources and explicitly promote messages of inclusion and equity. Promoting the work of lesser-known campus resources, highlighting unique offices and supportive staff, celebrating students' volunteer work, promoting wellness activities, and centering student voices (and advocacy efforts), especially those from historically marginalized communities, are some examples of how Topping uses social media strategically. The Topping staff are constantly innovating – arranging guest speakers and launching new gatherings and groups – in response to students' needs. Combining efforts across student affairs and academic affairs allows the program to build an interconnected web of support as a social and academic safety net.

Activating our connections on behalf of students opens the doors to all kinds of knowledge and resources across campus. For example, scholars who won national or international fellowships were warmly introduced to our partners in Honors and Fellowships, because staff from that office facilitated a developmental workshop on "your values and goal alignment" at the Annual Topping Retreat. Topping creatively brings in campus partners, not to just plug their programs, but to build trust, build relationships, nurture motivation and goal development, and build the bridges to social capital that first-generation students came to college to access. Collaborations purposefully bring resources *to* students, as opposed to just referring students to an office or service. The philosophy behind this practice is to "call in" people, not "call out." Students trust the Topping "family," and when we endorse a colleague, it is meaningful to our students.

Collaborations with campus resources are fruitful in building a strong web of support because we vet the services, and students trust us to connect them to institutional agents that will respect and validate their concerns. Cited most often as the top three services used due to referrals from Topping were financial aid liaisons, mentor programs, and staff at career services, with academic coaching and community service programs following closely behind. Topping's culture of care is what makes this such a unique and powerful program for supporting FGLI retention, success, and well-being. Topping partners with dozens of student services offices (Table 6.1) to expand each student's network of support, and widen the access to unique opportunities for growth. The expert staff also advise colleagues on a variety of campus initiatives to increase access and support for this population (First Generation Student Union, First Generation Orientation, College Academy, First Generation Plus Center, Graduate Admissions, and others), and in so doing create symbiotic relationships across campus.

Impact of the Pandemic

When the university moved to remote learning due to the COVID-19 pandemic, the advising practices, success programming, and campus partnerships that we built over many years were tested. Topping adapted nearly all signature events, student success workshops, and community-building programs to virtual

Table 6.1 Campus Partnerships and Collaborations

Campus Partner/Collaboration	Delivery
Academic Coaching Center (study skills)	Retreat workshop
Campus Crisis Support Team	Retreat workshop
Basic Needs Office	Pop-up info session
Campus Activities (Leadership Development)	Retreat workshop
Financial Aid Office (outreach staff)	Retreat workshop and pop-up
Research & Fellowships (for first-years and transfers)	Retreat workshop and pop-up
B.E.A.T. – Black Excellence at Topping	Monthly gatherings with guest speakers
First Generation Professionals Program (for grad students)	Retreat workshop
Progressive Degree Graduate Programs	Pop-up info session
Career Services	Various workshops
Pre-health Pathways Advisors	Retreat workshop
Office of Religious Life	Guest keynote at Grad Celebration
Faculty members (across the disciplines)	Various workshops; Lunch & Learns
Cultural Centers	Welcome sessions, workshops, mixers
DACA and Undocumented Student Services	Retreat workshop and pop-up
Counseling Center Multicultural Outreach Team	Dialogue sessions; workshops

platforms. Professional staff utilized Zoom to provide social programs, academic and well-being workshops, and one-on-one advising, continuing to fully engage students and meet our learning objectives. One of the main goals for Topping is to create a sense of belonging among students. In order to foster belonging, the annual New Scholar Welcome Breakfast become three separate virtual events, where each new cohort (freshmen, transfers, and graduate students) could more intimately connect with peers, staff, and continuing students. Breakout rooms allowed students to answer icebreaker questions in small groups and begin to share their apprehensions and their goals. Based on the program evaluation, 82% of respondents reported that they *strongly agreed/agreed* that the welcome session helped them "feel like they are part of the Topping Family." Additionally, 73% of respondents reported that they *strongly agreed/agreed* that they felt "more connected to the overall USC community." Topping's annual retreat also transitioned to an online conference model, offering students 12 unique workshop and social sessions, as opposed to four prescribed workshops over a single day. Campus partners from 12 different departments collaborated for the online retreat "conference" – double the number of campus partners typically able to participate in an on-site retreat. This provided students with a greater diversity of topics and the ability to widen their networks.

Hosting events online such as the Faculty Lunch & Learn Series, alumni panels, or the end-of-year Graduation Celebration, the program was able to host a wider variety of guests from outside of the region. For example, one of the co-founders of the Topping program, Mr. Ron McDuffie, joined the speaker series as a featured guest in 2021, joining by Zoom from the East Coast, negating the need for travel. Of course, there is a downside to online programs – Zoom fatigue. Virtual lounges and social mixers provided students with a sense of the culture and environment of our office and study space, but attendance was often low at these events. The students who did come to mixers and workshops had positive feedback and enjoyed the opportunity to connect with peers. Even if the number of students impacted through an online event was small, the need was clear. Those who attended or visited online office hours to talk *needed* to connect with staff and resources.

Another big shift due to the pandemic was loss of in-person impromptu advising. Trust and rapport are built during frequent and informal interactions in the Topping office. Students in the program feel at home in the physical space and often drop by between classes. Prior to the pandemic, it was common for students to have informal meetings with the staff where they shared updates on classes and life overall, while grabbing a coffee in the lounge. During the pandemic, staff utilized email to recreate informal, conversational check-ins and reached out to students multiple times throughout each semester. Personalized emails addressed to the student (by name) were more likely to get a response: the average response rate to email "check-ins" was about 65%. The staff also made it easier for students to book appointments by using web-based scheduling tools, making staff more accessible.

The pandemic required educators to test new ways to reach and serve students, and we now have an opportunity to continue to offer services virtually. The New Student Welcome is one signature event that will continue to be virtual, as well as alumni panels and faculty speaker events. For many commuters, student parents, and students with health concerns or disabilities, among others, virtual appointments and events offer more accessibility and flexibility, and this practice will continue. In-person interactions are highly valued at Topping, since this contributes to a sense of belonging, but there are also benefits to thoughtfully offering workshops, social events and advising online, such as increasing reach, access, equity, and inclusion.

ASSESSMENT AND OUTCOMES

The Topping Program uses continual assessment to improve programming, advising, and other student services in a feedback loop model. Regular assessment is part of Topping's best practices and helps demonstrate our value to the student body who fund the scholarships with their fees, and to the student-led Governing Board, who help write the policies that steer our objectives. Topping's unique model of shared governance, and student-funded, ensures assessment and accountability in a way that few programs can match.

Topping utilizes both quantitative and qualitative data to measure the outcome of each educational activity and ensure we are meeting our student learning objectives. Using the program's macro goals (the mission), professional staff design activities with learning and development objectives specific to each activity and evaluation surveys are collect feedback data. Topping gathers longitudinal data also; using Arslan and Duru's (2017) school belongingness scale, we assessed student's sense of belonging at the beginning of the first term, after early engagement activities (university orientation, Topping welcome, Topping retreat, academic workshops), at the end of their first year, and mid-year annually, with an exit survey near graduation. Results confirm that the supportive environment and community contribute to a strong sense of belonging to a campus "family" (Pascarella & Terenzini, 2005).

Topping's comprehensive view of student success means supporting the whole student to reach their academic and personal goals, as well as their skill-building, intersectional identity formation and exploration, and interdependence and community responsibility. Topping pushes on these developmental levers through program design and holistic advising, all of which are tied to strategic learning objectives. For example, one advising learning outcome is *students will collaborate with staff to develop strategies for improvement in areas of concern*. The validation we provide empowers students and staff to work as partners – both parties shaping strategies and action plans to keep students making progress and developing.

Outcomes support the use of a three-pronged approach to supporting FGLI students. Topping's graduation rate surpasses the university's overall rate, giving credence to our high-touch and highly structured approach (Figure 6.5). Graduating students also reported feeling more committed to their studies, more committed to serving their communities, and that they had the support needed to reach their fullest potential because of the resources and people they connected to through Topping. Topping students have gone on to hundreds of advanced degrees, Fulbright placements, Truman Fellowships, Schwarzman Scholars, Schaeffer Fellows for Government Service, and even a Rhodes Scholar,

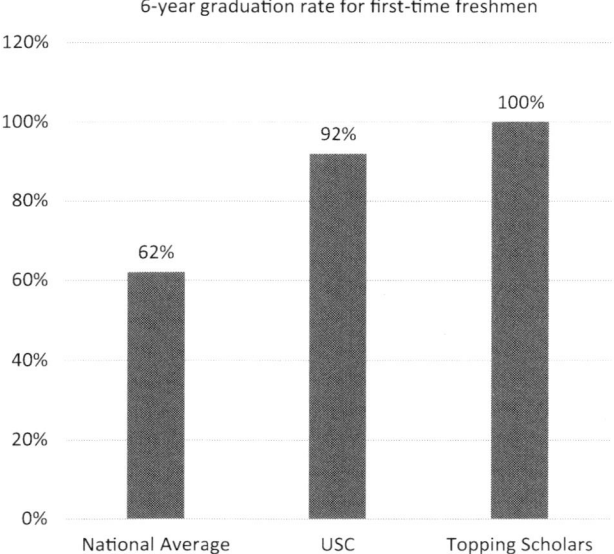

Figure 6.5 Graduation rates comparison. Note: National data from National Center for Education Statistics (NCES, 2020); USC Data from USC Fast Facts (2020); Topping Data from Norman Topping Student Aid Fund Annual Report (2020)

the oldest and most prestigious international scholarship program in the world. We measure our success not in these accolades, although they support the positive contribution of the Topping Program and its strong partnerships and prevalent place on campus. Topping's most promising practice is the focus on the development of students. From the time we welcome them to campus, and into the "Topping family," we ask ourselves, "Do they feel they belong in college? Do they have a safe 'home-base' to seek resources and ask questions? Do they have a place and people they can rely on for support while they face the challenges of academic, social, and professional growth?"

Increasing social, aspirational, navigational, and resistant capital through connection to the Topping community affects students' ability to persevere. For FGLI students, it is not only potential academic setbacks they may face, but also hardships in their personal lives that they have to navigate. Validating students, affirming that they belong, and building their capacity to overcome challenges (through support networks and skill-based programs), advances the resiliency they already possess. Topping explicitly communicates to students that they have limitless potential for growth, and the program ensures that students connect to the resources and tools they need to succeed in their academic, personal, and professional growth.

CHALLENGES

In this chapter, we have highlighted the Topping Program's guiding mission and philosophy, and explained how we operationalize theory and values into promising practices that support FGLI students. While the program has been successful in achieving high completion rates, increasing sense of belonging and community through a variety of levers, and keeping well-being at the forefront of holistic development, the program has its challenges as well. One such challenge is differentiating educational activities and interventions for our growing graduate student population. The strategic interventions of the last ten years, focused myopically on undergraduate students. Across the student affairs landscape, nationally, there is a gap in services for graduate students specifically, but Topping is innovating to serve first-generation graduate students in new ways that help them develop community and support networking outside of their academic silos, and with other emerging first-generation professionals. Topping trains them as mentors for first-generation undergrads, hosts a Fellows Forum gathering each semester to foster peer support and belonging, and holds a mini-retreat in winter to engage them in presenting their research, preparing for job searches, financial literacy, and mental health care strategies. There is still more work to be done in building up unique networks of support for graduate students, especially focused on professional development, identity formation and expression (in their field, across the university, and into professional spaces), and navigating the bicultural experiences of being first-generation and pursuing an advanced degree.

Another challenge is the attachment students build to the office, services, and staff. Topping does not offer psychological counseling and does not assess students' early development for insight into individual attachment styles (Brennan et al., 1998). What we have experienced is a resistance to connecting with resources outside of the Topping center, as well as receiving regular requests from students to offer a duplicate resource in the office. Specifically, requests for an in-house therapist, tutoring service, career counselor, and basic needs coordinator are common and recurring. Structurally, covering the costs to replicate resources already offered at the university would reduce the aid and resources we *do* offer, and so we must push the student to take advantage of the wider network. It becomes incumbent on the staff to have strong, positive relationships with campus partners so that warm hand-offs are possible, or students will be less likely to use resources outside of our office. To empower students to make the most of their (and our) campus network, we must build trusted relationships across campus, and make it easy for students to utilize them.

Lastly, students may feel conflicted about identifying as a Topping Scholar: celebrated for extraordinary community awareness, but also being "outed" as low-income. Only alumni have reported this struggle to us after their time in

Topping, but the threat of judgement by peers is still there. For many students, being as a Topping Scholar is uplifting and a cause for pride, but also may expose students as FGLI in classroom spaces before they are ready to share their class identity. We seek to combat any shame or stigma attached to class by speaking about it openly and celebrating the assets that FGLI students often bring with them to college. Fostering peer support through early engagement activities promotes a stronger sense of inclusion and belonging that reduces feelings of imposter syndrome and mediates class-related minoritization. Hiring staff with first-generation identities is also helpful. Lived experience as a first-generation and/or low-income college student allows for some foundational understanding between students and staff, but staff and faculty must be willing to share their struggles and triumphs with students to remain credible and trustworthy models and mentors.

LESSONS LEARNED

The Topping Program is nationally recognized as a successful model for offering holistic support to FGLI college students, fostering community and belonging that is integral to persistence. To implement a similar program on another campus is possible, but will depend on the culture of that campus. The three levers (refer back to Figure 6.2) of support that Topping offers – scholarship funding, academic and social support, and a strong community-care identity – are already levers used to uplift FGLI students on many campuses. However, very few programs or offices utilize all three in a highly structured program. Begin with these questions when considering a restructure of support services: where can student services be combined and/or offered in a central location – a "hub" – for FGLI students? Where do FGLI students go with questions or concerns (e.g. academic, social, personal, financial, and career)? Is a robust collaboration between two existing offices possible to cover the gap in culture, services, or funding? Defining the desired outcome and related success measures will determine the priority of investment for student/academic affairs leadership. Use a logic model as a starting point, as opposed to at the evaluation stage of a program, to gain consensus and buy-in from a variety of stakeholders needed to launch such a community-minded program (Kaplan & Garrett, 2005).

The tenets of the Topping program are transferable, of course, with the investment of student leaders or institutional funding. Having first-generation students as part of the student government can help to raise the profile of this special population. While not all first-generation students are low-income, a large percentage of students meet both criteria; the median family income for first-generation college students is less than half the average for continuing-generation college students (PNPI, 2021). Because administrative leaders still struggle to speak openly about economic class and class diversity, having

FGLI student groups active on campus allows space for identity formation and celebration of a working-class identity. Student activism around class identity can create a critical mass that will bring attention to the need for inclusive equity programming, making FGLI students more visible. As part of student government, FGLI students and their allies can lobby administrators for a student seat on the college's board, a seat on the campus diversity and equity council(s), and/or propose a fee referendum earmarking a few dollars per semester to go towards a FGLI scholarship and student services office.

If a financial investment avenue seems arduous, due to political, structural, or cultural barriers, the ability to dedicate a staff person and office space to a FGLI Success Initiative may be more feasible. One critical component of Topping is a culture of care that celebrates community identity. Values such as mutual aid, interdependence, counter-narratives, and asset-based equity thinking underlie the programming and advising initiatives. The costs to the institution do not have to be high, but finding and training the right people and building the culture takes time and strategy. Branding the "ideal" of the FGLI Scholar on one's campus is an important step to cultivating this cultural change. Utilize language, symbolism, purpose, and a sense of prestige to motivate staff and students to realize the vision for the program (Bolman & Deal, 2017).

To best utilize the academic and social support lever and community-building lever, leaders must be able to attract people to the initiative: students, faculty, staff, and alumni who *want* to be a part of this special scholar community. Consider a variety of options for building coalitions and alliances across and beyond the campus, such as participation in National First-Generation Celebration Day, launching a first-generation student awareness week or conference, sharing stories of FGLI students through a variety of social media, hosting cohort workshops for subsets of first-generation scholars to create a sense of honor, creating fellowships that provide leadership trainings, and connecting students to institutional leaders that will inspire them and advocate for them across campus. As the community of brokers and bridges grows, so does the visibility of the program or office, and the likelihood the initiative will become institutionalized with dedicated staff, space, and funding.

CONCLUSION

In supporting the progress and growth of FGLI students, the Topping Program serves as a promising model providing three types of integrated support: equity-based funding, educational (skill-building) programs and holistic advising, and community-building opportunities. Building on core values — well-being and belonging — sets a solid foundation for the development of inclusive advisement protocols and strategic student learning objectives. The end goal for the institution is to prepare students to graduate and fully engage as global citizens, both as professional and civically minded community members. Institutional agents must now focus on the "black box" of college life, and work to create new pathways for equity and inclusion, upsetting old paradigms. Providing funds for FGLI students to access academic opportunities with attached costs, facilitating and modeling network-building activities, and exposing the hidden curriculum to students are essential actions to propel first-generation students through higher education and onto the professions.

Informal and formal peer mentoring programs also facilitate community-building and resource sharing. Newsletters and social media platforms open lines of communication and increase trust in the hub, or "home base," that Topping has become. We recommend that programs for first-generation students communicate *explicitly* about expectations for growth, help-seeking behaviors, and the cultural wealth students already bring to campus. Pushing students (gently but firmly) to use their resources, practice self-advocating, and take initiative to test their new skills will complement their classroom learning and prepare them for facing real world challenges. The investment in first-generation students is worth our time and effort, in order to increase the promise of diversity and inclusion at our universities. The students impacted by our program are the change-makers of tomorrow, and we have a duty to help them navigate all the university resources so that they may reach their fullest potential.

APPENDIX

Scale Items Difference between New Topping Students and Continuing Students

	New students after 4 interventions	Returners after 2+ years	Variance
Social Acceptance Scale			
I can be myself in this program.	3.25	3.55	.3
I have close/sincere relationships with advisors and peers in this program.	2.6	3.45	.85
I feel I am accepted by other people in this program.	3.45	3.45	0
I see myself as part of a community.	3.15	3.36	.21
I think people care about me in this community.	3.4	3.55	.15

(Continued)

(Continued)

	New students after 4 interventions	Returners after 2+ years	Variance
Social Exclusion Scale (reverse-scored)			
I feel like I don't belong in this program.	1.6	1.55	.05
I think I am not involved in most activities of this program.	2.6	2.6	0
I feel excluded in this program.	1.85	1.55	.3
My peers and advisors often ignore me.	1.4	1.18	.22
I have no close connections in this program.	2.35	1.64	.71

Note: Adapted from Arslan and Duru's (2017) School Belongingness Scale.

REFERENCES

Arslan, G., & Duru, E. (2017). Initial development and validation of the School Belongingness Scale. *Child Indicators Research*, *10*(4), 1043–1058.

Beard, T. (2018). Toward a local student success model: Latino first-generation college student persistence. In A. Rondini, B. N. Richards, & N. P. Simon (Eds.), *Clearing the path for first generation college students: Qualitative and intersectional studies of educational mobility* (pp. 319–341). Lexington Books.

Beard, T. A. (2021). Emerging Social Capital in the Lives of Latinx First-Generation College Students: The Case for "Apprentice Agents" in a Social Capital Framework. *Journal of First-generation Student Success*, *1*(2), 92–110.

Bolman, L. G., & Deal, T. E. (2017). *Reframing organizations*. Jossey-Bass.

Bourdieu, P. (1986). The forms of capital. In J. Richardson (Ed.), *Handbook of theory and research for the sociology of education*. Greenwood.

Brennan, K. A., Clark, C. L., & Shaver, P. R. (1998). Self-report measurement of adult romantic attachment: An integrative overview. In J. A. Simpson & W. S. Rholes (Eds.), *Attachment theory and close relationships* (pp. 46–76). Guilford Press.

Dynarski, S. M. (2003). Does aid matter? Measuring the effect of student aid on college attendance and completion. *American Economic Review*, *93*(1), 279–288.

Goldrick-Rab, S., Kelchen, R., Harris, D. N., & Benson, J. (2016). Reducing income inequality in educational attainment: Experimental evidence on the impact of financial aid on college completion. *American Journal of Sociology*, *121*(6), 1762–1817.

Hausmann, L. R. M., Schofield, J. W., & Woods, R. L. (2007). Sense of belonging as a predictor of intentions to persist among African American and white first-year college students. *Research in Higher Education*, *48*(7), 803–839. https://doi.org/10.1007/s11162-007-9052-9

Jack, A. A. (2019). *The privileged poor: How elite colleges are failing disadvantaged students*. Harvard University Press.

Kaplan, S. A., & Garrett, K. E. (2005). The use of logic models by community-based initiatives. *Evaluation and program planning*, *28*(2), 167–172.

Loots, A. G. J. (2009). Student involvement and retention in higher education: the case for academic peer mentoring programmes for first-years. *Education as Change*, *13*(1), 211–235.

Maslow, A. (1943). A theory of human motivation. *Psychological Review*, *50*(4), 370.

Mehta, S. S., Newbold, J. J., & O'Rourke, M. A. (2011). Why do first-generation students fail?. College Student Journal, *45*(1), 20–36.

Museus, S. D., Yi, V., & Saelua, N. (2017). The impact of culturally engaging campus environments on sense of belonging. *The Review of Higher Education*, *40*(2), 187–215.

National Center for Education Statistics. (2020). *The Condition of Education 2020 (NCES 2020-144)*. U.S. Department of Education. https://nces.ed.gov/programs/coe/indicator_ctr.asp

National Wellness Institute. (n.d.). The six dimensions of wellness. https://nationalwellness.org/resources/six-dimensions-of-wellness/

Parkman, A. (2016). The imposter phenomenon in higher education: Incidence and impact. *Journal of Higher Education Theory and Practice*, *16*(1), 51.

Pascarella, E. T., & Terenzini, P. T. (2005). *How College Affects Students: A Third Decade of Research* (Vol. 2). Jossey-Bass.

Postsecondary National Policy Institute. (2021, February 1). First-generation students in higher education. *Fact Sheets*. https://pnpi.org/first-generation-students/

Rall, R. M., & Maxey, D. B. (2020). "A Steeper Hill to Climb": The role and experience of student trustees in public higher education governing boards. *Journal of Power*, *8*(2), 12–27.

Rendon, L. I. (1994). Validating culturally diverse students: Toward a new model of learning and student development. *Innovative Higher Education*, *19*(1), 33–51.

RTI International. (2021). *First-generation college graduates' participation in extracurricular and co-curricular activities as undergraduate students*. NASPA. https://firstgen.naspa.org/files/dmfile/FactSheet-021.pdf

Sharf, R. S. (2016). *Theories of Psychotherapy and counseling*. Cengage Learning.

Stanton-Salazar, R. D. (2011). A social capital framework for the study of institutional agents and their role in the empowerment of low-status students and youth. *Youth & Society*, *43*(3), 1066–1109.

Strayhorn, T. L. (2018). *College students' sense of belonging: A key to educational success for all students*. Routledge.

Terenzini, P. (2020, July 29). Rethinking effective student learning experiences. *Inside Higher Ed.* https://www.insidehighered.com/advice/2020/07/29/six-characteristics-promote-student-learning-opinion

Topping, N. H. (1990). *Recollections*. University of Southern California.

University of Southern California. (2020). Facts and figures. https://about.usc.edu/facts/

Yosso, T. J. (2005). Whose culture has capital? A critical race theory discussion of community cultural wealth. *Race Ethnicity and Education*, *8*(1), 69–91.

Chapter 7

Capitalizing on Networks of Support

A Review of the Georgetown Scholars Program's Peer Mentor, Alumni Mentor, and Regional Network Programs

Yasamin "Yasi" Mahallaty and Albert Ramirez

GSP PROGRAM DESCRIPTION

The Georgetown Scholars Program (GSP) was created in 2004 to recruit and support first-generation and low-income students at Georgetown University. Georgetown defines "first-generation" as a student whose parents did not complete a traditional four-year college degree. Understanding that each college-going experience or family context can be unique, GSP thinks of first-generation a bit more broadly to encompass students who may self-identify as first-generation from their lack of familiarity or exposure to experiences like obtaining a four-year degree at a residential, four-year, college in the United States immediately after high school. For "low-income," there is no specific income level that is used to determine eligibility, but most students participating in GSP have zero or limited expected family contributions as part of their financial aid. With an inaugural class of 50 in 2004, GSP's first students were awarded substantial scholarships, grants, and federal loans to attend Georgetown. In the last 16 years, our program has grown substantially in terms of number of students, available scholarships, program staff, and student-focused programming. As of Fall 2020, GSP is a community serving over 700 undergraduates, 1,600 alumni, and countless supporters. A total of 100% of GSP's student population still receive significant amounts of need-based financial aid, 85% are the first in their families to attend college, and 85% are students of color. Thanks in large part to students' advocacy efforts, the number of program staff has grown from one half-time employee in 2004 to seven full-time program staff members. GSP's mission is to support first-generation and low-income students at Georgetown so they can thrive during their time in college, from their transition into university life through completion. While GSP continues to grow and adapt to student needs, we currently categorize our work into four key areas: Community Building; Mentorship and Advising;

Advocacy and Empowerment; and Financial Resources. We use these pillars to inform the ways in which we work toward our mission of working toward a more equitable college experience for first-generation and low-income students at Georgetown.

Funded in large part by the generosity of our philanthropic community, GSP is widely regarded as one of the foremost programs of its kind in the country – supporting students during their time at the "Hilltop" and working to ensure their successful graduation from Georgetown. John Rosenberg, Editor of *The Harvard Magazine*, wrote in his October 2017 article *Mastering the Hidden Curriculum*, that Georgetown and GSP "established the playbook" for supporting undergraduates from under-resourced high schools (Rosenberg, 2017). Our students graduate at a rate of 96.4%, a percentage comparable to their Georgetown peers, and we have over 1,100 alumni/ae.

Our full-time staff include professionals with diverse backgrounds and skill sets including education, marketing, event planning, and counseling. The Executive Director leads strategic partnership building and fundraising approaches; the Associate Director serves as deputy director and oversees day-to-day operations and programming; two Assistant Directors lead student advising/engagement and operations/communications work; and two Program Coordinators support the Assistant Directors in each of these areas. Our students have access to our Necessity Fund, a fund that offers small grants to students for emergencies and essentials that fall outside of the traditional university cost of attendance. Our student engagement team coordinates our community building events, one-on-one and group advising sessions, and mentorship programs. Our goal is to help to make Georgetown University a more inclusive place for first-generation and low-income students. This work is realized and prioritized at all levels and areas of campus life, and not merely driven by a collection of student affairs offices. We work toward facilitating a *whole institution approach* – building relationships across all departments, both inside and outside the classroom, while consulting with other offices to ensure that their spaces are welcoming of our students. All of our work is done with our students in mind and we ensure that the student voice is heard in all of our decision-making. All aspects of membership in GSP are opt-in for students, which we believe makes for higher quality engagement and participation since students self-select into participating in any particular aspect of our programming. Students receive their scholarship funding no matter how involved they choose to be in the programmatic elements of our work.

Given our student population and available resources (number of staff, space on campus, etc.), our program staff must be creative and collaborative in order to holistically support our students. Outside of our full-time staff, we have developed – and are continuing to grow – a network of wraparound volunteer support, completely funded by our donors, with the help of three signature programs: Peer Mentor Program, Alumni Mentor Program, and Regional Network Program.

PEER MENTOR PROGRAM

Peer Mentor Program Mission, Goals, and Objectives

Much research has shown that a range of academic and social factors support a sense of belonging during the first year of college (Strayhorn, 2012) and that positive interactions with peers are especially significant (Means and Pyne, 2017). As such, our Peer Mentor Program has served as one way to welcome and support our students, particularly in their first year on campus. Through one-on-one meetings and social events, students join a strong community while discovering the resources available to them as GSP and Georgetown students. Our hope is that our first-year students find support in having at least one older GSP student in their corner.

For **mentees**, the goals of the Peer Mentor Program are that they:

1) Demonstrate an increased sense of belonging at Georgetown
2) Exhibit an increased sense of belonging in our program, GSP
3) Build skills to utilize campus resources to navigate the Georgetown community
4) Develop strategies that enhance participation in the student curricular and co-curricular experience

For **mentors**, the goals of the Peer Mentor Program are to:

1) Improve mentors' relationship building skills
2) Refine mentors' communication skills
3) Provide meaningful leadership experience to help them self-identify as leaders on campus
4) Give meaningful leadership experience to help them self-identify as leaders within GSP

Mentors' primary responsibilities include mentor training, monthly check-ins, and student referrals to staff for additional support.

Peer Mentor Program Implementation and Stakeholders

Given the significant amount of research that points toward the importance of first-year peer relationships, we have built, grown, and modified our Peer Mentor Program each year to best accommodate our students. As of the Fall 2020 semester, our program includes 169 peer mentees and 85 mentors. The program's timeline is as follows:

- **May:** All returning GSP students are invited to apply to serve as a peer mentor for up to two incoming first-year students, including new transfer students.

- **July:** Incoming students receive information about GSP including the Peer Mentor Lookbook, an electronic publication that includes mentor information and profiles, as well as a survey to rank their top five mentors of choice based on mentor descriptions.
- **August:** GSP staff uses student surveys and narratives to match mentors and mentees. Peer Mentors and Mentees are "e-introduced." Mentors receive training on how best to engage their mentees and the expectations of the program. We encourage monthly interaction for the students and facilitate opportunities through our office should students want to take part. Additionally, we offer $50 per semester of funding for on- or off-campus events and outings that mentors and mentees would like to attend together.

Peer Mentor Program Assessment Plan

Assessment (see Table 7.1) for the GSP Peer Mentorship Program includes both summative and formative approaches aimed at assessing outcomes for both mentees and mentors, and to provide ongoing feedback to program staff to ensure that mentorship pairs have the resources and support necessary to meet their shared goals.

The summative assessments include two surveys of GSP students. One is aimed at first-year students (i.e. the mentees) and is conducted as part of GSP 101, the orientation series provided to students during their first semesters on campus that is intended to onboard students to GSP. In this survey, students have the opportunity to share about their early experiences with their mentors and the role mentors may have played in supporting their transitions to campus. Year-end surveys sent to mentors and mentees also allow an opportunity for students to assess their experiences against the program's stated goals and outcomes. Qualitative and quantitative analyses are utilized to create a fuller picture of students' experiences and any trends that may have emerged during the year.

Summative assessments provide students an opportunity to give formal evaluations of program staff and provide informal feedback. The feedback is used to calibrate program implementation throughout the academic year. For example, program staff reaches out to students who have expressed concerns in their GSP 101 survey about their early experiences with their peer mentors. Students are then asked if they would like to a) provide greater details about their concerns via a check-in with program staff; b) be reintroduced to their mentor (if the challenge is that the mentor and mentee have not yet connected; c) be assigned a different mentor; or d) withdraw from the mentorship program. Students are also invited to offer feedback or concerns in response to each monthly e-newsletter distributed to mentors and mentees.

Table 7.1 Peer Mentorship Assessment Plan

Outcome	Evidence Collected	Method of Collection
Peer Mentorship Program – Mentees		
1) Demonstrate an increased sense of belonging at Georgetown	• Self-reported by students	• Year-End Survey • GSP 101 Self-Reflection Survey
2) Demonstrate an increased sense of belonging in GSP	• Number of 1–1 mentor/mentee experiences reported • Self-reported by students	• Tracking 1–1 experience funding requests • Year-End Survey • GSP 101 Self-Reflection Survey
3) Develop skills to utilize campus resources to navigate the Georgetown community	• Self-reported by students	• Year-End Survey • GSP 101 Self-Reflection Survey
4) Develop strategies that enhance participation in the student curricular and co-curricular experience	• Self-reported by students	• Year-End Survey • GSP 101 Self-Reflection Survey
Peer Mentorship Program – Mentors		
1) Improve mentors' relationship building skills	• Self-reported by students	• Monthly check-ins with program staff • Year-End Survey
2) Improve mentors' communication skills	• Self-reported by students	• Monthly check-ins with program staff • Year-End Survey
3) Provide mentors with meaningful leadership experience to help them self-identify as leaders on campus	• Self-reported by students	• Year-End Survey
4) Provide mentors with meaningful leadership experience to help them self-identify as leaders within GSP	• Self-reported by students	• Year-End Survey
5) Help mentees develop skills to utilize campus resources to navigate the Georgetown/GSP community and enhance mentees' participation in the student curricular and co-curricular experience	• Self-reported by students	• Monthly check-ins with program staff • Year-End Survey

Peer Mentor Program Outcomes

Mentee Outcomes

Mentees were asked to fill out a year-end assessment and feedback survey distributed at the end of the 2019–2020 academic year. The majority of mentees found that their mentors helped them feel a sense of belonging in GSP (73%), provided guidance in accessing campus resources (73%), helped them feel a sense of belonging at Georgetown more broadly (54%), and provided guidance in accessing GSP resources (54%). A smaller percentage of mentees reported that their mentors helped them by finding specific ways to get involved on campus (42%), but we understand that this may be due to Georgetown's transition to a virtual learning environment. In addition, mentees identified academic (classes, professors, studying, etc.) and social issues (friends, roommates, etc.) to be among the most prevalent topics discussed during conversations with their mentors (77% of respondents identified these as prevalent topics of discussion).

Based on the GSP 101 surveys distributed to first-year students early in the fall semester, 78% of respondents indicated that their mentors had been helpful in their transitions to college, and 22% indicated that their mentors had not been helpful. In many cases, understandably, mentees shared that they had not yet had the opportunity to reach back out to their mentors during their naturally busy transitions to campus life. When considering satisfaction with the program, about three out of four mentees (73%) indicated that they intended on applying to be peer mentors once they were eligible as upperclassmen.

Mentor Outcomes

Peer Mentors were also asked to fill out a year-end assessment and feedback survey at the end of the 2019–2020 academic year. The vast majority of mentors reported that participating in the Peer Mentorship Program as mentors gave them a sense of leadership in GSP (93% of respondents), gave them a sense of leadership on campus (86%), and improved their relationship building skills (86%). A smaller majority reported that serving as mentors had improved their communication skills (57%).

In terms of areas of support provided to their mentees, mentors identified academic issues (93%), social issues (86%), and wellness issues (71%) as the most prevalent topics discussed during their conversations with mentees. A smaller percentage (57%) named financial issues as among the most prevalent topics discussed.

ALUMNI MENTOR PROGRAM

Alumni Mentor Program Mission, Goals, and Objectives

While GSP's peer mentors serve as a crucial component of our first-year support strategy, our Alumni Mentor Program offers upperclassmen the opportunity to connect with a Georgetown and/or GSP alumnus for the remainder of their time at Georgetown and beyond. Our hope is that students have the chance to broaden their network by forming a strong relationship with their mentor, facilitating a mutually beneficial system of mentorship. Research has shown that undergraduate students who participated in mentor programs reported developing the skills and behaviors necessary to succeed professionally (Schlosser et al., 2003) and that longer mentor relationships have a higher likelihood of having a positive impact on the mentee (DuBois et al., 2002). Mentors provide one-on-one guidance to GSP students on a wide range of topics including: navigating Georgetown and the college experience; encouraging career and academic interests; pursuing extra-curricular opportunities; and providing a caring, supportive, and informed perspective.

For mentees, the goals of the Alumni Mentor Program mirror those of the Peer Mentor Program with a few additions:

1) Demonstrate an increased sense of belonging at Georgetown
2) Build skills to utilize campus resources to navigate the Georgetown community
3) Develop strategies that enhance participation in the student curricular and co-curricular experience
4) Improve upon their ability to network and professionally socialize
5) Grow their personal and professional community

Alumni Mentor Program Implementation and Stakeholders

As GSP has grown, so too has our Alumni Mentor Program. Students have the opportunity to sign up for an Alumni Mentor at the end of their first year. Alumni mentors are Georgetown alumni/ae who complete an online application and pass a phone interview with GSP staff. The majority of our non-GSP alumni mentors learn of this program through word of mouth. Many are donors of our program or friends of GSP alumni. A small number of alumni mentors are also alumni/ae of GSP with the hope that one day GSP alumni will serve as the majority of mentors. Alums of GSP are recruited through email, social media, and word of mouth.

Timeline:

- **May:** Students attend an informational session and complete an online survey asking what they are seeking in a mentor

- **June:** GSP Staff complete the mentor/mentee matching process. Mentors and mentees receive a handbook with helpful tools on how to get the most out of the relationship
- **August:** Pairs are "e-introduced" and encouraged to connect prior to the beginning of the academic year
- **October**: Mentors and mentees are invited to connect at the annual GSP Community. Mentors are also encouraged to join for a training session where pertinent topics are discussed

We encourage monthly phone, text, or in-person interaction but understand that each mentor/mentee relationship is different. As many of our students prefer to lean on their mentors for professional support and advice, certain times of the academic year are more relevant and filled with these types of conversations.

Alumni Mentor Program Assessment Plan

As with the Peer Mentorship Program, the Alumni Mentorship Program also provides formal and informal opportunities for participants to provide feedback to program staff (Table 7.2). Historically, owing in part to the fact that the alumni mentorship program has been heavily supported by alumni volunteers, summative assessments were primarily targeted at mentors' experiences in the

Table 7.2 Program Assessment

Outcome Assessed	Evidence Collected	Method of Collection
Alumni Mentorship Program – Mentors		
1) Form strong relationships with mentees	• Self-reported	• Year-End Survey
2) Develop longer term relationships that stretch over several years of mentees' college careers	• Data collected on return rate of mentors each year	• Year-End Survey
3) Provide mentees with guidance and perspective on a broad range of topics, including: navigating Georgetown and the college experience, encouraging career and academic interests, pursuing extra-curricular opportunities, and providing a caring, supportive, and informed perspective	• Self-reported	• Year-End Survey

program. We keep track of these engagements through Google Sheets with hopes of one day incorporating these engagement touchpoints on our university's formal database system. Future assessments will allow for more formal evaluation of mentees' experiences in the program.

Alumni Mentorship Program Outcomes

Alumni mentors and mentees were asked to submit year-end feedback and assessment forms during the 2019–2020 academic year. The vast majority (93%) of respondents reported that they were in regular contact with their mentees, and the same percentage reported that they hoped to serve as a mentor again (either to the same student as the past year, or a new student if their mentee was graduating) in the coming year.

In keeping with the goals of supporting mentees' growth in professional networking and expanding their professional and personal communities, 95% of mentors identified "Careers and Internships" as an area in which they provided support to their mentee. A total of 84% provided support related to academics; 77% provided support related to finding greater life balance (alongside academics and other obligations); and 63% provided support related to navigating Georgetown and GSP resources.

Qualitative assessments provide a snapshot of students' experiences in the alumni mentorship program. Students shared feedback that ranged from overly positive or negative, to indications that program staff could do more to set expectations, and to provide additional support in helping mentor/mentee pairs to uncover areas of shared resonance and build stronger relationships more quickly.

REGIONAL NETWORK PROGRAM

Regional Network Program Mission, Goals, and Objectives

The GSP Regional Network Program was created to support students as they build their personal and professional networks around the country and world. With 11 regional hubs around the United States and one international hub, Georgetown alumni and GSP supporters serve as connectors for GSP students during and after their time as undergraduates. Our Regional Network Coordinators aid in student recruitment by calling our students to congratulate them on their acceptance to Georgetown and GSP; and help in welcoming students with our annual new student "Welcome Receptions" each summer. Most importantly, Regional Network Coordinators build community among their local students and assist with internship and job help for students who are looking for a new set of connections.

Regional Network Program Implementation and Stakeholders

Given that most GSP students hail from hometowns outside of the Washington, D.C. area, our Regional Network allows students to connect with Georgetown and GSP alumni in their respective hometowns. These coordinators were recruited through our GSP Advisory Board, a group of Georgetown alumni committed to GSP's mission. Many of our regional coordinators serve on the Board or serve as alumni mentors. A small group of these coordinators are also GSP alumni who identified that they would like to remain deeply involved. Our coordinators also serve as local "experts" in terms of social services and professional networks. While each region may only have a few "official" coordinators, these volunteers serve as a gateway for students to connect with the larger Georgetown community that spans all over the world. Thanks to the vast Georgetown alumni network, regional coordinators can capitalize on the general Georgetown alumni base and recruit volunteers through the various alumni clubs around the country and the world. This is our newest network of support, and our implementation is still in its pilot stage. Like everything else in our program, students are not required to take advantage of this resource, but our hope is that by offering them access to these coordinators early and often, students can grow in relationship with them throughout their undergraduate careers.

Timeline:

- **Spring and Early Summer:** Regional Network coordinators call prospective accepted students to congratulate them and offer to answer students' questions
- **Late Summer:** Regional Network coordinators host "Welcome Receptions," opportunities for incoming GSP students to meet others in their area and connect with returning local students and alumni
- Throughout the academic year, coordinators host Zoom or in-person meetings during the Thanksgiving, winter, spring, and Easter breaks to meet and check-in with students

Regional Network Program Assessment

Given that our Regional Network Program is relatively new and still growing, the 2020–2021 academic year will be the first year where we formally assess its effectiveness. Our Regional Network Program is our most prominent opportunity for students to receive informal mentoring. Informal mentoring involves the provision of general guidance and support and, in some instances, helping a student learn something new. Research shows that mentorship also promotes students' sense of well-being by challenging the negative opinions they may have of themselves and demonstrating that they can have positive relationships with adults. The relationship may be short- or long term, but in both instances, mentoring has a lasting positive impact on the student (Rhodes et al., 2000). Given the flexibility of these relationships, our evaluations may vary year-to-year.

Our assessment plan will include feedback surveys and interviews with regional coordinators and students. Our goal is to ensure that students are *aware* of the resources available to them through the Regional Network so that, when the time comes, they can effectively utilize their coordinator(s). Like the Alumni Mentor Program, we want to ensure that students feel comfortable reaching out to coordinators. We believe that the networking muscles students begin to build and flex in their first year with their peer mentor can translate to their alumni mentor and regional network coordinators.

Lessons Learned

As the Georgetown Scholars Program continues to evolve, so do our network of support. We know that our first 15 years have been formative in the development of our program, and we believe that the next 15 will continue to challenge the status quo and improve our effectiveness in supporting students. Our lessons learned can be categorized into three buckets: staff time and capacity; volunteer time and capacity; and capitalizing on additional opportunities.

All three of our support programs were inspired by stakeholders outside of our immediate staff. Students, alumni, and volunteers, respectively, each identified opportunities for programs such as these, proposed the visions and missions of these programs, and provided early iterations of each program's current implementation. Each of these programs had their own growing pains, especially when it came to scaling opportunities for a larger student population over time. Another reality includes the natural challenge of life transitions and the loss of institutional and historical knowledge that is often deeply entrenched into grassroots initiatives such as our mentorship programs: students graduate, alumni take on other responsibilities, and volunteers relocate or experience other life events. Our staff quickly learned that support from a full-time staff member in the GSP office was key to ensuring the success of each program and to guarantee consistency. We now have one full-time staff member that facilitates all three programs. We believe that this dedicated position benefits all stakeholders and will ensure the programs' sustainable future.

Another challenge has been to create and offer helpful tools and resources that allow each mentoring relationship to "self-manage" themselves to a certain degree, when it comes to having a shared vision, expectations, boundaries, method of communication, etc. For example, one mentee shared feedback about "not knowing what to talk to [their alumni mentor] about, or what to ask for, or what to update them on." The program needs to move in the direction of having a more layered approach in terms of goals and outcomes to support mentors and mentees in co-creating shared "agreements." We believe that doing so will allow each mentorship pair to maximize their time together and more precisely assess their relationship progress based on the agreements they have created together.

We also quickly learned that, while mentors are equipped to provide support to students on a myriad of levels and topics, certain circumstances require mentors to escalate concerns to the level of staff attention. That is, mentors are not trained to be "experts" on *all* things Georgetown, nor are they mental health professionals. To ensure that both students and staff remain healthy and not burn out, we learned that mentors need to be made aware of – and encouraged to use – the many resources available to them and their mentee. While a peer or alumni mentor is a great listening ear to whom students can vent, sometimes the help of a mental health clinician can provide a more appropriate space for certain topics, especially when trauma is involved.

If you are looking to build out one or all of these programs at your organization or institution, we suggest starting small with a committed group of volunteers. While there are *many* people willing to give their time and energy to our students, we must ensure that they are well-supported and informed. One of our future goals is to restart our faculty and staff mentorship program. This program was created in GSP's beginnings but, due to staff capacity, has been sitting on the bench for a few years now. While many students have unofficial mentorship relationships with their faculty, deans, and advisors across campus, we believe that a more built out program could benefit our students and allow for non-GSP staff to become more involved with our office. As an example of one of our core values of building out supportive programming that utilizes a *whole institution approach*, we hope that the university's recently formed First-Generation Faculty and Staff Initiative can help offer the leadership and capacity needed to reinvigorate this particular mentorship offering and ultimately provide another opportunity for our students to experience greater senses of belonging and support in our campus community.

We must acknowledge too that we have truly seen the positive effects of these programs in light of the COVID-19 pandemic. Given Georgetown's virtual learning environment, engaging students in the same ways proved incredibly difficult. Without our Peer Mentor, Alumni Mentor, and Regional Network Programs, our students would not have experienced the wraparound support that is a part of the GSP experience. The virtual environment proved beneficial for these programs as it allowed more flexibility for relationship building and allowed for a video call to be less intimidating to all involved. We believe that the lessons learned in the last year will help inform our work in the future.

APPENDIX

Outcomes – Peer Mentees

Which topics did you find most prevalent in your conversations with your mentor? (Choose all that apply.)

Academic issues (classes, professors, studying, etc.)	77%	20
Social issues (friends, roommates, etc.)	77%	20
Financial issues (financial aid, GSP grants, work study, saving, etc.)	46%	12
Wellness issues (mental health, physical wellness, etc.)	42%	11
Total	100%	26

My GSPeer Mentor... (Choose all that apply.)

helped me feel a sense of belonging at Georgetown	54%	14
helped me feel a sense of belonging in GSP	73%	19
provided guidance in accessing on campus resources	73%	19
provided guidance in accessing GSP resources	54%	14
supported my getting involved on campus	42%	11
Total	100%	26

Will you apply to serve as a peer mentor next year?

Yes	73%	19
No	27%	7
Total	100%	26

Outcomes – Peer Mentors

My participation on the GSPeer Mentor Program... (Choose all that apply.)

improved my communication skills	57%	8
improved my relationship building skills	86%	12

(Continued)

(*Continued*)

gave me a sense of leadership on campus	86%	12
gave me a sense of leadership in GSP	93%	13
Total	100%	14

Which topics did you find most prevalent in your conversations with your mentee? (Choose all that apply.)

Academic issues	93%	13
Social issues (friends, roommates, etc.)	86%	12
Financial issues (financial aid, GSP grants, work study, saving, etc.)	57%	8
Wellness issues (mental health, physical wellness, etc.)	71%	10
Total	100%	14

How often did you connect with your mentee this year?

Weekly	7%	1
Monthly	57%	8

Outcomes – Alumni Mentors

Are you in regular contact with your mentee?

Yes! We have been in regular contact.	93%	40
No, we have not been in contact.	7%	3
Total	100%	43

I would like to serve as a mentor again

Yes	93%	40
No	7%	3
Total	100%	43

(*Continued*)

(Continued)

In what areas did you provide support to your mentee?		
Academics	84%	36
Georgetown and GSP resources (i.e. Necessity Fund, tutoring, mental health resources, advising, etc.)	63%	27
Careers and internships	95%	41
Life balance (i.e. exercise, nutrition, social life, hobbies, clubs, etc.)	77%	33
Finances	26%	11
Total	100%	43

REFERENCES

DuBois, D. L., Holloway, B. E., Valentine, J. C. et al. (2002). Effectiveness of mentoring programs for youth: A meta-analytic review. *American Journal Community Psychology* 30, 157–197.

Means, D. R., & Pyne, K. B. (2017). Finding my way: Perceptions of institutional support and belonging in low-income, first-generation, first-year college students. *Journal of College Student Development* 58(6), 907–924.

Rhodes, J. E., Grossman, J. B., & Resch, N. R. (2000). Agents of change: Pathways through which mentoring relationships influence adolescents' academic adjustment. *Child Development*, 71, 1662–1671.

Rosenberg, J. (2017). "Mastering the 'Hidden Curriculum'." *Harvard Magazine*. https://harvardmagazine.com/2017/11/mastering-the-hidden-curriculum (accessed June 10, 2022).

Schlosser, L. Z., Knox, S., Moskovitz, A. R., & Hill, C. E. (2003). A qualitative examination of graduate advising relationships: The advisee perspective. *Journal of Counseling Psychology*, 50(2), 178–188.

Strayhorn, T. L. (2012). *College students' sense of belonging: A key to educational success for all students*. Routledge.

Chapter 8

Faculty Mentoring Dinners

Facilitating High-Impact Practices

Malaphone Phommasa,
Yasmine Dominguez-Whitehead,
Angelica Caudillo and Kari Weber

FACULTY MENTORING DINNERS: FACILITATING HIGH-IMPACT PRACTICES

First-generation college students succeed despite living and learning within institutional structures that were not originally designed to support them, demonstrating strength and persistence. They navigate uncharted territories in their higher education journey, including but not limited to building relationships with faculty, participating in high-impact practices, and finding community among peers. Research on first-generation college students examines experiences of isolation and marginalization at predominantly white institutions, a lack of cultural validity in the curriculum, and cultural mismatches between home and the university (Azmitia et al., 2018; Jehangir, 2010; Rendon, 1994; Stephens et al., 2012). If they are transfer students, they may also perceive further marginalization due to their transfer student identity and negative perceptions of transfer students' academic abilities (Kodama, 2002; Laanan, 1996; Wood & Moore, 2015). Despite these institutional barriers, first-generation college students also bring resilience and cultural capital to the university (Yosso, 2005). The onus is on institutions to build policies and structures that work toward more inclusive experiences and equitable academic outcomes. The writers of this chapter, three of whom are first-generation college graduates, created the Faculty Mentoring Program as a way to honor the first-generation college student experience and provide more equitable opportunities in the face of institutional barriers.

INSTITUTIONAL CONTEXT

Guided by Hurtado and colleagues' (2012) Model for Diverse Learning Environments, our aim as professionals working in academic and student affairs units at the University of California, Santa Barbara (UCSB) is to develop programming that cultivates a sense of belonging for students, increases their cultural capital, supports high-impact practices, and contributes to their academic success (Kuh, 2008). UCSB is one of ten campuses in the University of California (UC) system; this four-year public, research-intensive university serves more than 23,000 undergraduate students, over 40% of whom are identified as first-generation college-going (University of California, 2020). First-generation college students are identified by the UC system as students who are the first in their families to earn a four-year degree (UCOP Institutional Research and Planning, 2017). UCSB also prides itself on its dual designation as both an Asian American and Native American Pacific Islander-Serving Institution (AANAPISI) and Hispanic-Serving Institution (HSI) by the US Department of Education. These institutional identities and the research on first-generation college students' experiences in higher education frame the purpose and drive for our shared work between the ONDAS (Opening New Doors to Accelerating Success) Student Center, Transfer Student Center, and the Educational Opportunity Program (EOP).

Despite being housed in separate divisions within the university, our units have a shared purpose – to serve student populations that have been historically marginalized and minoritized in higher education. This includes lower income students, first-generation college students, transfer students, and black, indigenous, and people of color (BIPOC). EOP (recently celebrating its 50th anniversary in 2017) is a foundational unit at UCSB that was created out of demands to support minority students during the Civil Rights Movement (Educational Opportunity Program, 2020). This legacy has resulted in an expansive unit that provides holistic counseling, peer mentorship, cultural resource centers, and social/cultural programming for income eligible, first-generation college students. EOP is housed in the division of student affairs and is primarily funded by student fees. In response to continually shifting demographics of the UCSB undergraduate student population, specifically increases in the number of Latinx students, first-generation college students, and transfer students, the ONDAS Student Center and Transfer Student Center were founded in 2015 in the division of academic affairs. The ONDAS Student Center was developed with a US Department of Education Title V Part A grant that sunset in 2020; both centers are funded through the Executive Vice Chancellor's office (or commonly known as the Vice Provost for academic affairs office). The ONDAS Student Center and Transfer Student Center provide first-generation college students and transfer students with academic advising, study space, peer mentorship, and programming to support successful transitions into and through the university. The missions of EOP, ONDAS Student Center, and Transfer Student Center are well-aligned for cross-campus collaboration to serve the needs of our diverse student body.

FACULTY MENTORING PROGRAM
Purpose of the Faculty Mentoring Program

The purpose of the Faculty Mentoring Program is to facilitate meaningful connections between first-generation college students and faculty at UCSB. Additional objectives include: 1) humanize professors to first-generation college students through opportunities for real conversations outside of the formal classroom, 2) provide transfer students opportunities to develop stronger relationships within their academic department in preparation for research and graduate school opportunities, 3) allow undeclared students an opportunity to learn about new disciplines, and 4) promote students' participation in high-impact practices (e.g., undergraduate research, learning communities, etc.) that positively impact their undergraduate experiences and career trajectories. In order to achieve these objectives, we have employed a detail-oriented, wraparound approach to support students and orient faculty throughout their participation in the Faculty Mentoring Program.

Program Design and Structure

The Faculty Mentoring Program consists of two subset programs, Table Talk and Dining with Faculty. Table Talk serves first-generation college students of all class levels and is led by an EOP Counselor and the ONDAS Student Center Coordinator. Table Talk provides an opportunity for students to get to know faculty in their discipline, but is open to students of all class levels. The intention is that undeclared students or students who are exploring additional majors and minors can get to know a faculty member in a different field. Dining with Faculty exclusively admits first-generation transfer students and is led by the Transfer Student Center Coordinator and an EOP Counselor. We understand that transfer students are on an accelerated timeline and many UCSB transfer students enter the university already thinking about their post-graduation plans. Dining with Faculty participants must be majoring in the same discipline as their faculty mentor so that students can build their academic network, learn about research and internships opportunities, and gain general academic insights about their major department.

Faculty mentors volunteer their time and are assigned five to seven students interested in their area of expertise or backgrounds. These groups engage in three dinners over the course of the academic quarter to develop a mentoring relationship with the potential to extend beyond the duration of the program. We focus our efforts on serving minoritized students, while simultaneously sharing administrative coordination and program costs, including student orientations, dinner arrangements, and exit surveys. The following sections describe the implementation process.

Funding Strategies

Our partnership became our strength in securing a budget to set a foundation and build longevity for the Faculty Mentoring Program. The ONDAS Student Center and Transfer Student Center have limited funding for food expenses but have staff members available to assist with program logistics. Logistical support includes creating and disseminating invitations, arranging for location set-up, and organizing meal delivery. EOP, which is funded through multiple sources including student fees, grants, and institutional funding, offers more flexibility and provides a larger budget for food expenses. Therefore, EOP funds the cost of the meals, allocating approximately $14 per participant for each dinner. The ONDAS Student Center and Transfer Student Center provide $500 annually toward drinks, desserts, and utensils for both the pre-program orientation and dinners. Our total budget for the academic year is approximately $3,380 for 36 dinners and three orientations, yet we historically come in under budget.

Marketing and Student Recruitment

Acknowledging that first-generation college students hold a variety of intersecting identities, we intentionally recruit faculty volunteers, who identify as first-generation college graduates and/or first-generation allies, former transfer students, and faculty of color. We aim to have representation from a variety of disciplines over the course of the year, expanding our reach among first-generation college students. Formal email invitations to faculty members outline program goals, expected time commitments, and a list of faculty who have previously participated. Faculty mentors who commit to participation are invited to select three dinner dates. Student staff then create flyers, disseminate information to academic departments and campus partners, post on social media, and encourage students to apply. It is important to note that the program allows students to self-identify as first-generation college students, acknowledging that definitions of the identity can vary across different programs and institutions. Using Google Forms, we collect basic demographic information from student applicants and ask questions that help us determine participation. In order to maximize the number of students we serve, we prioritize students who have not previously participated in the program or similar mentoring programs. Selected participants' applications are shared with faculty mentors before the first dinner to help them learn about their participating group of mentees and what they would like to gain from the program.

We conduct an orientation for participating students to provide them with tools and skills to enhance their navigational capital (Yosso, 2005). We discuss the culture of academia; how occasionally, there are processes and protocols that a student will not find in a handbook or on a website – commonly referred to as the "hidden curriculum" of higher education (Chatelain, 2018; Delgado, 2020). Our intention is for first-generation college students who participate in this program to gain access to this hidden curriculum so they can use these tools to engage with faculty and teaching assistants. The orientation also provides students with an opportunity to meet their peers, allowing them to build rapport with each other before the first mentoring dinner. Students are tasked with working together to develop questions for their faculty mentor and are encouraged to utilize their agency to drive conversation topics during the dinners. We suggest topics that are not limited exclusively to academia, which has resulted in rich and dynamic conversations between students and faculty mentors.

Stakeholders

The stakeholders for this program fall into three categories: students, faculty, and funding sources. Students serve as the largest stakeholder group to this program. As the intended beneficiaries of the program, student feedback is imperative. We elicit feedback in the form of exit surveys to modify and make the program as accessible and equitable as possible. It could be argued, based on evaluation data, that faculty are also indirect beneficiaries of the program. The program is invested in seeing students succeed, which aligns with the overall goals of our funding sources. Accordingly, we create and share our data in the form of quarterly and annual institutional reports highlighting areas of success and challenges.

Assessment Plan and Outcomes

The program was initiated in 2017; the data presented spans from 2017 to 2020. A total of 197 students and 40 faculty members have participated. Two transfer students participated in both Table Talk and Dining with Faculty. Program assessment consists of student and faculty exit surveys upon completion of the three dinners. The exit surveys are developed by the team using Google Forms and periodically scrutinized in order to determine the extent to which the program's objectives are being met. The surveys were designed in order to 1) learn about the ways in which the program impacts participants and 2) provide opportunities for students and faculty to suggest improvements to the program. Quantitative and qualitative data indicate that students benefit from the mentorship relationship and that faculty find their participation meaningful. While the program has not examined student and faculty engagement that takes place after the dinners, in the future our goal is to assess long-term impacts. Program assessment and outcomes are further discussed below and take into consideration the two unique programs: Table Talk and Dining with Faculty.

Table Talk

A total of 108 students and 21 faculty members have participated in Table Talk. The program is specifically designed for first-generation college students with the intention of introducing them to information about a specific major and allowing undeclared students an opportunity to learn about new disciplines. Student reports indicate that program participation was beneficial in helping them approach faculty. For example, one student reported, "I felt like the professor was a real person, not someone unapproachable and scary." Approximately 95% of student participants reported that they felt more comfortable approaching faculty members after participating in the program. The following comment further suggests the program helped students approach faculty:

> For the first time since attending UCSB, I feel like I really got to know a professor on a personal level. From the Table Talk, I feel more motivated to seek out opportunities and go to office hours for my other professors as well.

Benefits were also apparent with respect to gaining a sense of belonging. A total of 78% of participants reported they felt their faculty member was "very helpful" when they were asked, "How helpful was the faculty member in helping you feel more confident about being part of the UCSB community?" Student comments further suggest that the program helped students build community. One participant shared, "It gave us an opportunity to learn from Professor Cooper's own experiences as well as from our peers (who I'd say have all bonded with each other and formed friendships)." Another stated, "Table Talk is a great program that allows for students to see a real perspective of professors while also utilizing time to build community at UCSB through meeting other like-minded students."

In addition to the student reports, faculty members also reported making connections with students. One faculty member reported, "It's a great opportunity to help students, particularly first-gen." The following faculty member also indicated the program was meaningful for them:

> It was a great opportunity for me to "pay it forward"...as an immigrant who wasn't properly documented and didn't speak English when I arrived, many people helped me along the way. So, I'm committed to bring people along in a rise up movement that levels the playing field.

Dining with Faculty

A total of 93 students participated in Dining with Faculty, exclusively for transfer students, and 19 faculty members participated from 2017 to the present. Student exit survey data reports indicate that participating in Dining with Faculty provided significant benefits to their academic experience. Benefits were apparent with respect to students' sense of belonging. When students were asked "How helpful was the faculty member in helping you feel more confident about being part of the UCSB community?" a total of 73% reported they felt their faculty member was "very helpful." One participant shared, "It was nice to interact with other students who share similar interests and who were in a similar position as myself. Having Professor West provide insights into how to navigate and approach education was priceless." The following participant reflected on her experiences navigating gender dynamics in her discipline and learning from others:

> I was scared of being the only female student in the group. I did not think I would have applied if it had been a male Economics Professor; and since the Professor was a woman, I presumed more girls would have applied. With that said, I was so grateful to listen to other students' talks: it opened my eyes as to how we were all different and yet were simultaneously so similar. I had crossed the gender barrier in communication that I formerly assumed was insurmountable and it was rewarding.

Students also reported increased confidence in approaching faculty, with 86% reporting feeling "more comfortable" approaching faculty in exit surveys. Making meaningful connections with faculty is especially important for transfer students given the short time they have at the university to develop and foster a meaningful relationship with faculty members to consider approaching them for letters of recommendation.

We ask faculty mentors to complete an exit survey regarding their program experience in order to conduct a well-rounded assessment of the mentoring program. Their reports suggest that participating faculty's values are consistent with the program's aims. As to be expected, critical feedback was also a part of the exit surveys received from the faculty including suggestions that the program exclusively serve incoming transfer students, a change in venue due to our conference room lacking windows and limiting the group to five students or less.

Table Talk and Dining with Faculty Combined Outcomes

As a whole, 90% of total student participants indicated they felt more comfortable approaching faculty members after participating in the program. When it came to promoting a sense of belonging, 74% of students indicated that the faculty member was very helpful with respect to feeling confident about being part of the UCSB community.

Although it was not a requirement of the program, it was not uncommon for faculty and students to continue their mentorship relationship beyond the program dinners. For example, some dinner groups independently organized outings to the theater, continued meeting for meals once the program ended, and other students became research assistants to their faculty mentor. While the program initiates first-generation college student contact with faculty members outside the formal classroom, student and faculty participants have the option to foster and further develop these relationships on their own.

Program Changes and Improvements

Throughout all four years of program implementation, multiple changes and improvements have taken place. Some of the changes have been a direct result of feedback from both faculty and students and other changes were the result of budget and staffing needs. In the inaugural quarter of the Faculty Mentoring Program, we held the dinners at the esteemed University Club but soon recognized that this option was not sustainable due to the high cost. We transitioned the dinners to the ONDAS Student Center and Transfer Student Center space after hours, which also serves the purpose of introducing students to the centers if they were previously unfamiliar with them. We initially offered dinners from a variety of local restaurants, but this proved to be challenging for staff due to payment limitations and pick-up locations. In order to facilitate the ordering, purchasing, and pick-up efforts, we now only use one restaurant for all three dinners in the course of a quarter. In that vein, we initially offered the entire menu from the restaurant to the participants, this quickly became untenable as participants were requesting complicated orders. Accordingly, we made adjustments to limit the number of choices and special requests while also meeting dietary needs.

Additional program improvements came by way of feedback from faculty mentors. Initially, we did not provide conversation starters because we designed the dinners as spaces where organic conversations could emerge. Faculty subsequently reported that, depending on the group, conversations were slow to start. We responded by creating and offering a "table prompt" or conversation starter at each of the dinners. Examples of conversation starters include, "Where did you grow up? And, what is the place known for?" and "If money or time were no object, I would study/research…" As a way to thank and acknowledge faculty's time commitment to the program, we provide faculty with both a handwritten thank you card and formal letter documenting their service. This formal letter was requested by a faculty mentor and could be included as part of the material presented for a faculty's personnel review, contributing to their career advancement.

In Spring of 2019, we organized a reunion event called the "Faculty Mentoring Program Rewind." All student and faculty participants of past programs (Table Talk and Dining with Faculty) were invited to reconnect and reinvigorate the initial mentoring relationship, while also enjoying a night of food and refreshments. This event had mixed results; many faculty members attended but few students were able to join. One complication was due to the fact that several Dining with

Faculty participants, who were transfer students, had already graduated from the university.

As we transitioned to remote learning due to COVID-19 restrictions, the program was paused for Spring 2020. We resumed the program remotely using the campus online meeting technology for Fall 2020, as data from students indicated that they desired faculty connections during remote learning. The program was designed similarly to the in-person dinners, allowing faculty members to select three consistent dates and times to meet with their mentoring group. Adjusting to the new environment, we considered implementation strategies for the dinner component including options for food delivery services, but opted for grocery store e-gift cards of $25 per student for each dinner to avoid service and delivery fees and to be inclusive of students who live in rural areas. We also transitioned funding for the program from EOP to temporary campus grant funds secured by the ONDAS Student Center and Transfer Student Center in order to ease the strain on EOP's programming budget during the pandemic. Program changes, improvements, and flexibility are essential to the continued success of our program. We embrace these changes in order to meet student, faculty, and staff needs through continued collaboration.

Exit surveys from students participating in remote programming indicate that the program can withstand variations that deviate from the original in-person dinners. One participant shared, "Getting to know my professor was very interesting, especially the insight he gave us in regards to the profession and graduate school…" The student also mentioned that the experience was "spectacular." The success of the remote mentoring dinners has opened up the possibility of implementing the virtual component when necessary. This also has implications for replicating this model at online universities and institutions where faculty and students need more flexible meeting options.

Lessons Learned

Four years of implementation has required our team to be flexible, adapt to unexpected changes, incorporate participant feedback from exit surveys, and commit to strengthening our partnerships. Employing these practices has led to smooth collaborative relationships and a successful Faculty Mentoring Program. For practitioners looking to design their own Faculty Mentoring Program dinners, we recommend: 1) open communication for sustaining equitable partnerships, 2) flexibility in program implementation, and 3) developing assessment or evaluation protocols like exit surveys.

Open, transparent communication is necessary from the onset of program design and throughout program implementation. We found it useful to establish clear lines of communication in order to determine the monetary and staffing resources that could be allocated to the program. For example, EOP had access to more programming funds than the ONDAS Student Center and Transfer Student Center, but the centers contributed with their access to faculty and academic departments. Therefore, EOP partners put effort into securing program funds while the two centers focused on the logistical work of securing faculty mentors. The centers were able to contribute financially, to a lesser degree, by funding a light meal at the Program Orientation. Being clear about contributions and expectations at the onset mitigates any financial and workload complications that may arise during implementation. Frequent communication throughout the duration of the program is also necessary for smooth operations. For example, team members email or text each other reminders about dinner pick-ups, communication to faculty and students, or requests for help if an emergency arises. This collaborative and communicative effort builds a strong partnership and collegial relationships.

A mindset of flexibility and adaptability is necessary when changes and complications arise, as they are bound to happen in the partnership and in program implementation. One example of a program adaptation due to the needs of partners is the shift from ordering meals from restaurants that required driving for pick-ups to ordering from a local restaurant that was accessible by foot or bicycle. This also allowed the team to rely on the support of student staff members to pick up meals when needed. Another example of required flexibility is when a faculty mentor requests a last minute reschedule of their dinner date and time. This requires team members to act quickly to inform students of the change, step in as a staff mentor during the dinners if meals have already been ordered, and work with the faculty mentor on rescheduling. Students are often understanding of these changes and appreciate the opportunity to continue the dinners.

Program evaluations allow teams to assess the impact of the program and understand how to better meet the needs of participants. Faculty Mentoring Program evaluation efforts included consistently conducting exit surveys in order to assess the impact of the Faculty Mentoring Program. Surveys were regularly updated to capture additional data when necessary. Assessment data allowed us to see similarly positive benefits (relating to networking, knowledge about research and graduate school, and connections with peers) in the remote faculty mentoring format as with the in-person faculty mentoring dinners, thus determining that the program can operate successfully in either format. The data collection efforts were beneficial for justifying sustained funding for the program; for instance, we secured more institutional and grant funding based on our data indicators. Lastly, the assessment data was used as a recruitment tool to encourage faculty participation.

CONCLUSION

The Faculty Mentoring Program is a staff-intensive program that requires detailed organization, frequent communication between collaborators, and robust financial support. Quantitative and qualitative data, derived from program evaluations from the last four years have demonstrated that our efforts have resulted in achieving the intended objectives of the program.

For example, quantitative data indicate that student participants overwhelmingly report feeling more comfortable approaching faculty members after participating. Additionally, we observed early signs of students' involvement in high-impact practices at the close of the program, with some student participants becoming research assistants for their faculty mentor. Qualitative data illustrate a more nuanced understanding of the program's impact on first-generation college students' experiences. One example is of the female-identified student in Economics who shared she was motivated to join the program because a female-identified Economics Professor (who is also a former transfer student) was serving as a faculty mentor. The student disclosed that she would not have applied if instead an Economics male-identified faculty was the designated mentor. Economics is a heavily male-dominated field, which is also the case in the major at UCSB. This example highlights why faculty mentors whose backgrounds and identities may resonate with first-generation college-going and transfer student populations are intentionally invited to participate in the program. The benefits of having faculty members who look like students or have similar backgrounds are well documented, especially for students who hold minoritized identities (Benitez et al., 2017), and it is our aim to promote these benefits.

Additional benefits of the program include the bonds formed by students within the mentoring cohorts. Connections were meaningful for both first-generation college students and faculty mentors, prompting some of the mentoring cohorts to continue meeting beyond the duration of the program. We intentionally designed an orientation so that student participants had an opportunity to meet each other in preparation for the first dinner with their faculty mentor, and we were also encouraged by the strong bonds and friendships that formed between the students as a result of the program.

While the Faculty Mentoring Program has become a successful, established program, we continue to envision what growth might look like for the program. Our long-term goals are to: 1) track student participants over the course of their studies at UCSB in order to accurately measure the program's impact on students' involvement in high-impact practices, 2) offer additional opportunities for mentoring cohorts to reconnect in future academic quarters, 3) provide a small stipend for faculty, acknowledging that first-generation faculty and faculty of color are often invited to take part in invisible mentoring labor (Cole & Griffin, 2013), and 4) scale the program to include more faculty and student participants. We recognize the current challenges: limited staff support to scale the program, stretched budgets, and hefty workloads for faculty. Notwithstanding this, we resolve to reach our goals of ensuring that more first-generation college students have opportunities to grow the tools and networks necessary to access and engage in high-impact practices.

REFERENCES

Allen, T. D., Lentz, E., & Day, R. (2006). Career success outcomes associated with mentoring others: A comparison of mentors and nonmentors. *Journal of Career Development*, *32*(3), 272–285. https://doi.org/10.1177/0894845305282942

Astin, A. W. (1999). Student involvement: A developmental theory for higher education. *Journal of College Student Development*, *40*(5), 518–529.

Azmitia, M., Sumabat-Estrada, G., Cheong, Y., & Covarrubias, R. (2018). "Dropping out is not an option": How educationally resilient first-generation students see the future. *New Directions for Child and Adolescent Development*, *160*, 89–100.

Benitez, M., James, M., Joshua, K., Perfetti, L., & Vick, S. B. (2017). "Someone who looks like me": Promoting the success of students of color by promoting the success of faculty of color. *Liberal Education*, *103*(2), 5.0

Chatelain, M. (2018, October 26). We must help first-generation students master academe's 'hidden curriculum'. *Chronicle of Higher Education, 65*(8), 1–3.

Cole, D., & Griffin, K. A. (2013). Advancing the study of student-faculty interaction: A focus on diverse students and faculty. In M. B. Paulsen (Ed.), *Higher education: Handbook of theory and research* (Vol. 28, pp. 561–611). Springer Netherlands. https://doi.org/10.1007/978-94-007-5836-0_12

Delgado, V. (2020). Decoding the hidden curriculum: Latino/a first-generation college students' influence on younger siblings' educational trajectory. *Journal of Latinos and Education*, 1–8. https://doi.org/10.1080/15348431.2020.1801439

Educational Opportunity Program (2020). http://eop.sa.ucsb.edu/

Gibb, S. (1999). The usefulness of theory: A case study in evaluating formal mentoring schemes. *Human Relations*, *52*(8), 1055–1075. https://doi.org/10.1023/A:1016983624755

Harper, S. R., Smith, E. J., & Davis, C. H. F. (2018). A critical race case analysis of black undergraduate student success at an urban university. *Urban Education*, *53*(1), 3–25. https://doi.org/10.1177/0042085916668956

Hurtado, S., Alvarez, C. L., Guillermo-Wann, C., Cuellar, M., & Arellano, L. (2012). A model for diverse learning environments: The scholarship on creating and assessing conditions for student success. In J. C. Smart & M. B. Paulsen (Eds.), *Higher education: Handbook of theory and research* (Vol. 27, pp. 41–122). Springer Netherlands. https://doi.org/10.1007/978-94-007-2950-6_2

Jehangir, R. (2010). Stories as knowledge: Bringing the lived experience of first-generation college students into the academy. *Urban Education*, *45*(4), 533–553. https://doi.org/10.1177/0042085910372352

Kilgo, C. A., Ezell Sheets, J. K., & Pascarella, E. T. (2015). The link between high-impact practices and student learning: Some longitudinal evidence. *Higher Education*, *69*(4), 509–525. https://doi.org/10.1007/s10734-014-9788-z

Kim, Y. K., & Sax, L. J. (2009). Student–faculty interaction in research universities: Differences by student gender, race, social class, and first-generation status.

Research in Higher Education, 50(5), 437–459. https://doi.org/10.1007/s11162-009-9127-x

Kodama, C. M. (2002). Marginality of transfer commuter students. Journal of Student Affairs Research and Practice, 39(3), 233–250. https://doi.org/10.2202/1949-6605.1172

Komarraju, M., Musulkin, S., & Bhattacharya, G. (2010). Role of student-faculty interactions in developing college students' academic self-concept, motivation, and achievement. Journal of College Student Development, 51(3), 332–342. https://doi.org/10.1353/csd.0.0137

Kuh, G., O'Donnell, K., & Schneider, C. G. (2017). HIPs at ten. Change: The Magazine of Higher Learning, 49(5), 8–16. https://doi.org/10.1080/00091383.2017.1366805

Kuh, G. D. (2008). High-impact educational practices: What they are, who has access to them, and why they matter. Association of American Colleges and Universities, 14(3), 28–29.

Laanan, F. S. (1996). Making the transition: Understanding the adjustment process of community college transfer students. Community College Review, 23(4), 69–84. https://doi.org/10.1177/009155219602300407

Padgett, R. D., Johnson, M. P., & Pascarella, E. T. (2012). First-generation undergraduate students and the impacts of the first year of college: Additional evidence. Journal of College Student Development, 53(2), 243–266. https://doi.org/10.1353/csd.2012.0032

Rendon, L. I. (1994). Validating culturally diverse students: Toward a new model of learning and student development. Innovative Higher Education, 19(1), 33–51. https://doi.org/10.1007/BF01191156

Ro, H. K., Lee, J., Fernandez, F., & Conrad, B. H. (2021). We don't know what they did last summer: Examining relationships among parental education, faculty interaction, and college students' post-first year summer experiences. Innovative Higher Education, 46(1), 21–39. https://doi.org/10.1007/s10755-020-09523-9

Stephens, N. M., Fryberg, S. A., Markus, H. R., Johnson, C. S., & Covarrubias, R. (2012). Unseen disadvantage: How American universities' focus on independence undermines the academic performance of first-generation college students. Journal of Personality and Social Psychology, 102(6), 1178–1197. https://doi.org/10.1037/a0027143

Trolian, T. L., Jach, E. A., Hanson, J. M., & Pascarella, E. T. (2016). Influencing academic motivation: The effects of student-faculty interaction. Journal of College Student Development, 57(7), 810–826. https://doi.org/10.1353/csd.2016.0080

UCOP (University of California Office of the President). (2017, August 23). UC kicks off systemwide effort to support first-generation students with new report [Press release]. https://www.universityofcalifornia.edu/press-room/uc-kicks-systemwide-effort-support-first-generation-students-new-report-website

University of California, Santa Barbara. (2020). *Through the years: A timeline of UC Santa Barbara.* https://www.ucsb.edu/about/history

Wood, J. L., & Moore, C. S. (2015). Engaging community college transfer students. In J. S Quaye, S. Harper, & S. L. Pendakur (Eds.), *Student engagement in higher education: Theoretical perspectives and practical approaches for diverse populations* (pp. 271–288). Routledge.

Yosso, T. J. (2005). Whose culture has capital? A critical race theory discussion of community cultural wealth. *Race Ethnicity and Education, 8*(1), 69–91. https://doi.org/10.1080/1361332052000341006

Part III

Learning Communities

Chapter 9

1st Gen Theme Community

Developing a Living-Learning Program for First-Year First-Generation College Students

Trebby L. Ellington

INTRODUCTION

This chapter will provide details about the design, administration, and implementation of University of Michigan's (UM's) 1st Gen theme community. The University of Michigan was recognized by the National Association of Student Personnel Administrators (NASPA) Center for First-Generation Student Success as a First-Gen Forward institution.

UM in Ann Arbor is a public flagship research institution that serves roughly 46,000 students where about 14% of the undergraduate population identify as a first-generation college student. UM defines a first-generation college student as any student whose parents do not have a bachelor's degree. As nearly 12,000 students reside on campus with about 10,000 undergraduate residential students, approximately 97% of first-year students live in the residence halls and over 30% of UM residential students live in a Living-Learning Programs (LLP) (J. Drolet, personal communication, November 19, 2020). Residence Education within Michigan Housing offers two types of LLPs for students living on campus known as Michigan Learning Communities (MLCs) and theme communities. These LLPs create opportunities for students with similar interests to live and learn alongside one another in a more intimate community. Residence Education's LLP offerings support Michigan Housing in living out its mission to foster holistic student development and cultivate inclusive communities where all students thrive. Ten MLCs exist across the UM campus and represent a more traditional LLP where students apply for membership to a specific MLC based on a particular academic field of study, career interest, and/or goals. Twelve theme communities exist in undergraduate housing across the UM campus.

DOI: 10.4324/9781003226321-12

THEME COMMUNITY STRUCTURE AND OVERARCHING LEARNING GOALS

Theme communities are structured through Residence Education and about half of the communities have partnership agreements with different units across campus. Campus partners provide expertise on community topics and themes. The assistant director of theme communities along with hall directors and theme partners manage each community. Communities provide meaningful programming that cultivates co-curricular learning, resource sharing, and opportunities for students to build connections with community members who live in a larger residential community. While this chapter will more specifically focus on the 1st Gen theme community and the 1st Gen experience scaffold, the overarching learning goals for all 12 communities are that students will be able to:

- Successfully recognize, navigate, and utilize resources connected to their theme and overall experience at the University of Michigan
- Navigate the building of relationships with diverse stakeholders (peers, faculty, and staff)
- Begin their journey to self-authorship through learning about themselves and others as they grow individually and as a community

1ST GEN THEME COMMUNITY PROGRAM DESCRIPTION

The 1st Gen theme community (1st Gen) began in 2017 and is a residential LLP of approximately 26–28 students that provides an additional layer of support for first-year first-generation college students. Through purposeful stakeholder collaboration and a formal partnership agreement between Residence Education and the director of first-generation initiatives, 1st Gen is dedicated to maximizing student success by creating a support system within the community that facilitates the development of helpful relationships between residents and UM staff and faculty. 1st Gen is currently located on the sixth (top) floor of Couzens Hall, which is a residence hall of approximately 520 mixed-academic level students. The sixth floor in its entirety in Couzens Hall includes all first-year students in double rooms with a floor lounge located at one end of the hall. One wing of the sixth floor includes first-year students who are not members of 1st Gen and the other wing of the floor includes the first-year students who are.

1st Gen is managed by the 1st Gen leadership team of one resident advisor, one hall director, one theme partner, and the assistant director of theme communities. The resident advisor role is a 20 hour per week commitment in which they fulfill all aspects of a traditional resident advisor role and simultaneously approach their work through the lens of their theme by engaging students with programming and resources around the particular topic area or related experience (first-generation college students) that the community is built upon. The hall director manages the daily administrative and programmatic operations of the entire residence hall they oversee, which encompasses leadership to 1st Gen and direct supervision of the resident advisor to meet goals and objectives of the program. The director of first-generation initiatives through the First-Gen Gateway office is the theme partner for the 1st Gen community and provides support for all undergraduate and graduate first-generation college students and allies. The theme partner supports the success of the 1st Gen leadership team and objectives of 1st Gen by serving as a needs-based resource and programmatic expert for first-generation college students collectively. Additionally, the resident advisor is required to collaborate at least once a term with First-Year Experience staff to provide an event or workshop for 1st Gen students.

MISSION, GOALS, AND OBJECTIVES

In its inaugural year, the initial proposal for students participating in 1st Gen included enrollment in the course ALA 171: *Making the Most of Michigan* during the first semester living in the community. This is a one-credit, seven-week course that helps students navigate their new environment, connect with other first-year students, and build skills for career and leadership opportunities. Participants are required to complete a segment of their electronic Michigan portfolio to help them articulate what they learned as a result of participating in 1st Gen.

Participants also have to attend check-in meetings twice a semester with the resident advisor. Finally, participants have to attend at least two 1st Gen programs each semester. While the initial proposal centered the focus of the community largely on academics, careers, and leadership, the realities of its first year predominantly focused on cultivating opportunities for 1st Gen students to build connections with each other.

As the overall direction and development of theme communities collectively at UM gradually became clearer with the hiring of an inaugural assistant director of theme communities in 2018, the goals and objectives of 1st Gen also evolved to their current state. With clearly defined overarching learning goals for all theme communities, 1st Gen is positioned to offer meaningful academic support and personal development programming with the implementation of the 1st Gen experience scaffold to address belonging and community building, utilization of campus resources, and exploration of social identities through student's transition, adjustment, and persistence.

CONCEPTUAL FRAMEWORK FOR 1ST GEN THEME COMMUNITY

Central to organizational operations and the residential experience, Residence Education functions through the interconnectedness of the following core values: diversity, equity, and inclusion; restorative practices; and community development. In congruence with these foundational values and the overarching learning goals of all UM theme communities, the conceptual framework for developing and implementing the 1st Gen Theme Community is centered through the critical theories of intersectionality and the community cultural wealth model. Leveraging these as the cornerstone for 1st Gen nurtures a perpetual praxis of criticality, collaboration, and human-centered design as a goal and process where 1st Gen's integrative approach provides a meaningful living and learning experience for all students participating.

Addressing support for first-generation college students through assumptions rooted in comparison to their continuing-generation college peers alone masks the complex realities of student experiences across multiple intersections of social life. One's status as a first-generation college student is an outcome of oppressive systems and structural barriers rooted in racism, classism, sexism, and so on (Garriott, 2020). Utilizing intersectionality as a frame to acknowledge and address how interlocking systems of oppression complicate the lived experiences of students at the interconnectedness of marginalized identities (Crenshaw, 1991), 1st Gen provides a structure through its resources, relationship connections, and programmatic efforts that include a difference-education intervention (Destin et al., 2014). This is important because the problem with the process of understanding issues as social and systemic is that it often conflates or ignores intragroup differences (Crenshaw, 1991) yet students are more than just their first-generation to college identity. A difference-education intervention highlights that understanding students' different backgrounds shape their college experience in positive and negative ways helps first-generation college students make meaning of their specific college experiences, increases students' comfort levels, improves their ability to navigate their new college environment by providing them with the strategies needed to address

background-specific obstacles, and ultimately leads to improved academic performance through seeking out appropriate resources (Destin et al., 2014).

Furthermore, community cultural wealth is a critical race theory that challenges antiquated understandings of cultural capital and centers an asset-based lens rather than a deficit-based lens on critical historical context that reveals accumulated assets and resources in the lives of Communities of Color (Yosso, 2005). Yosso (2005) asserts that traditional ideas of cultural capital, which are narrowly defined by white, middle class values, are more limited in concept than all of what truly encompasses wealth. The community cultural wealth model highlights six forms of cultural capital: aspirational, linguistic, familial, social, navigational, and resistance. These forms of capital are not mutually exclusive and build on one another as "an array of knowledge, skills, abilities and contacts possessed and utilized by Communities of Color to survive and resist macro and micro-forms of oppression" (Yosso, 2005, p. 77). To center the humanity and dignity of first-generation college students in all of their multiple and/or compounding experiences, it is integral to the empowerment, success, and living environment of the program to permeate intersectionality and community cultural wealth frameworks throughout design, implementation, and evaluation.

MARKETING, RECRUITMENT, AND STUDENT SELECTION

Marketing and recruiting for student participation in 1st Gen requires a variety of collaborations to provide targeted outreach to first-year first-generation college students. Throughout the fall term, staff participate in admissions panels titled "Finding Your Fit at Michigan: Theme Communities & MLCs." Throughout winter term as students are admitted to UM, a Michigan Housing/LLP flyer is included in their acceptance packages, separate targeted emails about 1st Gen are sent, and first-year student housing applications include the links to the 1st Gen website page. The 1st Gen website page includes: updated program descriptions, a list of signature opportunities and resources provided by participating in the program, testimonials from previous program participants, and responses to frequently asked questions. Additionally, vlogs regarding 1st Gen are shared on Michigan Housing's Facebook and Instagram pages and reshared by the Office of Enrollment Management and UM-Social. Information about 1st Gen is also highlighted on the central UM website for first-generation college student resources with links to the direct Michigan Housing website for 1st Gen. Moreover, in-person marketing and recruiting takes place through tabling during campus visit days which includes postcards and 1st Gen specific brochures for incoming students.

Students interested in 1st Gen complete an application process which includes two or three short essay questions about their interest in the program and generally opens in late January with a priority deadline of mid-May. Priority for 1st Gen is given to students who apply by the mid-May deadline, although the application may remain open through July. All students interested in 1st Gen must also complete the general housing application when it becomes available to them in April (see Appendix A for Theme Roadmap Year Review). Interested students can apply for up to two theme communities. Currently, if a student applies to both an MLC and a theme community and they are accepted into the MLC, their theme community application will be removed as their MLC application is automatically considered their first preference. This policy has a noticeable effect on the application pool for 1st Gen and the selection process because it significantly decreases the initial number of candidates available for 1st Gen.

The hall director and theme partner are responsible for selecting participants for 1st Gen based on centralized instructions for the selection process from the assistant director of theme communities as well as specific considerations due to the program's identity. This process includes: individual review of applications, selection of residents, and identification of an alternative list. The hall director and theme partner examine the following when admitting candidates into the program: clear assertion of interest in 1st Gen, alignment between expressed desires and what the theme can offer, and evident connections to Residence Education's core values and community standards. To ground the conceptual frameworks of 1st Gen in practice, the hall director and theme partner are deliberate in application review and selection of candidates to understand and consider:

- Short application responses do not necessarily mean the candidate has a poor application
- As incoming first-year students, candidates do not know what they do not know and that can influence some vagueness in applicants' responses and/or clarity of what they are hoping to gain from the theme
- Student needs vs. student wants – students are socialized in specific ways regarding how to approach applications, so candidate responses may focus on what they can bring to the theme rather than what they need and/or are hoping to gain even if the questions explicitly ask the latter
- Storytelling in application responses is a form of cultural capital as highlighted through Yosso's community cultural wealth model and it is important to not provide negative evaluations of candidate responses who do not answer in a linear format for example

Funding

Funding for the 1st Gen community comes from the hall director's fixed programming and training budget to support engagement and programming where, at minimum, $100 of that budget is reserved specifically for 1st Gen. If there are costs that cannot fit within the fixed programming and training budget, the hall director assesses whether additional communities could benefit from a joint function with shared costs, works with the resident advisor to submit a funding proposal(s) to the community's hall council, multicultural council or the Residence Hall Association for additional funding, reaches out to on-campus partners for sponsorship, or connects with the assistant director of theme communities to see if there are more funds available within the department. With proper strategic management of the fixed programming and training budget, the hall director generally reserves roughly $200–$300 to cover the costs of 1st Gen's key annual signature events whereas resources and events outside of those can be funded through the aforementioned methods if necessary or grant opportunities.

1st Gen Experience Scaffold

The 1st Gen experience scaffold (see Appendix B for 1st Gen Experience Scaffold Snapshot) serves as the resource and programmatic curriculum which gradually builds upon itself as the academic year progresses to meet the goals and objectives of 1st Gen. Through strategic cross-collaboration with the 1st Gen leadership team and various campus offices, the experience scaffold provides a combination of casual opportunities as well as structured resources and programming to promote community building, utilization of campus resources, and exploration of social identities. The 1st Gen experience a scaffold that provides at least a biweekly programming schedule. Additionally, the resident advisor is required to collaborate with First-Year Experience staff and the 1st Gen leadership team on at least one event or workshop each term.

To enrich the 1st Gen experience scaffold, the resident advisor hosts frequent casual community building activities to foster authentic student connections whereas the experience scaffold is largely supported by the 1st Gen leadership team in planning and facilitation. With the experience scaffold, the resident advisor is either working with the leadership team or supporting the theme partner events through the First-Gen Gateway office by advertising and taking students to them. Key annual signature resources and events integral to 1st Gen are briefly described below:

- **Kick-Off Event** – 1st Gen students move into campus housing a day earlier than the rest of campus. Resident advisors begin building meaningful connections through a floor dinner and the first floor meeting. Students are introduced to the 1st Gen leadership team and learn about program offerings and expectations.
- **First-Gen Parent-Family Open House** – Hosted by the theme partner in the First-Gen Gateway office, this is an opportunity for students and their family to meet faculty, staff, and students and learn about campus resources for first-generation students.
- **UM's First-Generation Week** – This week of events celebrates first-generation college students as part of a community of over 4,000 students who share this identity, acknowledges the different ways that first-generation college students thrive at UM, and highlights campus resources.
- **National First-Generation Day** – This celebration is an opportunity for the 1st Gen resident advisor to facilitate an intimate, celebratory community building activity for the students and begin deepening dialogue about their first-generation college student experience.
- **1st Gen Faculty & Staff Mixer** – The purpose of this event is to cultivate an intimate, informal space for the 1st Gen students to connect and engage with faculty and staff who identify as first-generation college graduates.

This mixer breaks down barriers that exist between faculty, staff, and first-generation college students and enhances students' success in connecting with faculty and staff beyond this space.
- **1st Gen Grad Student Networking Opportunity** – This networking event provides activities that allow the 1st Gen students to connect and engage with current graduate students who identify as first-generation. Graduate students offer advice and insights into their experiences navigating college, discuss their graduate school experiences along with their personal and career journey, and answer any questions/address topics of interest from the 1st Gen students.
- **1st Gen Fridays Biweekly Newsletter** – This newsletter provides students with important residence hall announcements/updates, 1st Gen and campus events, and resources.

ASSESSMENT PLAN

The 1st Gen leadership team has enhanced the structure of 1st Gen by addressing a variety of content to inform residential and campus-wide resources, culturally relevant connection points, informal programming, and formal signature events. This is supported by: the UM student support task force final report created in 2019 to bring together faculty, staff, and students to develop recommendations for addressing challenges that low-income and/or first-generation college students face on campus; extensive research on first-generation college student's needs; campus-wide residential survey assessments; and community engagement themes from Sessions – an online platform that allows for event registration, attendance recording, and survey distribution. As a fairly new LLP evolving with consistent organizational changes within Michigan Housing, a formal assessment plan exclusively for 1st Gen is necessary to further attest to the success of the program as one does not currently exist. A 2018–2019 campus-wide residential survey assessment on belonging within the residence halls also confirms this due to limited sample size of respondents in theme communities overall and thus limited representation of 1st Gen.

Through 2018–2021, the 1st Gen leadership team has assessed the effectiveness of the program and its initiatives through various informal quantitative, qualitative, and experiential analyses in relation to: belonging and community development, utilization of campus resources, and identity development through social identity exploration. Pre-move-in, mid-year, and end-of-year surveys as well as student testimonial opportunities are provided to all theme communities across campus. While response rates vary, this information has been useful in informing ongoing practices and indicating where the program is meeting its intended goals and where the program needs to shift. Some additional analyses come from individual program evaluation based on attendance and student experiences, trends regarding community conduct and well-being case management, ongoing qualitative feedback from students and program staff, and retention through the first year within the residence hall community.

A formative assessment is recommended as most beneficial to know whether 1st Gen is achieving the learning outcomes it was created to accomplish. This requires an evaluation of the full course of the program where all goals are directly linked to the activities, connections and resources developed for participants (Banta & Palomba, 2015). Keeping the program's specific learning outcomes in mind, which include belonging and community development, utilization of campus resources, and identity development through social identity exploration, the short-term goals are meant to be achieved upon student completion of the program at the end of their first year. The medium- and long-term goals are meant to further the short-term goals after program completion, optimize leadership, enhance social capital networks, and increase belonging to assist students in positively navigating the UM community over the course of their undergraduate trajectory. It is recommended to evaluate qualitative and quantitative data in this assessment comparing rates of students participating in 1st Gen to their first-generation college student peers not in 1st Gen as well as the general student population. A comparative analysis of GPA, community engagement, and retention rates from first year to second year are metrics that will also be helpful to understand.

OUTCOMES

In the 2018–2019 residential survey assessment on belonging in the residence halls by community type, students in LLPs showed more engagement than students who are not involved in LLPs which also presumably shows an increase in sense of belonging (J. Drolet, personal communication, November 19, 2020). For theme communities specifically, the average belonging factor scores for themes did not differ significantly from that of students not involved in themes, which reduced the ability to detect a difference in mean belonging scores (J. Drolet, personal communication, November 19, 2020). However, the latter does not solidify that LLPs are not effective. A national study of LLPs during spring 2004 indicated that first-generation college students in LLPs revealed a more successful academic and social transition to college than their first-generation college student peers living in a traditional residence hall community (Inkelas et al., 2007).

Aside from the 2018–2019 residential survey assessment, some outcomes of students' participation in 1st Gen include students' involvement in leadership positions on campus beyond their time in the theme community and retention living on campus after their first year. A few specific examples of these outcomes include: involvement in the First-Gen College Student organization on campus through Executive Board positions or general membership, leadership in the

Returner Residence Hall Association representative positions in the residence hall, and participation in the returning student theme communities across campus. 1st Gen students experience an increased sense of ownership over their community as evidenced by their initiative to organize student-led programming and collective responsibility towards community standards. Additionally, a number of students each year express a desire to continue to be involved in the program beyond their first year. These types of outcomes would indicate program success towards its intended learning outcomes (belonging and community development, utilization of campus resources, and identity development through social identity exploration); however, a formal assessment plan exclusive to 1st Gen is necessary to accurately affirm whether or not the objectives are being met and how.

LESSONS LEARNED

While many lessons have been learned developing and managing the 1st Gen Theme Community over its four year existence, five of the most important lessons to be considered when developing an LLP for first-generation college students of this nature include:

- Do not believe the LLP has to address all first-generation college students' challenges as indicated through literature, research, and campus data. What is necessary is to remain steadfast in understanding the role the LLP plays as just one component of the student experience and thus cannot address everything in its offerings in one year. Be accountable to the LLP's goals and objectives and clearly communicate the purpose of the program to stakeholders to avoid overwhelming students and staff.
- The LLP is home to the students. With a continued increase in interest in the experiences of first-generation college students across the country (Rashne, Williams, & Pete, 2011), the student's home needs to be honored and protected by LLP leadership as many different staff, departments, and organizations on and off campus may try to get facetime with the students. Be clear and decisive about which opportunities and connection points align with program goals and objectives because students need space to simply be present in their home without constant intervention.
- The location of the LLP within the residence hall is important to the student experience in many formal and informal ways. In using an asset-based lens about the community and through student feedback, students consistently expressed a desire to have their own intimate space while still able to easily access others living in the halls not a part of the LLP.
- When the program experience scaffold is deliberate in design and implementation, students want to continue their participation beyond

their first year because of the meaningful experiences they had while participating. For the 1st Gen theme community, it currently only offers opportunities for first-year residents. This contributed to the integration of targeted opportunities in the 1st Gen experience scaffold to connect residents to leadership opportunities across campus and networking/relationship building opportunities across various shared identities such as the First-Generation College Students@Michigan student organization or the multicultural center.

- There is a distinct difference in what the 1st Gen theme community students wanted and expressed a need for during the fall term versus winter term. Students generally want to focus more on community building and learning how to engage with residence hall and campus resources in their transition and adjustment to the year with a gradual increase throughout the fall term in exploring their social identities. This does not mean there are not or should not be identity exploration opportunities early in the fall, as the 1st Gen experience scaffold offers these as early as move-in week, but a matter of how to engage those spaces with students appropriately. In the winter term, students return to campus with various experiences from their break as home-life and college-life may collide in unexpected ways. Students return with a greater desire to engage more deeply how they are experiencing life as a first-generation college student. Winter term affords more opportunities to reflect and make deeper connections about all of their social identities and thus, offers a deepening to the experience scaffold around these explorations.

RECOMMENDATIONS FOR IMPLEMENTATION

In summary, five key recommendations are provided for those desiring to implement a similar model as the 1st Gen theme community at their institution:

- **Formal Partnership Agreement and/or Cross-Collaboration:** If the institution houses an office and/or administrator(s) established for the purpose of providing expertise, resources, and support in service of first-generation college students, it is integral to the success of the LLP to develop a formal partnership agreement or standards for cross-collaboration. According to Garriott (2020), "Importantly, the CCWM [community cultural wealth model] requires that practitioners attend to environmental, structural, and political influences on [first-generation college] students' well-being and success. This means that college personnel…must step out of the confines of their one-on-one roles with [first-generation college] students and intervene at institutional and policy level (p.90)." To disrupt silos and dismantle the many structural barriers first-generation college

students navigate in education, it is a necessity to build collective capacity, consensus, and coalition(s) that accurately support their needs.
- **Key First-Generation College Student Literature and Critical Frameworks:** Familiarize all LLP staff with foundational key literature and research regarding the experiences of first-generation college students as well as the oppressive structures and practices of higher education institutions that further marginalize them. This is especially necessary in the likely event that there are staff managing the LLP who were not first-generation college students themselves. To address root issues contributing to student experiences, critical and intersectional frameworks are essential to ground the LLP in for accurately responding to student needs individually and systemically. There is a disservice to the student and their holistic experiences when programming, support, and resources are solely about their first-generation to college status alone and must also center their multiple and intersecting identities.
- **Nuances in First-Generation College Student Experiences across Institutional Types:** While there are similarities in first-generation college student experiences across higher education, it is necessary to understand the nuances of experiences across various institutional types and contexts to best design and implement the LLP in ways that accurately address each institution's students' particular needs. An example includes acknowledging the differences in how first-generation college students experience and navigate the cultural, among other, aspects of private Ivy institutions as described by Anthony Abraham Jack (2019) in his book *The privileged poor: How elite colleges are failing disadvantaged students*.
- **Peer Mentor or Other Added Staff Component:** The LLP would benefit from additional student staff positions to supplement the resident advisor, like a peer mentor role, to allow second-year students and beyond to continue their involvement with the program through leadership acceleration. Program alumni want to be more involved when they have a meaningful community experience as a participant. It is essential to think about what it means for first-generation college students when they have had an intimate communal experience with targeted support and resources in their first year and then that potentially does not exist afterwards. An embedded mental health professional who can provide support to program staff and students would be an asset to the LLP leadership team.
- **COVID-19 Implications:** During the COVID-19 pandemic, there were minor adjustments to the 1st Gen experience scaffold, which predominantly included shifting in-person opportunities to virtual opportunities and increasing the frequency of casual, community building activities facilitated by the resident advisor and leadership team. Additionally, some students who were admitted to 1st Gen chose to stay home instead of moving into the

residence halls as originally planned so the program expanded to allow for continued participation of those admitted regardless of whether they chose to live on campus or not. As institutions transition to increasing in-person formats, it is recommended to continue to offer the options of access to resource and programmatic opportunities virtually as well as in-person.

APPENDIX A

Theme Road Map Year Review

Fall Term	
July	Theme Hall Director (HD) Training (historically)
Mid-August	Theme Resident Advisor (RA) Training (historically)
Late August	HDs schedule fall Leadership Team Meetings
Late August	Theme residents move in early/the first day of move-in (historically)
Late August	Theme Kick-Off Events: expectations are shared, residents sign photo release forms, Theme Ambassador Program announced, etc. Theme RA, Partner, & HD expected to participate
September	Theme Ambassadors are nominated/apply/are selected and start meeting monthly
September/October	HDs & Partners submit nominations for future Theme RAs
October	Updating Theme RA job description, essay/interview questions
November	Theme RA interviews
November/December	Mid-year Theme survey sent out
December	Fall semester ADTC (Assistant Director of Theme Communities) check-ins with HDs & Partners (separately), Updates to Theme Websites
December/January	Advertising for returning student Theme Communities, Updates to first-year Theme application

Winter Term	
December/January	Advertising for returning student Theme Communities, Updates to first-year Theme application

(*Continued*)

(Continued)	
January	HDs schedule winter Leadership Team Meetings
January/February	First-year Theme application live
January - April	Theme Committee & Theme Ambassadors attend Campus Visit Days
April	End of the year survey sent out, Theme RA transition documents are due
May	First-year Theme application review
May/June	Winter semester ADTC check-ins with HDs & Partners (separately)
June	HD Theme handbook updates are due

APPENDIX B

1st Gen Experience Scaffold Snapshot

Fall Term	
Newsletters *key annual signature resource	1st Gen Fridays biweekly newsletter
August Move-In Day	Theme partner welcome in hall, 1st Gen Kick-Off Event
August Move-In Week	Housing required events, First floor meeting with 1st Gen leadership, First-Gen Gateway student-parent open house
September	Student 1:1 meetings with resident advisor, Community building activity, First-Generation Welcome Fall Dinner through First-Gen Gateway
October	Monthly community meeting/event, Workshop with First-Year Experience or Counseling and Psychological Services
October/November *key annual signature events	UM First-Gen Week
November	Monthly community meeting/event

(Continued)

(Continued)

November *key annual signature event	National First-Gen Day celebration
December	Final Exams: de-stress & academic support, Monthly community meeting – fall closing

Winter Term

Newsletters *key annual signature resource	1st Gen Fridays biweekly newsletter
January Return to Campus/New Student Move-In Week	Welcome (back) community email, Welcome (back) community meeting
January	Student 1:1 meetings with resident advisor, First-Gen Winter Community Dinner through First-Gen Gateway
February	Student 1:1 meetings with resident advisor, Monthly community meeting/event
February *key annual signature event	1st Gen Faculty & Staff Mixer
March	Monthly community meeting/event, Workshop with First-Year Experience or Counseling and Psychological Services, Advertise First-Generation College Student organization elections
April *key annual signature events	1st Gen Grad Student Networking opportunity, Monthly community meeting with activity to pass on to next year's 1st Gen cohort, Advertise First-Generation College Student organization elections
May	Attend or volunteer for First-Generation Graduation Ceremony

REFERENCES

Banta, T. W., & Palomba, C. A. (2015). *Assessment essentials: Planning, implementing, and improving assessment in higher education* (2nd ed.). Jossey-Bass.

Crenshaw, K. W. (1991). Mapping the margins: Intersectionality, identity politics, and violence against women of color. *Stanford Law Review, 43*, 1241–1299.

Destin, M., Stephens, N., & Hamedani, M. (2014). Closing the social-class achievement gap: A difference-education intervention improves first-generation students' academic performance and all students' college transition. *Psychological Science*, *25*(4), 943 953.

Garriott, P. O. (2020). A critical cultural wealth model of first-generation and economically marginalized college students' academic and career development. *Journal of Career Development*, *47*(1), 80 95.

Inkelas, K. K., Daver, Z. E., Vogt, K. E., & Leonard, J. B. (2007). Living learning programs and first-generation college students' academic and social transition to college. *Research in Higher education*, *48*(4), 403 434.

Jack, A. A. (2019). *The privileged poor: How elite colleges are failing disadvantaged students*. Harvard University Press.

Rashne, J., Williams, R. D., & Pete, J. (2011). Multicultural learning communities: Vehicles for developing the self-authorship in first-generation college students. *Journal of the First-Year Experience and Student in Transition*, *23*(1), 53 74.

Yosso, T. J. (2005). Whose culture has capital? A critical race theory discussion of community cultural wealth. *Race Ethnicity and Education*, *8*(1), 69 91.

Chapter 10

Living Learning Communities for First-Year First-Generation Students

Kiley Moody, Gregory Eiselein, Rebeca Paz, Tamara Bauer, and Kevin Cook

Research in higher education indicates that living learning communities (LLCs) on college campuses impact students' retention (Cambridge-Williams et al., 2013; Kuh, 2008; Purdie & Rosser, 2011; Zhao & Kuh, 2004), including first-generation students. Significant scholarly attention has also been given to the ways that fostering a sense of belonging and building community are critical to first-generation students' success (Strayhorn, 2012). Moreover, first-generation students often feel they do not belong in college and may experience imposter syndrome – an internal feeling of intellectual phoniness or having deceived others of one's ability (Clance & Imes, 1978). Addressing feelings of alienation and imposter syndrome and creating a sense of belonging and understanding of the first-generation student identity are critical to retention and persistence to graduation (Strayhorn, 2012). Less often practiced and studied are living learning communities designed specifically for new first-generation students.

PROGRAM DESCRIPTION AND CONTEXT

K-State is a public, land-grant institution established in 1862 with the passage of the Morrill Act, focusing on a mission of providing quality education for all. With an overall enrollment of ~20,000 undergraduate and graduate students, the last decade has provided intentional efforts to focus on the success and retention of first-year students. As these efforts developed, a specific focus on supporting first-year, first-generation students emerged, which deeply connects to our overall university mission of providing access and educational opportunities to all individuals. A key part of the university's Strategic Enrollment Management plan has been to improve graduation rates and student success generally, but also particularly among first-generation students. The university's newly created

Office of Student Success, which includes, among other units, an Office of First-Generation Students and a first-year experience program (FYE), has been charged to lead and support these improvements.

K-State First: First-Year Experience at Kansas State University

The FYE program, known as K-State First, is a university-wide effort to support new students with the transition to college-level learning and college life. The first-generation LLCs are a part of this larger effort and follow the program's objectives of fostering feelings of belonging, supporting campus community and involvement, and academic engagement. All K-State First programs have been developed for students to achieve success during their first year, and they emphasize four learning outcomes: 1) critical thinking, 2) communication skills, 3) community building, and 4) application of learning. These learning outcomes are the same across all CAT Communities (the CAT acronym stands for Connections Across Topics, which alludes to the university mascot, the Wildcats or Cats), including the first-generation communities. The focus throughout the program is on small-sized learning experiences (no more than 22 students per class) that feature clear connections to a vibrant student life experience and inspiring faculty members. K-State First includes a common reading program, a mentoring program, a robust set of First-Year Seminar courses (FYS's), and a learning community program called CAT Communities. Participation in a K-State First course is voluntary, and on the K-State campus from 2015 to 2019, 38.03% of first-time, full-time, degree-seeking undergraduate students enrolled in a FYS or CAT Community.

CAT Communities: Learning Communities at Kansas State University

A signature program within K-State First, CAT Communities are interdisciplinary learning communities based on majors, students' interests, future careers, and/or a common identity. The objectives include learning in a small community, earning credit toward general education requirements, receiving mentorship from an advanced undergraduate peer mentor known as a Learning Assistant, attending campus co-curricular events together, meeting new people, and creating lasting bonds through shared interests and study opportunities. From 2015 to 2019, first-generation students accounted for 23.98% of the first-time, full-time, degree-seeking students in the CAT Communities, a percentage that is just slightly higher than the first-time, full-time, degree-seeking cohorts over the same period (23.10%). The overall goal of the program is to help new students establish a strong foundation for the rest of their college career. There are a wide variety of CAT Communities on the K-State campus, typically more than 40 each year, including non-residential offerings in which the students take classes together but do not live in the same residence hall, study abroad communities that feature an overseas learning experience, student success CAT Communities that provide additional academic support and encouragement, and the living learning communities (LLC) known as our residential CAT Communities. These LLCs meet students where they are by providing an opportunity for students to take a set of three or more classes together and to live near one another in a residence hall or community of residence halls.

First-Generation Themed CAT Communities

Among the LLCs at K-State are a set of first-generation themed learning communities. They have been divided into two basic kinds: (1) first-generation friendly CAT Communities, which focus on first-generation needs and content but allow continuing-generation students to enroll alongside first-generation students, and (2) first-generation only or first-generation specific CAT Communities, marketed specifically as a community for first-generation students and focused on their needs. Both sets of learning communities have a maximum enrollment of 22, and an average enrollment closer to 20. From the fall of 2014 through the fall of 2020, K-State hosted 21 first-generation friendly CAT Communities and 11 first-generation specific CAT Communities.

The first-generation specific LLCs enroll students in the same three classes for a total of seven credit hours. The classes focus on the transition to a four-year university, exploring the first-generation identity from an asset-based lens, and honing academic skills. In its current design, the first-generation specific LLCs at K-State aim to accomplish these goals through three different primary venues: a University Experience class, based on academic skill building; an Introduction to Leadership Studies course, where students explore leadership identity utilizing the CliftonStrengths tool; and a one-hour learning community class that connects content from both classes by focusing on the strengths, assets, and identity of first-generation students. While the benefits of FYE programs and LLCs are widely known (Pascarella & Terenzini, 2005), experiences designed specifically for first-generation students can also be a vital component of students' transition to university life.

UNDERSTANDING AND SUPPORTING FIRST-GENERATION STUDENTS

At K-State, first-generation students are defined as those who did not have a parent or guardian complete a four-year degree. Because their parents did not attend or complete college, first-generation students often encounter institutional barriers and do not bring with them social and cultural capital related to higher education (Dumais & Ward, 2010). This lack of capital translates to them not having prior knowledge and experience of support systems to navigate the complexities of higher education nor decode the university's hidden curriculum. Not having parents or guardians who have navigated the college system successfully places first-generation students on an uneven playing field compared to their continuing-generation counterparts. Thus, making them less likely to graduate compared to their continuing generation counterparts.

Entering college involves social, emotional, and academic transitions. When first-generation students attend college, they may realize that they do not understand a complex system, which can be overwhelming. This feeling can be internalized as feelings of lack of belonging, which can take the form of imposter syndrome and may result in a student not persisting (Clance & Imes, 1978). Common university lingo may sound like a foreign language to a student who has not developed that vocabulary nor familiarity with the system. These barriers can compound and impact the students' ability to adjust, develop a sense of belonging and succeed academically. Effective support systems that assist first-generation students in navigating college culture and decode curriculum are necessary to their persistence and success.

Investing in curricular and co-curricular experiences and support for first-generation students early in their college journey is critical to addressing the unique challenges they experience during this transition period. Through our work with the first-generation LLCs, we seek to break these barriers to level the playing field for first-generation students. We firmly believe that first-generation students enrich our campus, and we develop our practices and pedagogies to meet their needs with an asset-based lens. First-generation students possess resiliency and bring diversity to our institutions; they have community cultural wealth and a host of intersecting identities (Yosso, 2005). Developing a strong first-generation identity and pride is also essential to the students acquiring a sense of belonging, and at the core of the first-generation CAT Communities' curriculum. Some of the core components of this experience aid in developing a strong first-generation identity. This includes intentional curricular components focusing on assets, building relationships among other students and faculty with first-generation identities, and connecting students with resources to support their academic and social needs. Investing time and resources in our first-generation students early on will assist in their transition to college, will impact their sense of belonging to the university, and ultimately, their overall academic success.

IMPLEMENTATION THROUGH COLLABORATION

The process of developing our first-generation LLCs is an evolving one. Most importantly, the strategic collaboration among many stakeholders across campus, who saw and understood the need for specific first-generation student programming served as the primary catalyst. As a result of strong retention rates with initial first-generation programs and initiatives it was decided to create additional first-generation specific CAT Communities to serve more first-generation students.

First-Year Experience Office

As shared earlier, all the living learning communities are managed by our first-year experience office, K-State First. This office is responsible for managing the curricular components of each community. This includes securing the instructor, holding the appropriate number of seats in each of the associated classes, collaborating on the selection and supervision of student learning assistants, and providing assessment and evaluation processes. The first-year experience office staff also supports the recruitment and marketing efforts by working with our admissions office and on-campus housing. This office also collaborates with academic advisors to manage enrollment of students in the affiliated courses for the living learning community.

On-Campus Housing

Establishing a strong link with on-campus housing is essential to the success of any living learning program. A mid-level housing staff member that works directly with the recruitment and admissions functions of the university provides additional marketing and promotion of the living learning communities. This is done by including the living learning communities in publications and presentations for prospective students and their families. The living learning community offerings, benefits, and process are also incorporated into all training that is done with university recruitment staff, both professionals and student employees. Mid-level housing professionals also participate in selection of the student learning assistants and aid in confirmation of the students housing room assignments. As a part of the assignment process, housing staff provide an appropriate perspective on what types of living arrangements might best suit the target population. Depending on the campus context, cost, room style, and location on campus should be factored into this decision-making. Staff in housing also manage the room reservation process and ensure that students in the LLC get assigned to the correct building or community. In addition, the full-time and graduate assistant housing staff in the associated residence halls provide supervision and support for the undergraduate learning assistant that lives close to the student residents. Throughout the semester, full-time and graduate assistant housing staff also serve as dependable mentors and provide check-ins to student residents if they are struggling. Housing staff also supports co-curricular programming for the LLC through funding, space, and other resources as needed.

Associated Academic Programs

Since each LLC has multiple academic partners, it is important for one academic area to take ownership for the LLC. This most often takes the form of leading the one-hour connections course for the living learning community. In the case of our first-generation community, our leadership studies program provides the academic home for our efforts. The faculty work closely with the learning assistant to ensure the students are making intentional connections and receiving adequate support. When considering what academic programs or faculty to invite to be part of the living learning community, ideally the faculty and their associated courses should be selected based on passion for supporting first-generation students and the incorporation of active learning techniques into their courses. It is also important that ongoing learning and education about the needs and characteristics of first-generation students be provided regularly to the teaching faculty.

First-Generation Support and Creation of an Office of First-generation Students

When our first-generation student LLC began, we did not have a dedicated first-generation student support office. However, the Office of Student Life in conjunction with the Office of the Provost designated an individual to serve as intentional support staff for first-generation students and to work closely with existing programs that supported first-generation students. This was a vital part of our program as this designated individual engaged in intentional outreach with students, developed rapport and trust, and provided a conduit for questions, concerns, and support. The initial data from the LLCs indicated that student participants developed a sense of belonging to the institution and had higher retention rates than their peers who did not participate. These data were critical to stating the need for a devoted office for first-generation students.

K-State established the inaugural Office of First-Generation Students in the fall of 2017 through a grant from the Suder Foundation. This office was launched in alignment with the university's Higher Learning Commission Quality Initiative's goals, required for accreditation. These goals focused on increasing the recruitment, retention, and graduation rates of first-generation students, thus, signaling an institutional commitment to close the equity gap between first-generation students and their continuing generation peers. LLCs are an example of intentional ways to impact the retention of our first-generation students.

Once a formal office was established, it became the crucial link to provide initial and ongoing support to the participants in the living learning community. Students enrolled in the first-generation LLCs participate in activities hosted by the Office of First-Generation Students with the goal of building early connections for engagement and support for subsequent years. Having professional staff who consistently connect with the students makes our living learning community more effective. For example, one of the LLC instructors is a member of the Office of First-Generation Students. This instructor builds strong connections with students and serves as a mentor. Through this direct connection to the office, this staff member also facilitates student engagement with the office's events and initiatives and listens to student voices and perspectives, as we build initiatives for first-generation student success.

Academic Advisors

To successfully ensure that students understand and embrace the curricular component of our living learning communities, academic advisors are key, as both our experience and previous research indicates (Priest et al., 2016). Cultivating positive relationships with academic advisors and their associated academic programs, colleges, and administrators has made our living learning programs more successful. When considering first-generation living-learning communities, it might be necessary for some members of the associated team to do some training and education on the needs and unique characteristics of first-generation students with advisors. Helping academic advisors understand the positive outcomes associated with living learning communities, particularly in relation to first-generation students, will provide additional incentive for them to recommend the living learning community to students. At our institution, academic advisors are key in getting students enrolled in the living learning communities. They do this by promoting LLCs to students in recruitment visits and recommending living learning communities to students and families at the time of enrollment. If you do not create a strong connection with advisors, it will be difficult to reach students during the crucial initial enrollment process.

Residential Learning Assistant

Each LLC has a residential learning assistant (RLA) who lives in the same residence hall or residence hall area as the students and attends the weekly one-hour connection class. The RLA is usually an upper-class, first-generation student who has successfully completed the two courses that are part of the LLC. The residential learning assistant helps plan and organize co-curricular activities and assists the instructor with planning and leading the one-hour connection class. These peer mentors are a key to the LLCs success because students often relate to the RLA more than the instructors and might feel more comfortable going to the RLA with their questions or when seeking resources.

Necessary Resources

As key as stakeholders are to success, it is also essential to understand the resources needed in order to create and sustain a successful LLC program. Our FYE office (K-State First) provides much of the necessary financial support and incentive on the curricular side of the living learning community. This includes a $1,600 stipend for the faculty LLC leader and $500 scholarship for the residential learning assistant (RLA). Housing and Dining provides in-kind support of a room and board waiver for the RLA and funds for co-curricular activities and programs. The FYE office provides logistical support and funding for co-curricular activities planned by the faculty member or RLA in addition to coordinating training and professional development related to active learning strategies and first-generation student characteristics and needs. Financial support for student participants might also factor into an LLC. For the first five years of the first-generation specific LLCs, one of the learning communities was supported with scholarships that were funded by an external grant from the Suder Foundation. When the grant support expired, the scholarships ended, though the first-generation specific LLCs continued.

Overall, the long-term success of our living-learning community programs have been a result of continual conversations and collaboration among partners. Collaboration of this nature requires substantial dialogue to sustain progress and adjust as necessary. Intentional reflection, evaluation, and planning with all stakeholders strengthens the program and ultimately provides better support and outcomes for the first-generation students involved.

DESIGNING THE EXPERIENCE

How we connect with students matters. The language we use and the messages we share are critical. It indicates we are ready to help them be successful and serve as their champion and advocate. Faculty and the RLA must have a student-focused mindset and willingness to engage with students in personal, individualized ways. Class time and co-curricular events must be carefully designed to build a community of belonging, and academic content must support student success in college. Asset-based approaches are essential, and faculty must be ready to outwardly share, then help develop the important success skills and tools. Asset-based approaches are grounded in what students can do, emphasizing individual and collective strengths, skills, and capacities, compared to a deficit approach that focuses on what the problem is, weaknesses, or what experiences one has not encountered (Mein, 2018). Highlighting when students have demonstrated resilience and perseverance through assignments and past experiences will help create a sense of belonging and persistence as they work toward graduation. Asset-based, student-centered practices create an experience where everyone feels supported and understood.

The one-hour connection course is intentionally designed to connect students to one another, the university, and their courses. We must meet students where they are and provide opportunities to apply, synthesize, and expand the learning they are experiencing in college. To do this, the class focuses on three primary objectives: understanding one's first-generation identity, identifying and leveraging personal assets utilizing CliftonStrengths, and building community among students within the university. We design asset-based learning experiences to specifically build capacity and work toward self-authorship.

Some examples of the asset-based exercises include the following:

- **CliftonStrengths** Students use this powerful self-discovery tool throughout the semester to aid in self-understanding and thinking critically about their assets. Grounded in positive psychology, students can apply their CliftonStrengths to how they see their strengths show up in their daily lives, the college experience, and how the talents they already have can be leveraged throughout the semester.
- **Personal Narrative Exercise** Students reflect on their first-generation journey prior to coming to college and identify significant experiences, people, and values that have shaped who they are today and why they are pursuing their college degree. Framed as "My Story – My Journey" we ask students to highlight the assets that have brought them to where they are today, along with proposing how the college journey will continue to impact their future. This autobiographical narrative empowers students to see their first-generation identity as an asset, thus, propelling them to feel proud of this intersecting identity
- **Campus Resource Scavenger Hunt** Students work in small teams to visit different parts of campus to solve clues that are related to resources they can utilize throughout their college experience. This out of classroom time often provides significant community building among the team, along with a shared experience of feeling more confident around campus.
- **Future Casting Exercise** Students verbalize their greatest aspirations for the future to one another and envision the potential paths ahead. Students are asked to connect their CliftonStrengths to the potential pathways and envision a purpose for their future. Sharing these visions with one another further develops a community of support and purpose among one another.
- **Peer-to-Peer Coaching** Students are asked to identify challenges they are experiencing, then consider how they can leverage their CliftonStrengths to address that challenge. They share this with peers and thus are more likely to be honest and vulnerable about the challenges they are experiencing. The coaching opportunities aim to empower students by providing them with an opportunity to be heard and to find support through asking questions.

Exercises like these teach students to better understand their own identities and how to use their self-identified skills and strengths to help them navigate their first year of college.

Co-curricular events provide opportunities to engage with students outside of the regular class hours. Selecting on-campus events that align with the objectives of the learning community encourages students to attend and engage with the range of university opportunities and activities. We have found that many students do not attend these co-curricular events if they do not have someone to attend with or if they do not understand why they should attend. Attending events with their peers in the CAT Community and with their faculty member and RLA creates a shared experience that can be built upon in future weeks.

Intentional collaboration among the living-learning community stakeholders is one of the ways we organize and offer student support. For example, the instructor in the CAT Community course may notice that the student is struggling to attend all their classes. The instructor could reach out to the RA and RLA and ask if one of them could check in with the student prior to class and encourage them to attend. Personal attention and support are important to helping students navigate individual challenges that may occur, and we have found that texting with students and meeting with them outside of class helps to achieve that goal. To help monitor where each student is, each class period includes a short check-in to identify what questions students have about resources, their college experience, and navigating life outside of school. These check-ins can be done anonymously, but then shared with the class to normalize feelings and ask questions. Faculty members and the RLA use this feedback to make pivots in course content.

Designing an experience for first-generation students requires faculty members to be flexible and to meet students where they are. While the semester will begin with learning objectives, a course schedule, assignments, and co-curricular events, it is important to remain flexible and open to adjustments once the semester begins. Each semester the CAT Community has taught us that there is not a standardized process; it requires getting to know the cohort of students and understanding their needs. In order to support faculty in this process, continued professional development is helpful. To that end, all K-State First faculty meet at the beginning of the semester and have opportunities to engage in professional development throughout the semester. All professional development opportunities focus on best practices and what is either new or most effective in the literature regarding students' needs and academic preparedness. This also creates a community of reflection and idea sharing among other faculty who are working with first-year students.

ASSESSMENT AND OUTCOMES

As mentioned earlier, one of the goals of the Office of First-Generation Students and K-State is to close the equity gap between first-generation and continuing generation students. First-generation LLCs play a critical role in achieving this goal. Data shows that fostering a first-generation community will ultimately affect students' ability to persist to graduation, and our experience with first-generation LLCs from 2014 to 2019 bear this out (see "Tracking Data" below). Our focus of the CAT Communities includes exploring the first-generation student identity and its intersectionality with other identities, understanding strengths through CliftonStrengths, and connecting students to campus resources and services. The CAT Community classes, co-curricular opportunities, and faculty and staff engagements all stem from an asset-based lens and inclusive pedagogies that foster a growth mindset and develop students' sense of belonging.

We use multiple modes of program appraisal to avoid over-reliance on just one data source. The assessment of the learning community program and the first-generation LLCs has happened in multiple ways. These modes include course evaluations and student feedback, learning outcome assessment, peer class observations, and tracking of student success.

Course Evaluations and Student Feedback

We collect anonymous student feedback informally and formally throughout the semester. We gather informal feedback by asking students to complete a one-minute reflection on a notecard sharing what they have learned and any questions that remain. Each student also meets with their RLA. These one-on-one meetings are crafted to gather feedback that the RLA will then share with the faculty member. Additionally, each week the RLA and faculty members meet and discuss observations about student engagement and well-being to consider additional ways of supporting or adjusting curriculum. At the end of the semester, students can share feedback about the student learning outcomes (see "Program Description and Context" above). Several years of student comments indicate that the students strongly believe that those key outcomes were achieved. In terms of community building, for example, students have written: "I wish I could take this course more than once. It connected me with friends (my best friend) and sources all over campus. Thank you!" (December 2019); and "I am glad I took this class because it gave me the opportunity to meet people and feel welcome here at my new home" (December 2017). Such comments are typical of the student feedback about the first-generation LLCs, and they highlight the importance of relationships, community building, and a sense of belonging that transcends their time at K-State. Other comments speak to the ways the learning communities generate excitement about their college experience: "This class was one of my favorites personally, I was always excited to go to this class because every class was so different, and the environment and people was [sic] so positive that motivated me to continue and keep being strong" [December 2020]. In addition to the student learning outcomes, it is apparent that the first-generation CAT Communities help introduce students to college-level learning, help with their transition from high school to college life, and inspire hard work. One student wrote: "I liked that the class was a way for us to learn the different options that we have here on campus. We were also shown the many ways we can get help, which will be useful when I need it" [December 2018]. Another student shared: "This class was important to my growth and I am very glad I took it. It helped boost my confidence" [December 2019]. Such comments suggest that students are applying their learning and practicing their communication skills by asking for help and knowing what resource(s) to seek out.

Student Learning Outcomes

Beginning in 2019, K-State First and its CAT Communities adopted a new student learning outcome (SLO) assessment process in which the CAT Community faculty leader scores each of their students using a detailed rubric covering the four core learning outcomes: application of learning, community building, communication skills, and critical thinking. The rubric uses a scale from 1 to 5. A score of 1 represents a failure to achieve the learning outcome, whereas a 2 indicates partial achievement. Students who are proficient or meeting expectations in terms of the specific learning outcome are scored with a 3. At the higher end, a 4 represents some distinction or an exceeding of expectations, whereas a 5 indicates clear mastery. The program goal is to have all students in the 3 to 5 range, and it's clearly understood that a 5 denotes a stretch goal, one that allows the process to record student work or student learning that is exemplary.

In 2019 and 2020, about 90% of K-State First students performed in the 3 to 5 range: application of learning (90%), community building (91%), communication skills (90%), and critical thinking (92%). Over that same two-year period, students in the first-generation residential learning communities performed slightly better: application of learning (92%), community building (96%), communication skills (96%), and critical thinking (96%). The program's attitude toward these assessment data remains exploratory and provisional. The initial year (2019) was one of calibration and recalibration of the assessment instruments and the new assessment process, while the more recent year (2020) was one significantly shaped by the global pandemic, whose effects on first-year and first-generation college student learning are not entirely clear. Nevertheless, even considering such qualifications and cautions, the assessment data appear to suggest that the students in the first-generation LLCs are achieving in terms of student learning outcomes at rates equal to or slightly higher than their peers in other FYE options at K-State. The 5% higher community-building percentages (the largest of the differences, 96% for first-generation residential learning communities, compared to the 91% for K-State First students in general) might suggest the real success that the first-generation communities have had in fostering a sense of belonging.

PERCENTAGE OF STUDENTS MEETING OR EXCEEDING LEARNING OUTCOME EXPECTATIONS, 2019–2020

Learning Outcome	All K-State First Students (%)	First-Generation Residential Learning Community Students (%)
Application of Learning	90	92
Community Building	91	96
Communication Skills	90	96
Critical Thinking	92	96

Peer Observation

The first-generation LLCs are observed at least once each year, usually by another professor who teaches in the CAT Community program or by a university administrator or member of the K-State First office. The program uses a common observation form that emphasizes observed strengths and goal setting for future classes. During the week after the observation, the CAT Community leader meets with the observer to discuss their feedback, the class, and pedagogical plans for future classes. These discussions are also an opportunity for CAT Community faculty leaders to raise concerns, request support, and sound out possible ideas for future classes. An examination of the learning community observation data shows that the first-generation LLCs have excelled at building community among the students and among the students and their peer mentors and instructors, at helping students discover their own intrinsic purposes or motivations for attending college, and at integrating and utilizing the peer mentor to support student success and feelings of belonging.

Tracking Data

From the start of K-State First and its first-generation LLCs, the program has tracked first-year to second-year retention, as well as year-to-year persistence, graduation rates, and grades, as one way to measure the overall success of the program. Entering ACT scores have also been included in this retention and graduation data tracking effort. Over the seven-year life of the first-generation

LLC program, the first-generation specific learning communities have had higher one-year retention rates than the CAT Communities program as well as the university first-year student population in general. From 2014 through 2019, first-gen specific learning communities have a first-year to second-year retention rate of 87.1% compared to a learning community program average of 86.0% and an average of 85.1% for students who did not participate in any K-State First programs over that same period. These higher retention rates happened even though the students in the first-generation specific CAT Communities had a lower average ACT scores (23.2) compared to the non-K-State First students (25.3 ACT). The highest retention rates were among the scholarship-supported First Scholars students at 88.1%, who also, nonetheless, had an average entering ACT score (23.9) below the 25.3 average of non-participants. The students in the first-generation LLCs did not outperform their peers in the other learning communities or in the university first-year population generally in terms of first-year grades; in fact, their first-year average grades (3.07) were in fact slightly below the non-participant average (3.11). Nevertheless, in terms of six-year graduation rates, the students who were a part of a residential first-generation LLC outperformed the students in the other learning communities, the students who did not participate in K-State First, and the overall university average. Students in the first-generation LLCs had a six-year graduation rate of 76.2%, compared to a six-year graduation rate of 73.4% for the CAT Communities program as a whole and a 65.1% graduation rate for students who did not participate in a K-State First learning community or FYS.

ACT SCORES, RETENTION RATES, FIRST-YEAR GPAS, AND SIX-YEAR GRADUATION RATES, 2014–2019

Metric	Non-Participants (Students Not Enrolled in a FYS or Learning Community)	All Learning Community Students	First-Generation Residential Learning Community Students
Average ACT Score	25.3	24.2	23.2
First-Year GPA	3.11	3.12	3.07
First-Year to Second-Year Retention Rate (%)	85.1	86.0	87.1
Six-Year Graduation Rate (%)	65.1	73.4	76.2

LESSONS LEARNED

Our work with first-generation LLCs throughout the last seven years has illuminated several important takeaways. Foremost, residential learning communities for first-generation students are a powerful intervention to help these students succeed in college and persist to graduation. Well-designed curricular and co-curricular experiences partnered with strategic and collaborative partnerships among university faculty and staff who care and engage in meaningful ways with first-generation students create transformational change across the higher education landscape. When beginning to explore if LLCs could be an option, it is imperative to identify the stakeholders and involve them immediately. Partnerships and collaboration are critical to creating buy-in and sustaining LLCs. If there is not buy-in or others willing to do this work, it may not be possible.

Data talks. As resources become scarcer, data and assessment are critical. Understanding how many students identify as first-generation, how many first-generation students live on-campus and identification of other data that is collected regarding first-generation students will be helpful to understand if an LLC is feasible. The assessment and feedback measures implemented share a story that these LLCs offer a value-added intervention to helping first-generation students succeed, and because of these initial successes, we are committed to the process moving forward.

As a result of COVID-19, changes were made to ensure these LLCs would continue. Safety precautions (masks, physical distancing, cleaning, and sanitizing, etc.) were incorporated into the living and learning spaces. Classes were offered in-person and via Zoom to accommodate students who may have been in quarantine or monitoring COVID-related symptoms. An even greater emphasis was placed on building community, creating a sense of belonging, and well-being. This included intentional classroom conversations, meals outdoors, and outreach and follow-up through one-on-one meetings, GroupMe, and our campus student success communication tool. Informal feedback from students and other teaching faculty indicated that the classroom experience and creating a sense of community could all be managed virtually but required additional time and intentionality. As the spring semester concluded, the instructors met with the students who participated in these LLCs in the fall of 2020. It was evident that the relationships formed as a result of the LLCs were the students' lifelines during the spring semester and ensured the students remained in college and persisted to the end of the year.

As we look ahead, however, there remain challenges that require ongoing reflection, dialogue, and action. This work is not linear, easy, or simple. In fact, one of the most enduring lessons we've learned is about the importance of persistence. In our first-generation LLCs, we see and develop such qualities in our students, and we've learned over the life of this program that such grit is also vital to sustaining an effective LLC. We've realized that a successful program cannot simply be created and then left to operate on its own, in part because the program itself depends not only on the quality of its faculty and student leaders, but on units and contexts outside the learning communities themselves. In other words, some of the most important recommendations we have to offer are closely related to our own ongoing efforts and relationships with partners and stakeholders.

Language Matters

We continue to experience challenges utilizing the descriptor of "first-generation." While this term is common among higher education professionals, most incoming college students and their families are not familiar with the term, especially if they are first-generation. This has proven problematic, as students must self-identify if they are a first-generation student on their admissions application. which in turn becomes the data utilized to recruit students into the LLC. Misreporting happens, which can lead to missed opportunities to connect with the students who might benefit most from a learning community for first-generation students. Moreover, some students do not identify with the term "first-generation," and therefore may not seek out nor understand a cohort experience like the LLC, which is challenging for recruitment and enrollment. Even if students understand the term first-generation, they may not resonate with that identity as it may feel embarrassing or lesser than their peer counterparts who have experience with the college system. Messaging must be carefully cultivated to be clear and inclusive in order to help students recognize what it means to be first-generation. Additionally, language that is asset-based and celebrates the identity of being first-generation will help in creating a culture where first-generation students feel valued.

Recruitment and Support

Recruiting first-generation students into the LLCs has been a continual challenge every year. Being proactive with our office of admissions is essential to identify the first-generation students enrolled at the university and crafting a marketing and communication plan to reach them. Given the challenges with identification of first-generation students, we have worked every year to better tailor specific and individualized messages to students, engaged in phone calling campaigns to recruit students, discussed reaching out to the families of first-generation students, and examined the marketing approach including adjusting the name of the CAT Community to see if it captures more attention. We also recognize an added barrier to enrollment in an LLC is the cost of an additional credit hour.

Research shows that first-generation students are concerned about money, will need to work more hours, and do not want to take extra credits (Davis, 2010), which could deter students from enrolling in this experience. Our most successful LLC experiences were when we were able to provide a scholarship to participants. This financial incentive allowed us full enrollment in the course and provided additional motivation for students to engage in strong academic behaviors to retain their scholarship. It also supported students financially, which provided a stronger connection to the university and the courses. Identifying and securing these funding resources is an important challenge. Unfortunately, the scholarship was discontinued at the end of the grant period. Opportunities for additional funding continue to be explored including partnerships with colleges to provide scholarships for first-generation students.

Community and Culture Building

While the LLCs are an important intervention in supporting first-generation success, it is not enough. It is essential that the university creates a campus-wide culture of supporting first-generation students. This begins with the collaborative partnership approach of integrating the knowledge and experience gleaned from working with the LLC and sharing the learning with the larger community. Faculty and student life professionals all can benefit from additional knowledge and context as to how to better identify and intentionally support first-generation students they work with across campus. One way to better share this information more broadly is to partner with the Teaching and Learning Center (TLC) to host professional development sessions about working with first-generation students. Another suggestion is to host first-generation focused training with academic advisors and housing staff to better equip individuals to identify and respond to needs. Additionally, an office dedicated specifically for first-generation students will continue to bring visibility and resources to first-generation students. Overall, more awareness and knowledge must be woven into the fabric of the campus community that supports creating a culture of first-generation success and support.

Purpose and Persistence

As we seek to address the challenges with language, find more success in recruitment, and work to create a culture of first-generation student success across campus, we arrive at our final and perhaps most important lesson learned: the importance of staying the course. There have been various reasons we could have abandoned a first-generation LLC model after the first year or two (when we didn't achieve all our intended goals, for example) or during the 2020–2022 pandemic (when both recruitment and community building became more difficult than ever, for example). Nevertheless, ongoing dialogue and collaboration among stakeholders helped us to realize the importance of recognizing key successes (retention and graduation rates, for example), while also using our assessment and reflection processes to help us design improvements and changes going forward. Our own experience has led us to changes in co-curricular event programming, to additional professional development opportunities for our faculty leaders and student peer mentors, and to increased campus-wide advocacy for first-generation students. These improvements and the reflection and dialogue that led to them have helped us understand the importance of our commitment to staying the course. It is essential to recognize that success cannot be judged on a single attempt. To evaluate program effectiveness, it is essential to gather assessment data, feedback from the program's range of stakeholders, including students, faculty, advisors, administrators, and more. Utilizing this data, key stakeholders can work together to identify growth areas and continue to design and mold the program within the context of the university setting.

Thus, just as we help our students understand the role and importance of a growth mindset within their own college learning experience (Dweck, 2006), we ourselves also must maintain a willingness to learn from setbacks and feedback, to embrace new challenges, to find inspiration in the success of our students and colleagues, and to realize that our own effort and our willingness to stay the course are critical to the success of our program.

REFERENCES

Cambridge-Williams, T., Winsler, A., Kitsantas, A., & Bernard, E. (2013). University 100 orientation courses and living-learning communities boost academic retention and graduation via enhanced self-efficacy and self-regulated learning. *Journal of College Student Retention: Research, Theory & Practice, 15*(2), 243–268.

Clance, P. R., & Imes, S. A. (1978). The imposter phenomenon in high achieving women: Dynamics and therapeutic intervention. *Psychotherapy: Theory, Research & Practice, 15*(3), 241–247.

Davis, J. (2010). *The First-generation student experience: Implications for campus practice, and strategies for improving persistence and success*. Stylus Publishing.

Dumais, S. A. & Ward, A. (2010). Cultural capital and first-generation college success. *Poetics, 38*(3), 245–265. https://doi.org/10.1016/j.poetic.2009.11.011

Dweck, C. S. (2006). *Mindset: The new psychology of success. How we can learn to fulfill our potential*. Random House.

Kuh, G. D. (2008). *High-impact educational practices: What they are, who has access to them, and why they matter*. Association of American Colleges and Universities.

Mein, E. L. (2018). *Asset-based teaching and learning with diverse learners in postsecondary settings*. Departmental Technical Reports (CS). 1271. Retrieved from: https://digitalcommons.utep.edu/cs_techrep/1271

Pascarella, E. T., & Terenzini, P. T. (2005). *How college affects students, volume 2, a third decade of research*. Jossey-Bass.

Priest, K. L., Saucier, D. A., & Eiselein, G. (2016). Exploring students' experiences in first-year learning communities from a situated learning perspective. *International Journal of Teaching and Learning in Higher Education*, *28*(3), 361–371.

Purdie, J.R & Rosser, V. J. (2011). Examining the academic performance and retention of first-year students in living-learning communities and first-year experience courses. *College Student Affairs Journal*, *29*(2), 95–112.

Strayhorn, T. L. (2012). *College students' sense of belonging: A key to educational success for all students*. Routledge.

Yosso, T. J. (2005). Whose culture has capital? *Race, Ethnicity and Education*, *8*(1), 69–91.

Zhao, C.-M., & Kuh, G. D. (2004). Adding value: Learning communities and student engagement. *Research in Higher Education*, *45*(2), 115–138.

Part IV
Exploration and Transition

Chapter 11

Global Leadership for First-Generation Students

Implementing Custom Study Abroad Programs

*Michelle L. Ashcraft and
Lisa Lambert Snodgrass*

Study abroad is considered a high impact practice in higher education (Kuh, 2008). Students with this experience earn higher starting salaries and are more likely to get into their graduate school of choice (IES, 2016). However, studies have found some students are less likely to participate in the experience. Various factors significantly impact students' intentions and decisions to study abroad, including financial support, cost, lost wages, length of program, personal safety concerns, family concerns about safety, family responsibilities, curriculum and degree plan restrictions, and cultural barriers (Berdan & Johannes, 2014; Vernon et al., 2017). These barriers disproportionately impact first-generation students.

In 2014, the Institute of International Education (IIE) launched *Generation Study Abroad* to double and diversify the number of US students studying abroad over a decade, and Purdue University (Purdue) signed on as a commitment partner (Institute for International Education [IIE], 2021). At that point, Horizons at Purdue had been coordinating study abroad for low-income, first-generation students since 2012. Purdue Promise, described below, launched a study abroad initiative in May 2017, and soon after Engle (2017) reported a significantly strong correlation between study abroad and graduation for first-generation students (defined as those whose parents have not completed a higher education degree), further justifying the experience.

PROGRAM DESCRIPTIONS

Purdue Promise

Purdue Promise is a four-year scholarship and support program for low-income Indiana residents who are part of the Indiana 21st Century Scholars (TFCS) program. TFCS students who enroll at Purdue as first-time, full-time, first-year students with a total family income up to $50,000 are automatically awarded the Purdue Promise award, a last-dollar scholarship that covers full financial need for up to four years. Purdue Promise scholarships are funded through donor and institutional funds. The program's mission is: "Champion access, affordability, and holistic support to facilitate opportunities for qualifying Indiana scholars to graduate on time, debt-free, and prepared for life after Purdue" (Purdue Promise, 2018). The four-year model is designed to minimize barriers to success and provide individualized care, and includes orientation, a first-year seminar, a senior seminar, coaching meetings and modules, optional study abroad, a senior survey, and other supports (Purdue Promise, 2020). Purdue Promise was established in 2009 to address a 10% four-year graduation rate gap for TFCS when compared to all Purdue undergraduates (Ashcraft et al., 2017), and the program has received campus, statewide, and national recognition for graduating students on time and debt-free.

To be eligible for TFCS, students qualify based on family income (eligibility for free- and reduced-lunch) in middle school and enroll in the program by June 30 after their eighth grade year. Currently TFCS must fulfill a scholar pledge (remain alcohol-free under 21, drug-free, and crime-free), graduate high school with a 2.5 GPA, file the FAFSA, and complete a high school scholar success program to earn a state scholarship that covers full tuition and regularly assessed fees for up to four years of postsecondary education (Indiana Commission for Higher Education [CHE], 2015; St. John et al., 2018).

Compared to their Indiana peers, TFCS are more likely to be low-income, first-generation, and from single-parent households (CHE, 2015). "Purdue Promise participants are historically more diverse than the Purdue-WL all-undergraduate population, and represent populations that are often marginalized in higher education" (Ashcraft et al., 2017, p. 2), with 28.0% of students enrolling from 2009 through 2018 identifying as students of color, 63.5% as first-generation students, and 97.1% Pell Grant eligible (Ashcraft et al., 2019). This compares to 9.1% of the Purdue all-undergraduate population identifying as students of color, 18.6% as first-generation college students, and 18.0% Pell Grant eligible during the same timeframe (Ashcraft et al., 2019). Since 2009, 57.9% to 72.6% of the Purdue Promise cohorts have been first-generation students, and they often graduate at higher rates than their Purdue undergraduate peers (Purdue Promise, 2020).

Horizons TRIO Student Support Services

Purdue's Horizons program is a federally funded TRIO Student Support Services program, as authorized by the Higher Education Amendments of 1968 (Horizons, 2020). The program's mission statement indicates that Horizons "assists students in developing academic, social, personal, and leadership skills through holistic services including tutoring, faculty mentoring, peer mentoring, career development, academic support, cultural enrichment, and access to global experiences" (Horizons, 2020). Horizons aspires to "retain and graduate its participants at the highest possible rate with the highest possible grade point average" (Horizons, 2020). Established in 1978, Horizons has served students for more than 40 years (Horizons, 2021a), and recently earned a $2.1 million grant from the US Department of Education to continue operations through the 2024–2025 academic year (Horizons, 2020).

To qualify for Horizons, students must: (a) enroll at Purdue, (b) have US citizenship or legal resident status, (c) qualify for federal financial aid and have a current FAFSA on file, and (d) apply for admissions to Horizons (Horizons, 2021b). Additionally, one of the following three criteria must be met: (a) students' families meet federal guidelines for income eligibility, (b) students are first-generation (neither parent completed a four-year degree), or (c) students have disabilities evidencing academic need (Horizons, 2021b). For cohorts enrolling from 2011 through 2019, the percentage of Horizons students that identified as first-generation ranged from 50.9% to 96.2%; and recent data indicates that Horizons first-generation students graduate at higher rates than their Purdue first-generation peers (Horizons, 2020).

PURPOSE, GOALS, AND OBJECTIVES
Purdue University

In 2013, Purdue established Purdue Moves, "a range of initiatives designed to broaden Purdue's global impact and enhance educational opportunities for students" (Patterson Neubert, 2016, para. 6). Purdue historically had a low percentage of students who studied abroad, despite being a top destination in the United States for international students (Purdue University [Purdue], 2020). Purdue set aspirational goals to be in the top 25 US institutions sending students abroad, and for "one-third of all undergraduate students to participate in an international study, internship or research credit-bearing experience before graduation" (Patterson Neubert, 2016, para. 6). Purdue Moves established six goals pertaining to: (a) doubling the number of undergraduate students studying abroad, particularly for a semester or longer; (b) making study abroad affordable through scholarships and financial aid; (c) enacting a cultural shift whereby students understood the importance of international experiences; (d) increasing semester-long immersive experiences; (e) incentivizing departments for study abroad programs and participation; and (f) embedding outcomes in the University Core Curriculum (Purdue, 2020).

The establishment of the Purdue Moves scholarship in 2013 to assist students in studying abroad has been vital to the success of the Purdue Promise and Horizons study abroad programs. Currently, there are two options – Purdue Moves Summer/Short Term Scholarship and Purdue Moves Semester Study Abroad

Scholarship – and scholarship amounts vary up to $3000 for short-term study abroad/away programs and up to $5000 for semester-long programs, based on program length and total family income (Purdue, 2015a, b). Purdue ranked 19th nationally for study abroad for the 2016–2017 academic year (Purdue, 2020). By 2018, nearly 70% more students graduated having studied abroad compared to graduates in 2013 (Purdue, 2020).

Purdue Promise and Horizons

The mutual goal of the Purdue Promise and Horizons annual study abroad experiences is to increase affordable access to study abroad for marginalized groups, including (a) low-income students, (b) first-generation students, and (c) students of color. Purdue Promise and Horizons have been recognized for significantly contributing to the Purdue Moves goals pertaining to affordability and diversifying study abroad (Purdue, 2020). All participants from both programs have been from low-income backgrounds, 61% of Purdue Promise and 64% of Horizons participants identified as first-generation, and 45% of Purdue Promise and 46% of Horizons participants identified as students of color (Purdue, 2020). Purdue Promise participants have traveled for less than $500 per student; and Horizons has reduced the cost of their study abroad programs to approximately 35% of typical short-term programs (Purdue, 2020).

These custom study abroad programs seek to explore how elimination of barriers to accessing global educational opportunities can have a positive influence on students' confidence levels, exposure to immersive cultural experiences, and enhanced cultural competency. The programs (a) develop understanding of global leadership success strategies, (b) foster skills toward enhanced leadership effectiveness, and (c) provide instruction on self-branding and marketing study abroad experiences for career development. The Purdue Promise study abroad program was recognized by NASPA (National Association of Student Personnel Administrators) with the 2019 Best Practices in International Education Award for study abroad programming. Horizons' (Purdue TRIO) study abroad program was selected as the 2020 recipient of the NASPA Region IV-E Innovation Program Award.

STAKEHOLDERS

The Purdue Promise and Horizons study abroad programs have been effective because of strong partnerships to fill gaps in knowledge and streamline planning processes. Horizons initiated study abroad programming in 2012 with assistance from two Purdue units, International Programs and Purdue Study Abroad. Since then, Horizons has annually rotated between five locations: Spain, Greece, Cuba, Peru, and Costa Rica. A true collaboration formed between Horizons and Purdue

Study Abroad to provide access at a reduced rate. The three-week programs are coordinated in partnership with third-party vendors for itineraries and travel.

Purdue Promise joined Horizons for the May 2016 program to Spain and Morocco to learn how to implement custom study abroad programs to further enhance access for first-generation and low-income students, as well as students of color. Based on the Horizons model, Purdue Promise commits funding annually to reduce the cost of the program, and helps students apply for financial aid to further cover costs. Since May 2017, Purdue Promise has offered an annual three-week program to Spain, also coordinated in partnership with third-party vendors.

Purdue University Partners

Purdue Promise is forever indebted to Horizons for paving the way. As Horizons explored options for study abroad to increase access for first-generation students, Purdue Promise began investigating the possibility and immediately encountered financial aid barriers (Ashcraft & Ramsey, 2019b). First, students cannot be over-aided, and Purdue Promise students receive grants and scholarships that cover full financial need; thus, extra funds to study abroad would simply reduce other aid meant to cover their expenses for the academic year (Ashcraft & Ramsey, 2019b). Secondly, scholarships are taxable if used for educational expenses beyond tuition, fees, and books, and Purdue Promise did not want to create a situation where providing funds for study abroad had negative tax implications (Ashcraft & Ramsey, 2019b). Horizons received internal and external grants to support their study abroad program, and created a true collaboration with Purdue Study Abroad to coordinate their program through an external provider. An account was set up within Purdue Study Abroad that allowed Horizons to pay providers directly to reduce the cost per student. Two years later, the restructuring of Student Affairs and Academic Affairs put both Purdue Promise and Horizons under the Access and Retention Team in Student Success Programs to streamline support for low-income and first-generation students. In 2015, Horizons invited Purdue Promise to pilot a study abroad program by co-sponsoring Horizons' 2016 program to Spain and Morocco. Purdue Promise sent ten students and a staff member who later helped co-lead the launch of the Purdue Promise Spain program in May 2017 with assistance from Purdue Study Abroad.

The executive director of Student Success Programs provides annual funding for Purdue Promise study abroad. The dean of International Programs at Purdue provides annual funding for Horizons study abroad. The dean committed funding for Purdue Promise to initiate a second experience to Scotland beginning May 2020; however, the program was cancelled due to the COVID-19 pandemic. The dean continues to be committed to collaborating with both programs to increase access to study abroad for first-generation and low-income students.

The dean also has historically provided opportunities for Purdue staff to certify as Intercultural Development Inventory (IDI) Qualified Administrators (QAs) through IDI, often paying 62.5% of the fees associated with the training. Most Purdue Promise and Horizons program leaders have been certified this way. In exchange, Purdue Promise and Horizons staff offer weekly time slots for Purdue students, faculty, and staff to schedule IDI debriefs, and thus support the rest of campus.

Within International Programs, both Purdue Promise and Horizons collaborate with Purdue Study Abroad to coordinate departmental programs and training for program co-leaders. While Purdue Promise and Horizons staff now collaborate directly with third-party vendors to coordinate travel and all in-country logistics, Purdue Study Abroad (a) approves program proposals; (b) registers participants for the associated courses; (c) coordinates billing with the Office of the Bursar; (d) directs the Division of Financial Aid to award study abroad scholarships; (e) serves as home-based emergency contacts for students, staff, and families; and (f) posts final grades for students, among other assistance.

Third-Party Vendor Partners

In order to increase efficiency and lower costs for students, both Purdue Promise and Horizons collaborate with third-party vendors to coordinate itineraries and travel. To capitalize on the expertise and relationships of host country leaders, the programs select organizations that specialize in hosting students from the United States abroad. To date, Horizons has collaborated with three vendors to plan the itineraries for annual programs: (a) IES Abroad for South Africa in 2012 and Costa Rica in 2013; (b) International Studies Abroad LLC (ISA, now a WorldStrides organization) for Spain in 2014, Greece in 2015, Spain and Morocco in 2016, Peru in 2018, and Spain in 2019; and (c) the Institute for Study Abroad (IFSA) for Cuba in 2017 (B. Corley, personal communication, September 22, 2020). Purdue Promise has always collaborated with WorldStrides ISA, beginning with the joint program with Horizons to Spain and Morocco, and continuing for annual Spain programs in 2017, 2018, and 2019. Both programs were partnering with WorldStrides ISA on May 2020 programs, to Spain and Scotland for Purdue Promise and to Costa Rica for Horizons, prior to the programs being cancelled due to the COVID-19 pandemic. Among other responsibilities, these vendors (a) coordinate ground transportation abroad; (b) place students in homestays to lower costs and increase cultural immersion; (c) book hotels for off-site excursions; (d) reserve classroom space in the host country; (e) book in-country guest lecturers; (f) plan tours, excursions, and activities; and (g) organize tour guides and interpreters.

Both programs also collaborate with third-party vendors to coordinate ground transportation in the United States and group flights. Purdue Study Abroad does not require a request for proposals for either form of transportation, but programs are allowed to submit them. Purdue Promise has always worked with STA Travel to coordinate group flights based on their long-standing relationship with Purdue Study Abroad. Horizons has historically had the vendor that coordinates the itinerary for the host country also book group flights (ex. WorldStrides ISA). Both programs have used two different local transportation companies to provide round-trip group shuttle service between Purdue and the airport.

PROGRAM IMPLEMENTATION
Funding the Program

The University President created the aforementioned Purdue Moves scholarship to subsidize the cost of study abroad. Presently, students can qualify for up to $2,500, based on total family income, for the three-week programs sponsored by Purdue Promise and Horizons. While these scholarships make study abroad more affordable, Purdue Promise commits to further advancing the priorities of the university, including affordability and accessibility. In order to further subsidize the cost of study abroad for Purdue Promise students, Student Success Programs annually contribute a $50,000 subsidy through carryforward funds (remaining funds from the Purdue Promise budget and the budgets of other Student Success Programs at the end of the fiscal year). Scholarships and subsidies, in addition to need-based summer aid options, have enabled Purdue Promise to create experiences that cost participants less than $500 out-of-pocket. Most participants have paid $0, particularly if they have $0 estimated family contributions (EFC) and register for additional classes upon return to the United States to maximize their summer aid.

The dean of international programs provides a similar annual subsidy to support reducing the cost of the Horizons study abroad programs. Horizons students are also encouraged to apply for the Purdue Moves scholarship and summer financial aid, though out-of-state students are limited in their options as need-based aid is reserved for in-state students. Horizons has limited funds to support program participants, but does use some of the funds to help further reduce the cost of participating in study abroad.

Both Purdue Promise and Horizons make programs affordable by partnering with Purdue Study Abroad to make arrangements for paying invoices directly to the providers. As many program costs as possible are built into contracts, including: (a) housing and meals, (b) ground transportation in the United States and host countries, (c) group flights, (d) insurance, (e) activities and excursions (including guest lecturers, tour guides, inerpreters, tips, and entrance fees), and (f) classroom space. Additionally, the programs are intentional about the timing of the experiences, which occurs during Maymester. This leaves students all of

June, July, and August to work, save money, gain internship experiences, and take summer classes. This timing helps mitigate concerns about program length, lost wages, degree plans, and family responsibilities.

Planning for Study Abroad

Selecting Program Leaders

Even with a study abroad planning committee, as Purdue Promise had in 2016, the program leaders do the bulk of the work for preparing students for study abroad and executing the experiences. At Purdue, proposals are due November 1 for summer programs, so Purdue Promise and Horizons select program leaders before the fall semester begins in August. That means once an annual program is up and running, travel happens in May, grades are submitted in July, new program leaders are selected in August, and the planning process starts again. Purdue Promise has program leaders sign participation agreements, ensuring that they will fulfill all responsibilities associated with planning and executing the program and submitting grades upon return to the United States. If program leaders choose not to participate in the program for any reason or leave their roles with the program, they are responsible for paying the full cost of their participation if their places cannot be filled by other staff members. Both programs have historically sent two staff members, sometimes three when trying to build a bench of "returners" who have gone before. The ideal situation is to annually send a returner and a new leader, and then have the new leader become the returner on the next trip, cycling through staff members in the programs. As the Purdue Promise team is much larger than Horizons, there is an application and interview process to select Purdue Promise staff to be program leaders.

Selecting a Country and Provider

Selecting a country and a provider could lead to a "which comes first" debate. Selecting the country first could exclude some providers. Selecting a provider first could exclude some countries. Options include (a) comparing a list of desired countries with a list of desired providers and seeing where they align, or (b) choosing a provider and selecting a country based on locations where the provider has local offices and teams. The relationship with the provider, both at the corporate level and the local in-country level, can significantly influence the experience for staff and students. Considerations for selecting a country may include: (a) option to do homestays, (b) affordability (such as cost of flights and exchange rates), (c) option for direct flights from the nearest domestic airport to the host country, (d) options for host cities and possible excursions to other cities, (e) closest in-country airport to the host city, (f) safety, (g) availability of a US Embassy near the host city, (h) possible language barriers, and (i) quantity of study abroad programs from the home institution that already exist within the host country.

Building the Itinerary and Contract

Assuming the decision to subsidize the cost of the program, being able to directly pay the provider has the most direct influence on making the experience affordable for students without causing financial aid issues or tax implications. Thus, it is important to collaborate with the provider to include as much in the itinerary and contract as possible. This includes, but is not limited to: (a) coordinating housing (preferably homestays) and corresponding three meals per day in the host city for students and separate accommodations for staff, (b) booking hotels for excursions outside of the homestay and allotting stipends for meals while traveling, (c) organizing all ground transportation within the country for official activities and excursions, (d) pre-booking group entry for various sites, (e) coordinating tour guides (especially if English-speaking is necessary) and interpreters, (f) pre-planning for gratuities for group meals and tours, (g) booking classroom space and guest lecturers, and (h) providing access cards for public transportation.

Making Travel Arrangements

Both Purdue Promise and Horizons collaborate with third-party vendors for round-trip shuttle service from Purdue to the airport as well as group flights. Both are reserved in September or October, as costs need to be built into the proposal for Purdue Study Abroad, including the budget for the Office of the Bursar and Division of Financial Aid. Details to consider when planning for transportation include: (a) time zones (institution versus airport), (b) direct flights versus layovers (direct is recommended, as many students will have never flown before), (c) cancellation policies, (d) deadlines to put names and passport numbers on flights, (e) surcharges for certain times of the year, (f) gratuity for shuttle drivers, (g) if the airline has its own terminal at the airport, (h) deadlines for checking in for flights, and (i) luggage limitations for shuttles and planes.

Understanding Financial Aid and Billing

Purdue Study Abroad collaborates with the Office of the Bursar to create a budget for each study abroad program, based on information Purdue Promise and Horizons submit in their proposals. This includes: (a) the Purdue Study Abroad fee, (b) the program fee from the third-party host country provider, (b) domestic ground transportation for staff and students, (b) flights for staff and students, (c) housing accommodations and per diem for staff, and (d) insurance for students. The budgets are then shared with the Division of Financial Aid to assemble financial aid packages and award Purdue Moves scholarships as directed by Purdue Study Abroad. It is important to know if summer is a header or trailing semester. Over the years, Purdue has switched from summer as a trailing semester to a header, which means students need to have the next year's FAFSA filed and cleared of all edits and verification to be packaged with summer financial aid. Purdue also has a summer aid application students must complete.

Student Recruitment and Selection

Marketing and Information Sessions

Purdue Promise introduces study abroad in the program's first-year seminar, GS 19700.

Both Purdue Promise and Horizons host information sessions in the fall semester, typically right after the Thanksgiving holiday. Attendance is required to be able to apply for the programs. Students are then able to use the remainder of the fall semester and winter recess to talk with their families, work on application materials, apply for a passport (if needed), and get money for a deposit. Many students will ask families for the deposit money as their holiday gifts.

Application Submission and Review, Interviews, and Selection of Participants

For Purdue Promise, applications are due in January at the end of the first week of the semester. Application review, interviews, and selection must be completed by the end of January, as the roster of participants is typically due to the third-party vendor in early February. In addition to collecting demographic information, students must complete several essay responses for applications for both programs. Both programs require proof of passport or a passport application and a deposit to apply. Purdue Promise also requires proof of filing the FAFSA to ensure the students will be eligible for summer aid. Horizons selects students based on the applications alone. As Purdue Promise has a much larger student population, the program selects students to interview from the applicant pool, and then makes final selections for the program. Once students are selected, they must sign participation agreements, as mandated by Purdue Study Abroad. The agreements are customized and outline the expenses that students would have to pay if they cancel their participation or are removed from the program.

Course Approval

Both Purdue Promise and Horizons have partnered with the College of Education to award three academic credit hours for completion of the Educational and

Psychological Studies (EDPS) 49000 course associated with the programs' study abroad experiences. The EDPS 49000 course is a variable title/credit course, and open to all majors. Permission to use the course was first gained by sending an e-mail to the department chair for Educational Studies. When planning for May 2020 programs, the course approval process was built into an electronic workflow for submitting proposals to Purdue Study Abroad, and getting the Educational Studies department chair's signature and approval from the director of study abroad for the College of Education.

In addition to the course approval process, both programs ensure that all course materials meet the standards set by the Center for Intercultural Learning, Mentorship, Assessment and Research (CILMAR). As the entire pre-program and in-country experiences contribute to students' earned grades in GS 49000, both the curriculum and activities are designed based on the Purdue-specific adaptation of the AAC&U (American Association of Colleges and Universities) Knowledge and Competence Rubric (Purdue, n.d.). Evidence of curriculum and activity alignment with the rubric are submitted as part of the program proposal. The curriculum for GS 49000 for both programs focuses on global leadership and intercultural competence. The program leaders and guest lecturers "develop students' understanding of their identity and role in a global context, as well as leadership strategies and cross-cultural skills to incorporate their experiences in personal, professional, and academic development" (Ashcraft & Ramsey, 2019a, p. 1). As students explore the host country together, they are "exposed to a breadth of diverse cultural experiences in which students are challenged to reflect on their emotional response and active participation" within the culture and "integrate these into their personal and professional world view" (Ashcraft & Ramsey, 2019a, p. 1).

ASSESSMENT PLAN

The overarching goal of the Purdue Promise and Horizons study abroad programs is to increase students' intercultural competence. The programs are designed to improve intercultural learning in the following areas based on the Purdue-specific adaptation of the AAC&U Knowledge and Competence Rubric (Purdue, n.d.): cultural self-awareness, knowledge of cultural worldview frameworks, verbal and nonverbal communication, and openness. These objectives target the "Emerging" level (level two) of intercultural knowledge and effectiveness. For cultural self-awareness, participants should be able to recognize new perspectives about their own cultural rules and biases (Purdue, n.d.). Pertaining to knowledge of cultural worldview frameworks, participants should be able to "demonstrate adequate understanding of the complexity of elements important to members of another culture in relation to its history, values, politics, communication styles, economy, or beliefs and practices"

(Purdue, n.d., p. 1). Related to verbal and nonverbal communication, participants should be able to recognize and participate in "cultural differences in verbal and nonverbal communication and begin[sic] to negotiate a shared understanding based on those differences" (Purdue, n.d., p. 1). Finally, with regard to openness, participants should be able to "initiate and develop interactions with culturally different others," and suspend judgment in valuing interactions with culturally different others (Purdue, n.d., p. 1).

Assessment Tools

The programs are assessed using two specific instruments. Students also complete written assignments throughout the programs, including journals, blog posts, and a final reflection paper. Through these assignments, students demonstrate their understanding of the course topics, reflect on their intercultural competence, and anticipate how their worldview will continue to develop.

Intercultural Development Inventory

The first instrument is the IDI that assesses changes in students' intercultural competence. The participants complete the assessment prior to departure from the United States, receive a debrief session from a qualified administrator (QA) and retake the assessment upon return, with the option to debrief the post-assessment. Additionally, QAs conduct a group debrief during one of the class sessions in the host countries.

Pre- and Post-Course Assessments

The second instrument is a pre- and post-course assessment administered via Qualtrics. This tool allows students to rate their confidence in several areas on a five-point Likert scale (1=Not Confident, 2=Somewhat Confident, 3=Confident, 4=Very Confident, 5=Extremely Confident). The 14 factors for Purdue Promise include: (a) navigation through unfamiliar environments, (b) cross-cultural communication, (c) intercultural competence, (d) ability to make a difference in the world, (e) adaptability to a new culture and interacting with people who are different, (f) ability to solve problems, (g) ability to solve conflicts, (h) knowledge and understanding of your own identity in a global context, (i) knowledge of your major/discipline in a global context, (j) ability to perform your job in a global context, (k) ability to lead others, (l) achieving your life's aspirations, (m) goal setting, and (n) taking action to decrease other peoples' suffering. Students' scores illustrate increased overall confidence in the assessed areas.

Course Components and Requirements

Participation

Participation is a significant portion of the course grade, starting with attendance and engagement at the pre-departure meetings, and continuing through the class lectures, activities, and excursions in the host country. On Purdue Promise programs, one co-leader is responsible for logging notes about attendance, participation, and engagement, including issues that would deduct points (such as tardiness) or boost points (such as asking questions in lecture and on tours). At the end of the program, the co-leaders award participation points for all participants.

Reflective Writing Assignments

Growth along the Intercultural Development Continuum (IDC) (Hammer, 2019), as presented in the IDI debriefs, is enhanced through reflection. Thus, the bulk of the in-country assignments are reflective writing assignments. Prior to departing for each program, the co-leaders create a blog, and participants sign up for days to author the blog. At the time they sign up, the students do not yet know the details of the itinerary, so what they will be writing about is often a surprise. On their assigned days, students document the experiences throughout the day, including taking photos that can be shared with their blog posts. The link to the blog is shared with participants' and program leaders' families, peers, and colleagues. Participants also complete journal assignments. There are typically five to eight journal prompts that are assigned throughout the in-country experience that allow students to reflect on their experiences, the IDI, skill development, (dis)comfort, and confidence. Often the journal prompts will have a few questions, frequently asking about class lectures, activities, excursions, homestay experiences, personal perspectives, and their futures. Typically the journal prompts are not pre-planned. Every few days, the program leaders assign a journal, and send the prompts out via GroupMe, e-mail, and the learning management system. Finally, upon return to the United States, participants complete final reflection papers. Program leaders typically write the essay questions after reflecting upon the experience and the students' journal and blog submissions. The questions will often ask about the IDI, their perceived growth, influential moments, their homestay experiences, and applying their learning toward future academic and career endeavors.

OUTCOMES

Horizons and Purdue Promise study abroad programs have yielded positive outcomes. Highlights of the IDI data demonstrate an option for measuring intercultural competency.

IDI Group Profile Reports

Annually, results typically reveal increases in participants' Developmental Orientation (DO), when comparing an IDI pre-score to a post-score. The most accurate indicator of the IDI® assessment is the DO scores. The DO scores indicate individual students' or group's primary orientation (or perspective) toward cultural differences. There are five stages on the Intercultural Development Continuum (IDC) (Hammer, 2019): Denial (score of less than 70 points), Polarization (70–85 points), Minimization (85–115 points), Acceptance (115–130 points), and Adaptation (a score of 130 or more points). The pre-test Group Profile Report shows each group's Developmental Orientation prior to their programs whereas the post-test Group Profile Report shows each group's Developmental Orientation after the conclusion of their programs. These are aggregate results, and the reports do not identify individual students' IDI® results. Annually, there has been an increase in Purdue Promise participants' Developmental Orientation. Most years Horizons see an increase in participants' Developmental Orientation.

LESSONS LEARNED

Prior to embarking on such program creation, particularly strong consideration should be given to lessons learned pertaining to recruitment, application, and selection processes. First, students often report in their essays and interviews that their primary reason for applying is a heritage connection to the host country. Thus, country selection appears to influence who will apply. Second, when students apply for study abroad programs at Purdue, they typically have to pay a $500 deposit by credit card. To make the Purdue Promise and Horizons programs more accessible, Purdue Study Abroad allows $200 deposits via checks that are only cashed if students are selected. Many students do not have checking accounts and would thus give $200 to someone to write a check on their behalf, which is problematic when depositing checks on the students' behalf, or returning checks for those not selected. Thus, consider requiring checks be in the students' names, and helping them set up bank accounts if needed. Third, while rubrics for applications and interviews are important, demographics should be reviewed through every step of the process. The first year of the Purdue Promise trip, all male applicants would have been eliminated based on application scores had adjustments not been made to ensure that the selected students mirrored the program demographics. Purdue Promise also provides the opportunity for students to have feedback meetings, and gives those students extra consideration for selection if they apply again in the future.

As previously mentioned, the COVID-19 pandemic caused the cancelation of the May 2020 Purdue Promise and Horizons study abroad experiences. Though emergencies should always be considered when planning for study abroad, the pandemic highlighted the need for emergency and contingency planning. Discussion of cancellation processes, timelines, and consequences with third-party providers will prepare program leaders for making key decisions about whether or not to run programs in pandemics or other emergencies, or respond accordingly should a future concern or university leadership decision force the cancellation of a program. While insurance is always key for study abroad experiences, determining whether the program or students should invest in additional cancellation insurance is a worthy discussion. Program leaders should also have a contingency plan in place for getting stuck in-country, including but not limited to: (a) who to work with for arranging extended lodging and other accommodations, (b) how to pay for extended stay in-country, (c) who to work with to arrange and pay for alternative flights, and (d) how to best communicate with others back in the US regarding a delayed return.

These study abroad programs exemplify best practices for supporting first-generation students. The programs not only provide access to global experiences to a population that is traditionally underrepresented in participation, but also leverages partnerships to make the experiences affordable. The creation of these study abroad programs illustrates Student Success Programs' commitment to access, affordability, and inclusion. Ultimately, the opportunity to go abroad is one way to improve student outcomes, particularly for first-generation students.

REFERENCES

Ashcraft, M., & Ramsey, J. (2019a). *2019 EDPS 490: Purdue promise in Valencia Syllabus* [syllabus]. Blackboard Learn.

Ashcraft, M., & Ramsey, J. (2019b, March 9 13). A whole new world: Planning affordable opportunities for low-income scholarship recipients to study abroad [Conference session]. In NASPA Annual Conference, Los Angeles, CA.

Ashcraft, M., Ramsey, J., Brodner, T., & Zhu, H. (2017, November 6 9). On-time and debt-free: A data-driven holistic coaching model for low-income student success at Purdue. In Proceedings of the 13th annual National Symposium on Student Retention [Symposium]. The Consortium for Student Retention Data Exchange, Destin, FL.

Ashcraft, M., Ramsey, J., & Stayback, T. (2019, September 11). On-time and debt-free: A data-driven holistic coaching model for low-income student success at Purdue [Paper presentation]. In 2019 20 webinar series of The Consortium for Student Retention Data Exchange, Norman, OK.

Berndan, S., & Johannes, W. (2014, May). *What will it take to double study abroad? A "green paper" on the big 11 ideas from IIE's Generation Study Abroad think tank*. Institute of International Education. https://p.widencdn.net/gbnycj/Generation-Study-Abroad-Green-Paper

Engle, L. C. (2017, October). *Underrepresented students in US study abroad: Investigating impacts*. IIE Center for Academic Mobility and Research Impact. https://www.iie.org/Research-and-Insights/Publications/Underrepresented-Students-and-Study-Abroad

Hammer, M. R. (2019). *IDI general information: The Intercultural Development Continuum (IDI™)*. https://idiinventory.com/generalinformation/the-intercultural-development-continuum-idc/

Horizons. (2020). *Horizons 2019–20 annual program report*. https://www.purdue.edu/studentsuccess/program-reports/hrz-2020.pdf

Horizons. (2021a). *An enduring, 40-year history*. https://www.purdue.edu/horizons/about/history.php

Horizons. (2021b). *Eligibility requirements*. https://www.purdue.edu/horizons/students/eligibility.php

IES Abroad (2016). *2016 career outcomes of study abroad students*. https://www.iesabroad.org/system/files/resources/career_outcomes_of_study_abroad_students.pdf

Indiana Commission for Higher Education. (2015, November 18). *21st Century Scholars: 25 years of supporting student success [PDF file]*. https://www.in.gov/che/files/25th_Anniversary_Brochure_11-18-15_Final_pages.pdf

Institute for International Education. (2021). *IIE Generation Study Abroad initiative*. https://www.iie.org/programs/generation-study-abroad

Kuh, G. D. (2008). *High-impact educational practices: What they are, who has access to them, and why they matter*. Association of American Colleges and Universities.

Patterson Neubert, A. (2016, November 14). *Purdue ranks 4th for international student population at public universities, places in top 25 for first time for study abroad* [Press release]. https://www.purdue.edu/newsroom/releases/2016/Q4/purdue-ranks-4th-for-international-student-population-at-public-universities,-places-in-top-25-for-first-time-for-study-abroad.html

Purdue Promise. (2018). *What is our promise?* https://www.purdue.edu/purduepromise/

Purdue Promise. (2020, December 10). *Purdue Promise 2019–20 annual program report*. https://www.purdue.edu/studentsuccess/program-reports/pup-2020.pdf

Purdue University. (n.d.). *AAC&U*VALUE** rubric for intercultural knowledge and competence*. https://www.purdue.edu/IPPU/CILMAR/Assessment/AdaptedBranded_nolines_rubric.pdf

Purdue University. (2015a). *Purdue moves semester study abroad scholarship*. https://www.studyabroad.purdue.edu/programs/aid/details.cfm?ScholarID=137

Purdue University. (2015b). *Purdue moves summer/short term scholarship*. https://www.studyabroad.purdue.edu/programs/aid/details.cfm?scholarid=228

Purdue University. (2020). *International experiences*. https://www.purdue.edu/purduemoves/initiatives/education/internationalExperience.php

St. John, E. P., Daun-Barnett, N., & Moronski-Chapman, K. M. (2018). *Public policy and higher education: Reframing strategies for preparation, access, and college success* (2nd ed.). Routledge.

Vernon, A., Moos, C., & Loncarich, H. (2017). Student expectancy and barriers to study abroad. *Academy of Educational Leadership Journal, 21*(1), 1–9. https://www.abacademies.org/articles/student-expectancy-and-barriers-to-study-abroad-6694.html

Chapter 12

Getting Career Ready at UC Riverside

The ORBITS Program

Thomas Dickson, Charlie Rodnuson, and Elizabeth Montgomery

Many first-generation students enter college with a singular goal in mind: obtaining a stable, high-paying job after graduation. The goal of college for some of these students has a singular focus on learning a skill or trade that allows for the acquisition of a stable vocation that comes with immediate and high levels of compensation (Davis, 2010; Housel & Harvey, 2009). Career counselors, advisors, and other faculty and professional staff often hear students state they have no idea what to do after graduation, have no concept of how they will get to that goal, and are uncertain about the processes involved in searching and obtaining employment (Davis, 2010).

For low-income, first-generation students a particular emphasis is placed on the role of a college degree as a vehicle for positive social mobility, or the change in personal, and sometimes familial, socio-economic status. We see this heavily in student major selections, experiential learning participation, career networking engagement, and job seeking behaviors. First-generation students seek out majors that are known in popular culture as having large salaries and long-term stability (Davis, 2010). Students are not seeking high-dollar careers alone, rather, they are opposed to taking any risk, any chance, that a lower-paying career path or a slower wealth-building career path will change their lives quickly enough after graduation (Davis, 2010).

First-generation college students see college as having a singular purpose of being a minimum credential required for higher-tier employment and as training for a future career (Housel & Harvey, 2009). In reality, there is a gap between employer perceptions and desires for college outcomes and the goals and learning outcomes colleges establish as part of degree completion. Research has shown that first-generation, and especially low-income, students are less likely to make experiential learning and professional development a focus of the college experience (Davis, 2010; Mochetti & Hudley, 2008). First-generation students may also be less likely to participate in internships, join clubs and student organizations, participate in leadership development programs, and to engage in career networking activities than their continuing generation peers (Mochetti & Hudley, 2008). With these factors in mind, the University of California, Riverside (UCR) designed a program called "Obtain Resources, Become Informed, Target Success" (ORBITS), to focus on the development and exploration of career and life skills for first-generation students.

The University of California, Riverside (UCR) is located in the Inland Empire region of southern California, approximately 50 miles inland from Los Angeles. UCR prides itself on being a regional, public, doctoral-granting, land-grant university that has a history of diversity, student access, affordability, social mobility, and a strong first-generation student population. Over 58% of UCR's 23,000 undergraduate students are first-generation (UCR by the Numbers) and more than half are Pell eligible. UCR is a Hispanic Serving Institution (HSI) with 39% of the student population identifying as Hispanic or Latino, along with a highly diverse student population that is 31% Asian, 13% White, 5.5% Two or More Races, and 3% Black or African American. UCR defines first-generation as "a student, faculty, or staff member with neither parent or guardian having graduated with a four-year degree or higher, in the United States" (Overview, 2018). UCR formulated this definition via a campus committee that looked at the prominent research conducted by the NASPA Center for First-Generation Student Success (Whitley, S.E., Benson, G., & Wesaw, A., 2018) and balanced it alongside the University of California's definition. In 2020, UCR was recognized as an institution actively advancing first-generation engagement, receiving "First-Gen Forward Institution" status from NASPA's Center for First-Generation Student Success. The campus identity and mission, along with the goals of the campus Career Center, helped to define how campus engages first-generation students and is a critical component for how the ORBITS program was conceived and implemented.

CAREER ENGAGEMENT OF FIRST-GENERATION STUDENTS

The Career Center at UCR originally designed the ORBITS program to support inclusive career communities and to craft career education and experiences for first-generation students. The program was designed based on staff observations of the needs of a heavily low-income, first-generation, and underrepresented minority student population. ORBITS was designed specifically for a rising first-generation population that often lacked access to the networks, knowledge, and resources of navigating campus and personal career development.

The ORBITS program was created in 2008 and has selected a new cohort each year since establishment. The program works with a cohort of 20–40 students each year who meet weekly in one-hour long sessions, equivalent to a one-unit course held both in the fall and winter quarters. Participants are all self-identifying first-generation students that are continuing into their sophomore year. As of 2014, first-year transfer students were incorporated into the program recruitment model to engage both entry admission points. The intent of structuring the program at this time in the student experience was to engage students early enough to allow for potential major changes, to allow for utilization of acquired knowledge, and to allow time for students to engage in internships and other career development programming prior to graduation. This timing also seeks to normalize early engagement in the utilization of career counseling services during the college experience. Historically, the majority of students at UCR tend to engage with career development activities later in their college timelines, often late in their junior and senior years. The timing of the program also aligns with best practices recommendations for career engagement, academic adjustment, social adjustment, affiliation, and navigation and understanding of campus culture components of the college experience (Ward, Siegel, & Davenport, 2012).

Career Decision-Making Process

In addition to learning about the career decision-making process, the ORBITS two-quarter (September through March) model supports students through personalized career assessments, resource exploration, career search processes, as well as short- and long-term planning. The ORBITS program further assists students with establishing informational, career, and resource networks through professional mentor assignments and the inclusion of both online and on-site visits with employers. ORBITS first focuses on obtaining resources (OR), providing first-generation students with the necessary campus and career resources for continued career exploration, major decision, and skill development. Students obtain resources on resume and cover letter writing, interviewing, graduate school preparation, job and internship search strategies, and major choice. Second, students become informed (BI) and engage in activities such as informational interviews, employer discussions, panels, and mock interviews in order to enhance their transferable skills focusing on communication, work ethic, leadership, and teamwork. Finally, students target success (TS) via development of long-term educational and career plans including their short-term target goals leading up to graduation.

MISSION, GOALS, AND OBJECTIVES

The mission and goals of the UCR Career Center include a focus on 1) social equity: engaging students of all identities as intentionally included and having their needs equitably served; 2) a robust career ecosystem: an environment with high quality, intentional, collaborative relationships with campus partners and industry stakeholders; and 3) inclusive career communities: scalable career exploration and education coupled with personal and professional development experiences. Secondary objectives include engagement of prior program participants as professional mentors, mentors in leadership roles from across campus, university alumni, and both regional and national partner employers.

NACE Career Readiness Competencies

At the core, the ORBITS program is designed around the National Association of Colleges and Employers (NACE) Career Readiness Competencies (NACE Staff, 2018) and three central learning outcomes that may be categorized as experiential learning, informational, and personal assessment and goals. NACE, or the National Association of Colleges and Employers, is a professional association connecting college career services, recruiting, and business solution professionals. Career readiness is a basis of demonstrating general core competencies that prepare college graduates for workforce success and career management. The competencies serve as a foundational piece of ORBITS in highlighting career goals, outcomes, and key transferable skills for students across varying job functions. Competencies are integrated throughout the ORBITS program content and course design, influence the structure of engagement activities, and inform stakeholder relationships. These, as well as the other five competencies, are assessed within the pre-and post- surveys.

Learning Outcomes

ORBITS is designed around four primary learning outcomes centered around the themes of vocational exploration, campus resource knowledge, career readiness skill development, and networking with stakeholders. The four learning outcomes include:

- Explore, evaluate, and analyze academic options and vocational trajectories utilizing career assessments, assessment results, and experiential learning opportunities
- Develop a series of goals and plans around college engagement, career development, and life
- Identify important campus resources critical for student success
- Engage with alumni, campus personnel, and employers to better understand career opportunities, trajectories, and networks

The experiential learning and information outcomes are centered around learning the career decision-making process, learning methods for investigating career options, clarifying career interests, testing ideas with employers and academic engagement, and engaging with campus programs. Emphasis is placed both on learning the campus ecosystem and learning to navigate the explicit and hidden curriculum of student success services that is critical for progression and post-graduation outcomes. Finally, a significant learning outcome is the development of personal goals through the intensive assessment of personal interests, values, strengths, and limitations for career and life planning.

IMPLEMENTATION

Design

The design of the original ORBITS program was modeled from staff observations of the ongoing needs of first-generation, low-income, and minority student populations at the University of California, Riverside. Since implementation, the ORBITS model has undergone repeated revisions on an annual basis, with the cornerstones of the model being built upon addressing the evolving NACE Career Competencies (NACE Staff, 2021) as discussed earlier in this chapter, and being heavily informed by Yosso's (2005) model of community cultural wealth.

In 2005, Yosso identified six forms of capital that form community cultural wealth as part of cultural capital. The ORBITS program heavily integrates aspirational capital, or future dreams and barriers, through personal career development planning, internship and graduate school application assistance, and a series of career assessments. Social capital, a network of people and community resources, is met through regular employer presentations that allow for expanded career knowledge bases and networks to form. Students learn from professionals in the marketplace, often alumni of UCR, who guide them on industry standards and get to know students on a personal level. Finally, navigational capital, or the skills acquired by traversing social situations, are addressed through a series of campus resource presentations and the integration of campus points of contact for participants. Mentor relationships allow for long-term connections to form and for each participant to know there is someone there to help them with any problem that may arise. These elements help students set personal goals and plans to meet those goals, and provide access to employers and campus leadership who help with navigating resources and the hidden curriculum.

The global pandemic created an opportunity to shift the method of program delivery to a virtual space while continuing to offer the same community building, career growth, connection to campus resources, and professional mentor relationships. Weekly cohort meetings were hosted in Zoom with students utilizing the Chat feature, reactions, annotation, and breakout rooms in addition to speaking on camera. This created more ways for students to engage than in the traditional in person environment. Additionally, the use of a Blackboard or

Canvas site for this program provided a place for student participants to access all program documents, submit assignments, and contribute to discussion boards. Offering the program virtually also created more access for on- and off-campus professional mentors as travel time to campus was eliminated and there were no location constraints.

Recruitment and Selection

For first-year students advancing to their second year, recruitment begins in the spring quarter, typically in May, and remains open throughout the summer. Transfer students are recruited during the summer quarter during transfer orientations. Recruitment is typically conducted with assistance from campus partners and via campus marketing and social media networks. Orientations for transfer students as well as critical partners coordinating each college's first-year success courses are used for marketing. Students are encouraged to apply with a simple survey containing contact information, demographic information and academic standing, and questions on current engagement on campus and with career development. In addition to the survey, students are also required to submit a resume and a one-page essay answering the following prompts: "What are your personal and career goals/dreams? What would you like to gain from ORBITS that can benefit both your personal and career goals/dreams?" Selection of students is limited to 20–40 participants each year. Historically, the applications have fallen in this range; however, a few years' budget and space constraints required that those selected were students who would benefit most from the programming. These "most benefiting" students were identified based on survey responses to campus and career engagement, with those possessing limited or zero prior campus and Career Center engagement selected to maximize program impact. Students are notified of selection and begin attending the first session in the fall quarter.

Mentor assignments are provided at the start of the first session. Mentors are recruited from campus, employer, and/or community partnerships with a focus of developing a pool of interested professionals who have a desire to mentor students. Of the interested professionals, an assessment of their career backgrounds are taken into consideration to evaluate if varying career functions were represented; if not, additional career professionals were sought out utilizing LinkedIn's Find Alumni tool to further identify mentors. Potential mentor career fields are then compared to the reported career interests and goals identified within the students' essays in order to facilitate a mentor and mentee match. However, it is emphasized that there is a lot to be learned and shared in a mentor and mentee match even when the professional and career goals of the students are not precisely aligned with the professional mentors. ORBITS mentors serve on a volunteer basis.

Course Content

The first quarter of the program is designed around career assessments and career development planning, mastering LinkedIn, resume writing workshops and review sessions, campus resources, professional etiquette and networking fundamentals, understanding and addressing impostor syndrome, understanding cultural capital, and connecting with alumni. The first quarter focuses on establishing an understanding of self through assessments, understanding career search fundamentals, establishing networks, and empowering students with resources and access to overcome potential barriers to success. The second quarter focuses on exploration of graduate education, interviewing skills and mock interviewing, networking and crafting meaningful connections, internship exploration, job searching fundamentals, job application strategies, and personal reflections. The second quarter is designed around continuation of relationships and networks, arranging graduate education and internships, and understanding where and how to search for employment. The ORBITS program is designed like a two-quarter course. Course topics from the ORBITS syllabus include:

First Quarter (Fall)

- networking with assigned mentors, navigating your career path, Strong Interest Inventory interpretation, mastering LinkedIn, resume writing fundamentals, resume reviews, campus resource panels, first-generation student supports, alumni networking, and impostor syndrome and first-generation students

Second Quarter (Winter)

- campus counseling resources, exploring and applying to graduate school, interviewing skills, mock interviewing, making meaningful connections, internship searches and applications, conducting a job search, and cultural capital and being first-generation in a job search

Students are required to attend the sessions like a regular course; however, at this time they do not yet receive academic credit. Students meet with their assigned mentors during scheduled in-class mentor events, as well as once per month outside of ORBITS meetings. They must conduct career assessments and write several reflections on assessment results/personal goals. At the end of the second quarter students conduct a final presentation detailing what they learned throughout the program and next steps. During the final session, students who complete all program requirements are presented with a Career Leadership

Certificate which they can include on their resume and LinkedIn profile as well as a professional notepad portfolio. Mentors are presented with Career Champion certificates.

Program Costs

The initial launch of the program was made possible by funding from the Career Center and a small grant for food as incentives that was received from an employer partner. The "food as incentive" model was quickly discontinued due to student requests, budgets, and significant food waste. The program costs have cycled between $1,000 and $2,000 over the last 12+ years, dependent on allocated funding from the Career Center and partnership grants. Expenses include $1,000 for a series of career assessments, bound notepad portfolios, and certificates of completion. Each student participant takes at least two of the following career assessments: Strong Interest Inventory (SII), Myers Briggs Type Indicator (MBTI), and StrengthsFinder. Additional expenses have included dinners with employers and alumni with occasional funding for transportation to employer site visits depending on the year. Travel and dining budgets traditionally have not exceeded $800 annually. Site visits focus on networking, professional etiquette, and career exploration. Employer site visits have included corporate offices of Target, Disney, Universal Studios, ESRI, Bourns Inc., and other regional partners. Program costs also include staff time of two Career Center personnel who serve as instructors, volunteer time of staff mentors recruited from across campus, and employer mentors from industry.

STAKEHOLDERS

Campus stakeholders have been critical in addressing campus resource navigation and networking. These stakeholders have included mentors and programming partners from TRIO, Ethnic and Gender Programs offices, Power of the Peers Network, Health Professions Advising Center, Education Abroad, The Well – the campus basic needs and wellness offices, Student Life, Academic Resource Center, Counseling and Psychological Services, and the office of Undergraduate Education's units of Student Engagement and First-Generation Initiatives. These units provide valuable knowledge about campus resources, support networks, basic needs and wellness resources, cultural connections, advising, undergraduate research, education abroad opportunities, and academic internships. These partners often present to each cohort and mentors are often recruited from these key programs to ensure students are matched with knowledgeable campus partners. In return, campus partners have a tangible way of giving back to students and seeing how their work directly impacts students.

ASSESSMENT PLAN

The ORBITS program maintains a series of quantitative and qualitative measures to assess the efficacy of Student Learning Outcomes and program goals. Formal pre- and post- surveys are designed to assess how well the following areas are addressed by programming: NACE Career Readiness Competencies, growth on Student Learning Outcomes, identification of resources to support career decision-making, knowledge of various job strategies and resources, and ability to articulate experience, education, and skills to potential employers and/or graduate programs. Additionally, participants are also asked to share how they believe the program will help (pre-survey) or has helped them (post-survey) personally and professionally as well as how they feel being an ORBITS member will support (pre-survey) or has supported (post-survey) their journey while attending the university. These criteria are measured on a mix of Likert scale questions where participants can identify between Strongly Agree, Somewhat Agree, Somewhat Disagree, or Strongly Disagree as well as free response questions to allow for further depth in information shared by students. Our pre-survey consisted of 16 questions and our post-survey consisted of 18 questions.

The program maintains data on post-program measures utilizing surveys of professional mentors as well as data analysis from career destinations surveys (local and national measures on career outcomes). The Career Center plans to conduct a review of program outcomes every five years, investigating ORBITS participants in comparison to other undergraduate and first-generation sub-populations. This evaluation will look at campus student success measures including persistence, graduation rates, grade point averages, post-graduation outcomes, student economics, first-generation status, and other student demographics to identify impacts and outcomes.

STUDENT SUCCESS OUTCOMES

In the last 12 years, the program has engaged over 240 student participants and 100 professional mentors. Exact counts remain elusive as complete student records and outcomes data were not transitioned to successive program coordinators. The program has over 12 years of student data and program effectiveness data collected from surveys that demonstrate successful completion of most program goals. Data has also shown a significant change in both student knowledge bases and career readiness behaviors. Pre-course surveys were conducted from 2008 to 2016, with the addition of mid-course and post-course surveys conducted from 2016 to the present. Most measures of the program show a positive, or strong positive, response from students on resource awareness, career choice knowledge, job search strategies, communication skills, professional outreach methods, professional network improvements, and greater confidence in life and career goals.

Post-survey results from the 2016–2020 cohorts yielded 47 responses out of 83 participants, a 56% response rate. These post-survey results measured the nine NACE Career Readiness Competencies and several additional measures of learning outcomes (ORBITS Post-Surveys, 2020).

NACE Competency Area	Agree to Positive Growth
Professionalism and Work Ethic	97.8%
Oral/Written Communication	95.7%
Critical Thinking/Problem-Solving	97.8%
Leadership	95.7%
Digital Technology	80.8%
Career Management	97.8%
Global/Intercultural Fluency	93.6%

The highest perceived student growth was experienced in the areas of professionalism, critical thinking, and career management with additional strong positives in the areas of leadership, and oral/written communication. The digital technology area was the lowest perceived growth. Student feedback concerning this score provided insights that strong positive growth was experienced in fluency and skill levels in LinkedIn for career development; however, this area was perceived to be a wider category and many students felt they still required development of their technological skills in other areas.

First Destination Survey

Utilizing the First Destination Survey from NACE, 83 students from the 2015–2019 cohorts confirmed graduations prior to the December 2020 survey collection point. The First Destination Survey (NACE FDS, 2021) captures new college graduates' data around career outcomes, job searching and acquisition, additional education or service, salaries, and intent to continue searching, pursue additional education, or service opportunities in the near future. Outcomes mapped for the 2014–2019 ORBITS cohorts were:

- 36% of ORBITS students had already secured employment, compared to 31% of the overall undergraduate classes of 2014–2019
- 20% of ORBITS students went straight into a graduate program, compared to 10% of the overall undergraduate classes of 2014–2019
- 8% of ORBITS students planned to enroll in a graduate program within a year, compared to 24% of the overall undergraduate classes of 2014–2019

- 6% of ORBITS students were participating in a year of service, compared to 2% of the overall undergraduate classes of 2014–2019
- 2% of ORBITS students reported not seeking employment, consistent with 2% of the overall undergraduate classes of 2014–2019
- 28% of ORBITS students were seeking employment, compared to 31% of the overall undergraduate classes of 2014–2019

Of the ORBITS students who had secured employment 59% had secured plans prior to graduation, 22% had secured employment in the three-month period after graduation, and 19% had secured employment within six months of graduation. These scores differ from campus wide averages as a greater percentage of ORBITS students experienced a transition to graduate programs, more secured employment prior to graduation, and there was a higher number of ORBITS students still seeking employment. It should be noted this data was for the aggregate of the entire campus, and not limited to first-generation populations. Further study is warranted to explore the potential differences between ORBITS participants and first-generation students who did not participate.

LESSONS LEARNED

A significant lesson learned is that first-generation cohorts have shifted their interests over time. Surveys from ORBITS participants have garnered positive results overall; however, there is always room for improvement. Several areas that have been enhanced due to student feedback are the length and depth of resume reviews as well as alumni and peer resume feedback sessions, expanding the length and depth of mock interviews and feedback sessions, and increasing sessions focused on email templates for networking and internship opportunity requests ORBITS' students provided feedback that the early years of the program relied too heavily on generic icebreakers to develop a group community, where students often felt sharing personal stories and doing peer reviews of resumes, personal statements, and career development plans created greater bases for bonding. Students also suggested less time be spent on organizational skill development, the content of which has been greatly reduced in more recent years.

Another factor to consider, which has informed the ORBITS program growth, is that first-generation students want tangible, clear results in order to participate. We must always understand that time is precious and students have many demands on their time – most that we cannot see. For low-income first-generation students, these demands only increase as available resources and temporal flexibility decreases. College is a matter of survival and any personal development activities and activities that do not directly relate to preparation for the world of work are considered superfluous and impractical (Davis, 2010). The ORBITS program has adapted lessons since its launch, reducing icebreaker length and frequency, focusing on the capital students bring with them, and adding more flexibility with absences and timelines for work completion. The program recognizes that anything that does not immediately advance the two primary goals of resource knowledge and personal career development should continue to be scrutinized heavily and reduced or removed wherever appropriate.

REFERENCES

Amaro-Jimenez, C., Pant, M.D., Hungerford-Kresser, H., & Hartog, J. (2020). Identifying the impact of college access efforts on parents' college preparedness knowledge. *School Community Journal*, 30(1), 139–159.

Blackwell, E. & Pinder, P.J. (2014). What are the motivational factors of first-generation minority college students who overcome their family histories to pursue higher education? *College Student Journal*, 48(1), 45–56.

Davis, J. (2010). *The first-generation student experience: Implications for campus practice and strategies for improving persistence and success*. Stylus Publishing, LLC.

Housel, T.H. & Harvey, V.L. (2009). *The invisibility factor: Administrators and faculty reach out to first-generation college students*. BrownWalker Press.

Moschetti, R., & Hudley, C. (2008). Measuring social capital among first-generation and non-first generation, working-class White males. *Journal of College Admission*, 198, 25–30.

NACE FDS (2021). The NACE first-destination survey. Retrieved from https://www.naceweb.org/job-market/graduate-outcomes/first-destination/ on 3/13/2021

NACE Staff (2018). Are college graduates "career ready"? Retrieved from https://www.naceweb.org/career-readiness/competencies/are-college-graduates-career-ready/ on December 12, 2020.

ORBITS Participant A (2020). Survey response, November 17, 2020.

ORBITS Participant B (2020). Survey response, November 17, 2020.

Overview (2018). Retrieved from https://firstgen.ucr.edu/about/overview on June 14, 2021.

Swanson, J.L. & Fouad, N.A. (2020). *Career theory and practice: Learning through case studies*. SAGE Publications, Inc.

UCR By the Numbers (2021). Retrieved from https://www.ucr.edu/about/ranks-and-facts on January 17, 2021.

Ward, L., Siegel, M., & Davenport, Z. (2012). *First generation college students: Understanding and improving the experience from recruitment to commencement*. John Wiley & Sons, Inc.

Whitley, S.E., Benson, G., & Wesaw, A. (2018). *First-generation student success: A landscape analysis of programs and services at four-year institutions*. Center for First-generation Student Success, NASPA Student Affairs Administrators in Higher Education, and Entangled Solutions.

Yosso, T.J. (2005). Whose culture has capital? a critical race theory discussion of community cultural wealth. *Race, Ethnicity and Education*, 8(1), 69–91.

APPENDIX A SAMPLE TIMELINE AND TASK LIST

Date	Task
Mid-March–Early April	Submit a WF request asking for a student list (Sharepoint: see "request first gen list guide" document located in the "Recruitment" folder in the ORBITS 2019–2020 folder) *May not need to do this with new label in Handshake
	Update the dates on ORBITS Online Application editable pdf (Sharepoint ORBITS 2019–2020 Application ORBITS 2019–2020 pdf)
	Submit WF request to update the ORBITS online app link once application has been updated, (link located on the career development program page and linked here, https://careers.ucr.edu/sites/g/files/rcwecm1726/files/2019-04/orbits_application_2019-20.pdf)
	Update the marketing email blast to be sent to student list end of April, early May (Sharepoint 2019–2020 Recruitment ORBITS Application Marketing Email to Students)
Mid-April–Early May	Send ORBITS application and marketing email to student list with the application deadline (deadline typically is the second week of September)
	Reach out to campus partners to share the ORBITS application and marketing email to student list with application deadline (refer to ORBITS Campus Partner document Sharepoint ORBITS 2019–2020 Application campus Partner document)
	Send thank you email to past Mentors and include updated ORBITS Mentor Survey (*Question on availability of dates). Ask if any mentors would like to return for the following year (Sharepoint ORBITS 2019–2020 Mentor Materials Thank you Mentors Survey and ask to Return as a Mentor)
	Begin planning and updating the fall 2020 ORBITS syllabus (Sharepoint ORBITS 2019–2020 Syllabus and Curriculum ORBITS Fall 2019 Syllabus)
	Send invitations to campus partners inviting them to present
	Review Pre and Post ORBITS Student Surveys in Qualtrics as well as Mentors survey and incorporate feedback in planning for the following year

(Continued)

(*Continued*)

Date	Task
	Once Mentor dates are confirmed on the syllabus, put in WF request for parking on those dates
	Put in WF request to reserve Meeting Rooms A & B for Fall on Tuesdays from 3pm – 4:15pm
	Put holds on calendar for ORBITS program and include 30 minute prep time before and after
	Place ORBITS marketing flyers out at the front and in resource room
Late May–Early June	Follow up with past mentors and look to identify new mentors (ideally to recruit at minimum ten mentors)
	Follow up on student marketing and send reminder emails for students to apply by deadline
June	Secure at minimum ten mentors (30 students) and send them program dates of when they will be participating in the program so that they can plan ahead of time (Sharepoint ORBITS 2019–2020 Mentor Materials Email template Mentor Outreach and Program dates)
	Invite any guest speakers on or off campus and put in WF parking request for any off-campus speakers
July	Update Blackboard and include finalized syllabus and passport once completed
	Update ORBITS Passport for Fall 2020 (Sharepoint ORBITS 2019–2020 ORBITS Marketing ORBITS Passport F19)
	Create new ORBITS 2020–2021 folder on Sharepoint and include all updated/new documents
August	Send last marketing email to student list sharing that the deadline is approaching
	Update Pre- (for first meeting) and Post-Survey for Students (Qualtrics) and Mentor Survey
September	Input ORBITS meetings into Handshake
	Schedule time to review applications after deadline and select applicants for the 2020–2021 program (ideally 30 students), call or email that they have been accepted, and give them a week to confirm their participation

(*Continued*)

(*Continued*)

Date	Task
	Add new students to Blackboard and send an announcement through Blackboard, welcoming them to the program
	Create student and mentor name badges (Sharepoint ORBITS 2019–2020 Marketing Mentor and Mentee templates)
	Match mentees and mentors based on the application materials and areas of support that students need. The matching is not based on major but more on how the mentor can best support the student with professional advice and support. We try to take into consideration the industry of the mentor and match them with potential mentees (max three mentees per mentor)
	Create an Excel document including all applicants who submitted applications and track those who have accepted and those who have not. This Excel doc is what is used to track attendance, and assignments (refer to Handshake check in) as well as mentor matching (Sharepoint ORBITS 2019–2020 ORBITS Applications 2019–2020)
October–December	Finalize winter quarter syllabus and send guest speaker invitations, update winter quarter passport, ensure parking requests for any off-campus presenters/mentors are put in WF

APPENDIX B SYLLABUS SAMPLE

Winter 2021: 1/5/21–3/9/21
Tuesdays 3:00 PM–4:15 PM
Meetings will take place over Zoom

PROGRAM DESCRIPTION

The ORBITS program is focused on the development and exploration of career skills and transferable life skills of first-generation, second/third year transfer UCR college students.

Obtain Resources

The first motive of the ORBITS program is to provide valuable campus and career resources to first-generation students. The second/third year of college is one of continued career exploration, major decision and skill development. Students will obtain resources on resume and cover letter writing, interviewing, graduate school preparation, job and internship search strategies, and major choice.

Become Informed

The second motive is for students to become informed with the resources they have already received continuing the development of their career and life skills. Students will engage in activities such as informational interviews, employer discussions, panels, on-site visits, and mock interviews. Students will also enhance their transferable skills focusing on communication, work ethic, leadership, and teamwork.

Target Success

The third motive of the ORBITS program is a long-term goal for students to graduate from UCR understanding the steps for pursuing graduate school or job search. Students will also develop a personal plan to include short-term target goals leading up to graduation.

STUDENT LEARNING OUTCOMES

- Participate in learning-centered activities and experiences leading to their own college, career, and life planning
- Become involved in campus activities and identify resources available
- Become familiar with the career decision-making process, including the role of self-concept, and apply to your own career and life planning
- Assess your own interests, values, strengths, and limitations pertaining to life and career planning
- Explore majors and careers related to your personal attributes
- Demonstrate effective career management and job seeking skills
- Participate in experiential and learning activities towards narrowing down career interests to a few options for further investigation
- Be able to explain why career decision-making is a lifelong process
- Be better prepared for the transition into a career or graduate school

BENEFITS

- Build a mentor relationship with community members: employers, alumni, staff, and fellow students
- Participate in employer on-site visits
- Build a community with fellow first-generation students
- Gain awareness of transferable life skills and how they relate to career choices
- Develop Life and Transferable Skills
  - Communication
  - Teamwork

- Leadership
- Work ethic
- Gain awareness of career planning skills and how they relate to life choices
- Develop core career planning skills
  - Create an effective resume
  - Understand how to interview effectively
  - Network
  - Recognize the steps for pursuing graduate school
  - Recognize the steps for an effective job search
- Receive a Career Leadership Certificate documenting your participation in the ORBITS program

ATTENDANCE AND PARTICIPATION EXPECTATIONS

Participants are expected to attend a minimum of eight of the ten scheduled winter course meetings as well as complete all program requirements (**Winter 2021: 1/5/21–3/9/21**.) Students are expected to have prompt, complete, and regular attendance as well as submit program assignments. If you are unable to attend a class session it is your responsibility to inform an ORBITS leader 24 hours in advance via email or telephone. Upon successful completion of ORBITS requirements, participants will receive a Career Leadership Certificate.

MENTORSHIP OPPORTUNITY

Participants will be matched with a mentor at the beginning of the quarter. The focus is on the interaction between mentors and mentees who will meet in the beginning of the fall quarter and throughout the winter quarter. The goal is to provide you with a means to form insightful and helpful relationships with professionals in order to enhance your growth, knowledge, and skills.

MENTEE RESPONSIBILITIES

Mentors and mentees develop relationships through phone or email communication, and face-to-face meetings.

CONTACT CALENDAR

January Reach out to mentor for tips on interviewing/initiated by **mentee**
February Share how your strengths can be used in the workplace/initiated by **mentee**
March Week before the End of the Year Celebration/follow up initiated by **mentee**

PROGRAM REQUIREMENTS

iLearn: Please refer to blackboard for program materials, inputting assignments in the discussion board and updates.

Social Media: All students will have a LinkedIn profile with at least five *new* connections. Must craft a personalized connection message

Internship: Participants are encouraged to apply to two to three internships by the final session.

Final Presentation – 3/9/21

Participants will present a three-minute PowerPoint presentation to include the following:

Presentation should include:

- Who am I now?
  - Reflect on the personal growth you've made after your ORBITS experience
- Where do I want to go?
  - Include the internships you applied to and future opportunities you see yourself becoming involved in your last two to three years at UCR
  - If you have secured an internship, how will you be successful? What skills have you learned that are important to employers?
- How do I get there?
  - How will you apply what you learned after the ORBITS program closes?

Winter, Tuesdays, 1/5/21–3/9/21

- The program will involve short readings, experiential exercises and activities, small group discussion, employer on-site visit(s), and reflective exercises
- Sessions will be led by Career Center Staff, and/or employers

Week 1:	1/5/21	Welcome Back!
		Career Brief on Syllabus and Expectations for Winter Qtr.
		UCR Counseling Center "Life as A First-Gen." Dr. Pitsavas and Psychological Intern Hunter D'Abundo
Week 2:	1/12/21	Graduate School Workshop Ft. The ARC, Jason Chou
Week 3:	1/19/21	Interview Skills Workshop Featuring Monica Cruz
Week 4:	1/26/21	Speed Mock Interviewing w/ Mentors
Week 5:	2/2/21	Making Meaningful Connections Featuring Derrin Ford

Week 6:   2/9/21   Personal Development
Week 7:   2/16/21   Internships
Week 8:   2/23/21 Where are the Jobs?
Week 9:   3/2/21   Reflections/Revisit Cultural Capital/What it means to be first-gen
Week 10: 3/9/21   Final Presentations/Networking

Chapter 13

First-Generation Transfer Students in an Honors College

Martha Enciso

Participating in an honors college or program at an institution could easily be a missed opportunity for some students. First-generation college students can be unaware of honors programs at their respective community colleges or choose not to engage in such programs due to stereotypes about honors or misperceptions about the "type" of student who can participate in these programs. As such, students may choose not to participate at university level. First-generation college students at San Diego State University (SDSU) encompass students whose parent(s) have some college and no college ("First-Generation Student Success," 2021). Some first-generation students may have applied to honors programs in the past but may have been denied or had higher education professionals serve as gatekeepers preventing them from applying. Some individuals may have an image of who can be in honors programs or colleges or who identifies as an honors student (Enciso, 2019). To change the perception of the types of students who participate in honors programs or colleges at university level, higher education professionals must take the time to reflect on the programmatic elements and examine ways to change existing structures which may be preventing first-generation transfer students from applying, being admitted, and ultimately graduating from an honors college.

PROGRAM DESCRIPTION

Public universities utilize special programs to attract the very best students to their campuses. These institutions "strive to create 'sub-environments' such as honors colleges and structured learning communities that can be used to set high expectations and create peer effects that reinforce these expectations" (Bowen et al., 2009, p. 234). The challenge with special programs such as honors colleges is that "the term 'honors' by itself carries an enormous amount of baggage around questions of privilege, elitism, and separateness" (Badenhausen, 2018, p. 11). Trying to engage students who may not view themselves as honors or have negative perceptions of students in honors can hinder certain populations such as first-generation transfer students from engaging in special programs. The Weber Honors College (WHC) at San Diego State University strives to change the image of the stereotypical honors student by developing a community of scholars from various backgrounds.

The Weber Honors College is an academic program available at San Diego State University. SDSU is the third-largest public university in California that currently enrolls nearly 34,000 undergraduate and graduate students ("About SDSU," 2020); a little over 30,000 are undergraduates. SDSU is one of 23 campuses which are part of the California State University (CSU) system. SDSU offers more than 90 majors for undergraduates to select from in addition to the honors opportunities ("About SDSU," 2020) and has a main campus located in La Mesa as well as a satellite campus at Imperial Valley. The urban setting provides students with the opportunity to utilize the information they learn inside the classroom and put it into practice. Students at SDSU have several honors options to select from at the institution. Students can participate in the following honors options: honors programs through select academic departments, single discipline and multi discipline honor societies, or graduate with honors and distinction.

The transfer student population at SDSU comprises 32.1% (9,673 students) of the overall undergraduate population. Of the transfer student population, 58.1% (5,617) of the transfer students identify as first-generation college students per the SDSU definition. WHC transfer students consist of 0.57% of the SDSU transfer student population and 62% (34 students) of the WHC transfer students identify as first-generation college students. The demographics of the WHC first-generation transfer students as compared to the SDSU first-generation transfer students are as follows: African American (3%–4%), Asian (3%–8%), Filipino (3%–2%), International (6%–4%), Hispanic/Latino (65%–56%), Multiple Ethnicity (3%–3%), Pacific Islander/Native Hawaiian (0%–0.2%), Other/Not stated (6%–3%), White (12%–19%), and Native American (0%–0.4%). Although much work has been done to change the composition of the honors population to reflect the SDSU student population, the WHC team realizes the equity work must continue.

The Weber Honors College was created in 2015 for students at the main SDSU campus. The WHC consists of an honors minor in interdisciplinary studies which helps students develop leadership skills and social responsibility, become global citizens, and engage in an international experience ("Special Programs," 2020). The Susan and Stephen Weber Honors College was named after the former university president and his wife. Funding for the Weber Honors College came from generous gifts from San Diego philanthropists, former President Weber, a former professor, and philanthropic efforts during President Weber's term as university President (SDSU News Team, 2015). Students in the WHC have access to the honors team which consists of a director, associate director, academic advisor, and administrative support coordinator. The WHC director assists with recruitment, mentoring, developing the honors curriculum, teaching honors courses, and ensuring the vision and growth of the WHC is aligned with SDSU needs. The associate director assists with recruitment, teaches honors courses, and mentors students on high-impact practices as well as national and international scholarships and fellowships. The academic advisor assists students with course planning, ensuring students are connected to resources, and ensures students' needs are met. The administrative support coordinator oversees the day-to-day needs of the WHC and assists with recruitment. The four team members ensure students have the information, resources, and support they need to graduate from the WHC.

Participation in the WHC requires completion of: a 16-unit honors minor in interdisciplinary studies, credit bearing study abroad experience, engagement in a high-impact practice (research, service, leadership, or creative activity), and a minimum cumulative 3.2 GPA at the time the student applies for graduation. Freshmen who enroll in the WHC are also required to live on the WHC floors in a designated resident hall with roommates who are also WHC students. In addition to the resident advisors who serve on each floor in the residence hall, academic mentors live on the honors floors only and serve as additional support for students. Academic mentors can help with students' academic needs as well as any other issues as they work with residential advisors to ensure that students have an enjoyable residential experience. Students can join the WHC as SDSU sophomores, juniors, and transfer students and are not required to live on campus.

Once students complete the honors minor requirements, they are invited to attend an honors graduation reception, receive recognition at commencement, a designation on their transcript, a medallion, and a WHC certificate. WHC first-generation college students also receive a pin to illustrate their distinction as a first-generation college graduate. WHC graduates are allowed to invite friends, family, and loved ones to the reception which is a smaller gathering compared to their college graduation ceremonies. As students walk across the stage, the WHC academic advisor reads a personal message for each student detailing some of their experiences at SDSU as well as their plans after graduation.

Conceptual Framework

The theoretical framework used to cultivate a more inclusive honors college for transfer students is a Transfer Receptive Culture (TRC). The focus of a Transfer Receptive Culture is a "commitment from the baccalaureate granting institution to provide the support needed for students to transfer and graduate successfully" (Jain et al., 2020, p. 12). Support for transfer students must continue beyond the community college in order for students to obtain a baccalaureate degree. The elements of a TRC (Jain et al., 2020) include the following:

1. Establish the transfer of students, especially nontraditional, first-generation, low-income, and underrepresented students, as a high institutional priority that ensures stable accessibility, retention, and graduation
2. Provide outreach and resources that focus on the specific needs of transfer students while complimenting the community college mission of transfer
3. Offer financial and academic support through distinct opportunities for nontraditional re-entry transfer students where they are stimulated to achieve at high academic levels
4. Acknowledge the lived experiences that students bring and the intersectionality between community and family
5. Create an appropriate and organic framework from which to assess, evaluate, and enhance transfer receptive programs and initiatives that can lead to further scholarship on transfer students

(p. 258)

This framework provides the elements required to create a program that promotes and assists in creating a transfer inclusive environment.

MISSION AND LEARNING OBJECTIVES

The mission of the Weber Honors College is to provide "an academic environment in which students experience a dynamic, interactive, and engaged education" ("Weber Honors College Viewbook," 2020). Participating in the Weber Honors College allows students to become a part of the honors culture at SDSU while meeting peers who are diverse, motivated, and have a curiosity for learning and share a responsibility for academic excellence ("Weber Honors College Viewbook," 2020). The Weber Honors College seeks to create "a unique atmosphere of creativity, interdisciplinary conversation, intellectualism, and collegiality" ("Weber Honors College Mission," 2020). The shared interest in intellectual endeavors allows for the creation and sharing of knowledge inside and outside of the classroom.

Through the honors minor requirements, students are expected to achieve nine learning outcomes. The structure of the Weber Honors College is intentionally designed to assist students in developing skill sets and obtaining experiences which will help them after graduation. Students who complete the Weber Honors College requirements will be able to:

1. Examine topics and issues from diverse perspectives and contextualize phenomena within cultural contexts.
2. Demonstrate self-awareness by identifying personal strengths, weaknesses, values, and goals.
3. Analyze phenomena not confined to a single academic discipline and make coherent connections among disparate disciplines.

4. Express ideas with clarity and purpose, both orally and in writing, and demonstrate these communication abilities in multiple contexts to a variety of audiences.
5. Demonstrate the ability to explore, and if feasible, experiment with possible applications of their learning toward the solution of "real-world" issues or problems.
6. Participate actively and collaboratively with faculty and peers from different fields of specialization in diverse, cross-disciplinary teams to analyze and/or solve applied, real-world issues and problems.
7. Participate in campus and community service as a component of active citizenship, community engagement, and social responsibility.
8. Evaluate issues of global significance from diverse cultural, political, economic, scientific, or technological perspectives and recognize the global context of the knowledge they produce and the decisions they make.
9. Demonstrate outstanding academic achievement.

("Honor 100," 2020)

The Weber Honors College learning outcomes are introduced in the Introduction to Honors course, are included in the syllabi of honors courses, and are reiterated at the honors graduation ceremony.

IMPLEMENTATION

The Weber Honors College team strives to provide various options and alternatives to satisfy the WHC requirements since they recognize that first-generation transfer students embody various intersecting identities (ex: veteran, parent, caregiver, etc.). "If we believe that honors programs and colleges benefit by engaging a diverse population of learners, we must make serious efforts to make honors accessible to transfer students" (Bahls, 2018, p. 75). First-generation transfer students must feel and see themselves represented in the program in order to consider viewing themselves as honors students and eventually applying to the program. The following describes how aspects of the WHC were modified to assist and allow for greater participation of first-generation transfer students in the WHC which can be utilized by similar programs.

Admission Process

Prospective students can apply to join the Weber Honors College at various points in their college career. Students can apply to join as incoming freshmen, current SDSU sophomores, juniors, or incoming transfer students. Students who apply to the WHC as incoming transfer students or as current SDSU students have a minimum cumulative 3.2 GPA requirement. Incoming freshmen are required to have a weighted 3.7 GPA. Transcripts and letters of recommendation are not required. The application consists of demographic information and a set of short answer questions which allow students to reflect on their previous experiences and identities. For transfer students, the short answer question focuses on why students want to join and what they hope to contribute to the WHC. The WHC team also asks about the applicants' first-generation identity by asking if their parents or guardians have attended college in the US. The team also asked for the highest level of education completed by either of their parents/legal guardians. Having both of these questions may reveal a more accurate account of first-generation applicants and participants since some applicants may have parents/legal guardians who attended college in the US but did not earn a baccalaureate degree. Transfer students are given three deadlines to apply: February 15, March 31, and July 2. The first deadline is a priority deadline and the second deadline is the final deadline for all students (incoming and current SDSU students) who want to join the WHC in the fall. The summer deadline was intentionally created for transfer students only since transfer students are admitted to the university at a later date than first time freshmen. The WHC admissions committee uses a holistic approach to admit students and recognizes the value of a diverse (in all senses of the word) honors student population that can benefit the overall campus community. The WHC should reflect the overall SDSU student population by representing the various identities of the students including the first-generation college student identity.

Intentional Recruitment Plan

Since first-generation college students may not be aware of honors communities or were excluded from similar honors opportunities, the WHC cannot only recruit transfer students who are honors program participants. Information regarding the WHC application and flyer are sent to transfer counselors, transfer directors, and honors program directors at the local community colleges. The WHC team offers community colleges the opportunity to schedule virtual information sessions to allow greater access for students. Applicants can also schedule individual appointments with the WHC team to learn more about the program. SDSU transfer admissions counselors are trained regarding the WHC requirements in order to publicize and create interest in the program during their community college visits.

Collaborating with the Office of Admission and the Transfer Student Success Office assists the WHC in increasing awareness of the WHC and participation in the program. The university holds an open house event in March titled Explore SDSU which serves as a yield event for the university. The associate director participates in the transfer workshops to inform students about the opportunity, benefits, and upcoming deadlines. The associate director works with the Transfer Student Success Office in recruiting honors transfer students to participate in the student panel which is part of the transfer workshop. Once transfer students submit their intent to enroll, the WHC sends an email invitation to the transfer students who have committed to SDSU and have a minimum cumulative 3.2 GPA. Since the summer deadline is July 2nd, students are encouraged to contact the WHC team to learn more about the program and application. The Transfer Student Success Office continues engaging with incoming transfers in May by hosting Transfer Tuesday sessions which offer information regarding special programs and opportunities for students to apply to since they have already committed to SDSU. Having the WHC associate director host a Transfer Tuesday session helps the students invited to learn about the WHC in a group setting while allowing other transfer students to learn about the program for the first time before the July deadline.

The WHC associate director works with the First-Generation Student Success team to conduct first-generation Friday sessions focusing on various academic topics throughout the month of June, late July and August leading up to the first week of classes. The associate director's participation helps students connect with a program they may not have previously considered. The sessions in June lead up to the WHC transfer application deadline in July. Having someone from the WHC team connect with first-generation students early on helps students recognize they have another person and team who believes and cares about their success.

The Transfer Student Success Office hosts a transfer summit in early July, a month before transfer orientation. The WHC associate director helps plan the summit and presents about the honors communities at SDSU. Since first-generation transfer students have had various touch points with the WHC team at this point, the summit serves as a refresher for some and for others as encouragement to apply for the following year. The transfer summit includes presentations from representatives from the following offices: career services, study abroad, undergraduate research, leadership minor, service learning, and financial aid. The keynote speaker is a faculty member who also identifies as a former first-generation transfer student. Having individuals who represent some of the attendees' identities helps create a congratulatory and welcoming environment for students.

Honors Courses

The Introduction to Honors course is a one-unit course which focuses on having students reflect on their academic journey, goal setting, interdisciplinary studies, and learning about resources at SDSU. Students enroll in the honors capstone course during the final semester at SDSU. The course is structured to allow students a space to reflect on their time at SDSU while making sense of their out of class opportunity. The WHC provides students the experience of a small liberal arts college by focusing on helping students develop an interdisciplinary mindset through courses which are exclusive to the WHC. The courses are taught by faculty from several disciplines across campus who represent various social identities, including the first-generation college student identity. Some of these courses include Hip Hop and Religion, Humanity's Journey Towards Evil or Hope, and Cardi B and Pop Culture Politics. The interdisciplinary courses are kept small in size and taught in a seminar style class to ensure the sharing of knowledge of ideas. Students learn how to view one broad topic from various disciplines and how working together they can strive toward solving a world problem. Developing an interdisciplinary mindset can assist students in working alongside their peers in class, in out of class opportunities, and with faculty and staff.

Academic Advising

The honors academic advisor supports approximately 1,300 students in the WHC. First-generation transfer student applicants also have the opportunity to meet with the academic advisor before they apply to ensure they have a sample of possible course schedules to assist with their decision-making process. By having access to advising that helps them reflect on the program requirements and how they align with their own personal goals and interests, students can begin to plan how they will succeed at the institution (Brown McNair et al., 2020, p. 92). If a student falls below a 3.2 cumulative GPA at any time during their academic journey, they are not removed from the WHC. The WHC academic advisor communicates with students via email and/or phone to ensure students are receiving the information they need and are directed to colleagues who can assist them. The academic advisor hosts group advising sessions for first-generation honors students and emails students individually to update them on their progress in the program.

Study Abroad Requirement

Beyond the courses, all WHC students are required to complete a credit bearing study abroad experience. The WHC offers a faculty-led study abroad experience exclusively for honors students with an honors faculty member. Although honors students can select the honors study abroad program as their international engagement option, they are not limited to this option. For students who are undocumented or are unable to travel outside of the country, the WHC team works with the student to identify an alternative to satisfy the study abroad requirement. A study abroad course in which students travel to Tijuana for class throughout the semester also serves as an option for individuals who may have difficulty leaving their family members behind or for those who serve as caretakers. Honors study abroad scholarships are available for honors students to support the requirement and these are offered in addition to the study abroad scholarships offered by SDSU and partner organizations.

High-Impact Practice

Students participating in the Weber Honors College are required to complete one high-impact practice (HIP) of their choice (under the categories of research, leadership, service, or creative activity). The WHC associate director serves as an advisor for students who need to identify a HIP opportunity or to learn how an out of class opportunity completed could satisfy the requirement. If students participated in a high-impact practice at their community college, the WHC team counts their experience as satisfying the honors HIP requirement. Some of the approved HIPs first-generation transfer students have completed at a community college include serving on a leadership position on a parent teacher organization and serving on the executive board for a student organization. Students are provided with a list of courses, on-campus programs, as well as campus organizations which contain HIP options. In order to receive credit for the HIP, students complete an online form. The form is reviewed by the WHC associate director to assess if the opportunity qualifies as a HIP. Students have the ability to submit an "other HIP" or a HIP they completed that is not listed as an option for approval. The flexibility in the types of HIPs which are accepted allows students the option to select an opportunity which will provide them with the skill sets and experiences they need to achieve their career goals. Furthermore, the flexibility in the types of HIPs first-generation transfer students can pursue allows students the opportunity to complete the WHC program requirements within the timeframe the student wishes to remain in college.

STAKEHOLDERS

The stakeholders include SDSU admission counselors, transfer counselors, transfer directors, and honors program directors. Additional stakeholders include first-generation transfer students themselves since a commitment to diversity, equity, and inclusion includes participation from such students. Senior administration also utilizes the WHC as a means to recruit and compete for high-achieving students who may be seeking a small intellectual community while still having the experience of a large public institution. Faculty on campus appreciate the opportunity to teach in the WHC as they can have flexibility in course topics while having a small class size. Faculty also recruit WHC students for internship opportunities, to serve as lab assistants, or to serve as teaching assistants.

ASSESSMENT PLAN

In order to evaluate the recruitment efforts and quality of the program, several assessments are conducted throughout the students' time in the Weber Honors College. The first-generation transfer students are asked for information about their perceptions of the WHC at the time of application, in the Introduction to Honors course, in their senior capstone course, and in the withdrawal process for students who decide to leave the program

At the time of application, transfer applicants are required to answer why they want to join which gives the WHC admission committee a sense of the applicant's understanding of the program as well as how students view themselves as honors students. In the Introduction to Honors course for sophomores, juniors, and transfer students, students were assigned a short assignment answering why they accepted their admission to honors. Since students have the option to decline their acceptance, the WHC team can utilize the information in the assignment to obtain insight into the students' decision-making process in regard to honors opportunities.

During the students' last semester in the WHC, seniors complete a graduation survey as an assignment for their capstone course which has been used since the creation of the WHC. Students are asked to provide information regarding the honors courses they took, describe their international experience, reflect on whether or not they achieved the WHC learning outcomes via the honors requirements, and to identify the strengths and weaknesses of the WHC. Lastly, students are asked if they would participate in the WHC again after reflecting on their experience. Students are also asked to describe their post-graduation plans which the WHC team recognizes may change by the end of the capstone course since the deadline to submit the survey is early in the semester. Students may receive an admission decision from a graduate program, or a job offer. The information received from the graduation survey is used to evaluate the quality of the program as well as to identify areas for improvement.

The WHC team realizes that some students may want to opt out of the program for a variety of reasons and these reasons are important sources of information. Students who participate in the WHC are not removed from the program at any moment regardless of their GPA. WHC students have the option of withdrawing from the program at any point in time. The withdrawal process (which was created in 2016) includes a withdrawal survey and an in person exit interview with the associate director. On the exit survey, students list reasons which influenced their decision to withdraw, any out of class involvements, if they met with any of the honors team during their time in the WHC, and to reflect on why they initially decided to apply and join the WHC. The exit interview was initiated for the WHC team to learn more about the student's reasons for withdrawing from the program which at times the student did not mention in their survey.

Some students initially appeared nervous about the interview; however, once the students were informed that the interview was meant for improving the program, students visibly appeared more relaxed. The information provided in the withdrawal survey and exit interviews allows the WHC team to identify areas for improvement, gaps in understanding between the program offerings and students' perception of the program, and to identify trends.

OUTCOMES

As a result of the efforts made by the WHC team, the number of first-generation transfer students has increased in the program. Nearly 62% of the Weber Honors transfer students identify as first-generation college students (34 out of 55 students). Of the first-generation college student population within the WHC, 16.3% of students identify as transfer students. Since the creation of the Weber Honors College in 2015, the growth of first-generation transfer students per cohort is as follows: zero students in 2015; one first-generation transfer student in 2016; four first-generation transfer students in 2017; 15 first-generation transfer students in 2018; 14 first-generation transfer students in 2019; and 28 first-generation transfer students in 2020. The number of first-generation transfer students continues to grow each year as more students are made aware of the program. The graduation rate for WHC first-generation transfer students who entered in cohorts 2015–2019 is 44%. The graduation rate has improved over time as programmatic changes were made as a result of the withdrawal survey. The WHC retention rate of first-generation transfer students who entered the program in cohorts 2015–2019 is 56%. The WHC team hopes to continue increasing both the graduation rate and retention rate as they learn more about the evolving needs of the first-generation transfer student population in each new cohort of students.

The increase in first-generation transfer students proves that "honors students know they are academically capable and expect to succeed at the university" (Dziesinski et al., 2017, p. 93). First-generation transfer students are starting to view themselves as honors students and encouraging their peers to do the same. The increase in first-generation transfer students has also resulted in the WHC team altering their recruitment of faculty to include individuals who share similar identities to the WHC population. As faculty begin to self-identify as first-generation and/or former transfer students, the WHC team will continue to meet with colleagues to encourage them to teach in the WHC.

As a result of course evaluations and verbal feedback during advisement sessions, a separate Introduction to Honors course was created for sophomores, juniors, and transfer students since their needs are different than first time freshmen. The course contains information regarding interdisciplinary studies, high-impact practices, scholar development, national scholarships and fellowships, as well as career development. The reflective course has given students the opportunity to learn more about campus resources, identify their goals, and contemplate ways the honors curriculum can assist them in their pursuit of their career goals. The course will continue to evolve based on course evaluation and the needs of the entering WHC cohort.

The unit requirement for transfer students was modified based on the assessment implemented in 2016. Students who withdrew mentioned not being able to complete 16 units in addition to their major and graduation requirement within a two-year timeframe. As a result, the WHC team modified the unit requirement to 13 units by waiving the lower division honors course for transfer students starting with the fall 2018 cohort. When students hear that they have completed an honors course prior to applying and participating in the WHC, they are more likely to begin viewing themselves as honors students. The information received from the withdrawal surveys has also assisted the WHC team in advocating for funding for additional sections of honors courses.

LESSONS LEARNED

In the last five years of the WHC, the WHC team has learned that in order to increase the number of first-generation transfer students, "the institution must also create a learning environment that promotes equity and inclusion by understanding the diversity of the students it seeks to educate" (Brown McNair et al., 2020, p. 4). Students need to know people care about their well-being and their success at the institution. Participating in workshops with the Transfer Student Success Office and the First-Generation Student Success team helped students not only learn about the WHC but also gave them an opportunity to engage with a person they could communicate with after the session. Since there is much overlap between students who identify as first-generation and as transfer, participation in first-generation and transfer student events/workshops is necessary. Assisting with the transfer and first-generation sessions, Explore SDSU, and transfer summit helped build rapport with the students and colleagues across campus. Students commented on how they remember receiving encouragement to apply after attending one of the transfer student and/or first-generation college student events. Although the time commitment is high for the WHC team, increasing the number of students who apply, enroll, and graduate from the WHC is worth the investment.

Individuals who would like to implement similar opportunities within existing honors colleges or programs should take the time to partner with similar offices or colleagues who focus their efforts specifically on working with transfer students. Creating cross divisional partnerships for transfer student success can assist honors staff in recruiting transfer students to the program. Additionally, honors staff should invest the time to learn more about the transfer students at their institution. Creating assignments, engagement opportunities (in person or on social media), or surveys to obtain information can provide useful insight to learning what programmatic modifications staff and faculty should develop that align with the needs of the current students. Understanding student motivation to remain in the program can expand the scope of what and how honors staff can improve the program.

The pandemic provided the honors staff with the opportunity to create virtual high-impact practice options for students and to rethink how a high-impact practice is defined. By working with colleagues across divisions, the honors team identified the following HIPs as possible options: a summer leadership program, diversity career conference, social justice summit, leadership conference, long term activism associated with an organization, and graduate school seminars. Creating alternative virtual options for students allowed them to participate in programs which they previously did not due to costs associated with attendance, date or time of the event, or inability to travel to campus. These virtual options allowed for students with varying abilities, students who are caretakers, and others who would not have been able to attend in person the chance to participate. Based on the participation and the feedback from students who engaged in the virtual HIP options, the honors staff plans to continue using them as possible alternatives to satisfy the high-impact practice requirement once the honors staff returns to campus.

Educating colleagues on campus on the new program requirements and helping colleagues and potential program participants deconstruct their image of what an honors student looks like requires time, especially when the students have had negative experiences with honors opportunities in the past. Since the First-Generation Student Success Initiative is relatively new, individuals on campus are still learning about the SDSU first-generation population as well as the first-generation identity. While the learning process continues on campus, the Weber Honors College demonstrates the effect of how programmatic and structural changes can lead to positive results pertaining to how students view themselves and their potential to succeed as honors students.

REFERENCES

Badenhausen, R. (2018). Making honors success scripts available to students from diverse backgrounds. *Journal of the National Collegiate Honors Council*, 19(1), 9–14.

Bahls, P. (2018). Opening doors: Facilitating transfer students' participation in honors. *Journal of the National Collegiate Honors Council*, 19(2), 73–100.

Bowen, W.G., Chingos, M.M., & McPherson, M.S. (2009). Completing college at America's public universities. Princeton University Press.

Brown McNair, T. Bensimon, E.M., & Malcolm-Piqueux, L. (2020). *From equity talk to equity walk: Expanding practitioner knowledge for racial justice in higher education.* Jossey-Bass.

Dziesinski, A., Camarena, P., & Homrich-Knieling, C. (2017). A privilege for the privileged? Using intersectionality to reframe honors and promote social responsibility. In L. L. Coleman, J. D. Kotinek, & A. Y. Oda (Eds.). *Occupy honors education*. (pp. 81–106). Lincoln, NE: National Collegiate Honors Council.

Enciso, M. (2019). Redefining Who Is An Honors Student. In E. Sandoval-Lucero & J.B. Maes (Eds.), *Case Studies in Equity*, *Diversity and Inclusion in Higher Education: An Intersectional Perspective* (82–87). Kendall Hunt Publishing.

Jain, D., Berlan Melendez, S.N., Herrera, A.R. (2020). *Power to the Transfer: Critical Race Theory and a Transfer Receptive Culture*. Michigan State University Press. doi:10.14321/j.ctvs09qkh

Martha Enciso. (August/2020). *Honor 100: Introduction to Honors* [Syllabus]. San Diego: Weber Honors College San Diego State University.

San Diego State University. (2020, August 19). *About SDSU*. Office of Admissions.

https://admissions.sdsu.edu/about_sdsu

San Diego State University. (2021, May 1). *First-Generation Student Success*. Faculty Advancement and Student Success. https://first-gen-at.sdsu.edu/

San Diego State University. (2020, September 9). *Special Programs and Services*. Office of Admissions. https://admissions.sdsu.edu/about_sdsu/special_programs_services

San Diego State University. (2020, June 16). *Weber Honors College Mission*. Weber Honors College Overview. https://honors.sdsu.edu/about-honors/college-overview

San Diego State University. (2021, May 1). *Weber Honors College Viewbook*. Weber Honors College Overview. https://honors.sdsu.edu/honors-admissions/application-information

SDSU News Team. (2015, February 23). *SDSU Honors College Named*. SDSU NewsCenter. https://newscenter.sdsu.edu/sdsu_newscenter/news_story.aspx?sid=75450#:~:text=At%20its%20current%20level%20of,SDSU's%20Division%20of%20Undergraduate%20Studie

Chapter 14

What We Learned from the Pandemic

Using Digital and Virtual Spaces to Support First-Generation College Students

Karen Jackson and Charmaine Troy

The onset of the 2020 COVID-19 pandemic required institutions to make significant changes in the ways they delivered instruction and services to students. The rapid transition to online learning, temporary closing of residence halls, and the absence of in-person co-curricular and extra-curricular engagement disrupted teaching and learning in ways never ever experienced by this generation. While all students were affected by this phenomenon, first-generation college students were some of the hardest hit, especially those whose first-generation identity intersects with the identities of other historically marginalized populations. A 2020 study conducted by the Student Experience in the Research University (SERU) indicated that first-generation college students were more likely to report being negatively impacted by the pandemic than continuing education students (Soria et.al., 2020). First-generation college students reported higher rates of financial hardships, academic challenges, and mental health concerns. This chapter will discuss how the COVID-19 pandemic impacted first-generation college students and ways institutions attempted to mitigate the challenges and support students in virtual spaces.

FINANCIAL IMPACT

The pandemic exacerbated already present financial shortfalls for many first-generation college students. The SERU study (Soria et.al., 2020) found that first-generation college students were more likely than their non-first-generation peers to report financial hardships during the pandemic and had greater concerns about their ability to pay for college. Three rounds of federal funding provided colleges and universities with emergency funds to provide increased support to students during the pandemic. Institutions used the funding in a variety of ways including, but not limited to eliminating tuition balances and providing book scholarships and direct grants to students.

Unsurprisingly, financial hardships also resulted in higher rates of food and housing insecurity for first-generation students. (Goldrick-Rab et al., 2020; Soria et al., 2020). To combat food insecurities institutions employed a number of strategies. These included the creation of food pantries, distribution of gift cards, and developing partnerships with local community organizations like food banks and religious organizations that distributed food. Students were also provided information on state and federal food assistance programs like SNAP and WIC. As many campuses closed residence halls and off-campus housing became unaffordable due to decreased wages, many students were displaced. A Hope Center Study with responses from over 38,000 students at 54 colleges and universities found that 15% of students at four-year colleges and 11% of students at two-year colleges experienced homelessness during the pandemic. (Goldrick-Rab et al., 2020) In addition to providing emergency funds and connecting students to community resources, some campuses allowed students who were experiencing homelessness to remain on campus.

Financial difficulties and housing insecurities also widened the digital divide between first-generation students and their continuing education peers during the pandemic. Results from a 2017 survey by the ACT Center for Equity in Learning indicated that 85% of the students who reported having access to only one device identified as low income, first-generation, or part of a minoritized population (Moore et al., 2018). Many of these students would have been in college at the onset of the pandemic which suggests the loss of on-campus technology limited their ability to be successful in online learning. Some first-generation college students who had to move home when institutions closed residence halls might have lost access to the technology needed to be successful. Moreover, first-generation students in the SERU study were more likely to report that they did not have access to the resources required to support online learning (Soria et al., 2020). In response to these technology disparities many colleges created or expanded loaner laptop programs and provided on-campus hot spots. Internet providers also provided discounted and sometimes free services to students.

ACADEMIC IMPACT

Many college students reported that the pandemic negatively impacted their academic performance. Financial hardships forced students to increase their work hours at the expense of class and study time. (Barber et.al., 2021). First-generation students were also more likely to move back to home situations where they had had additional responsibilities of taking care of younger siblings who had also transitioned to online learning (Soria et.al., 2020). These additional responsibilities also detracted from time dedicated to academics which resulted in decreased academic achievement. Campus closings also decreased access to suitable quiet spaces that are required for online learning.

In addition to the challenges associated with limited access to technology, remote instruction left students feeling disengaged with some stating they felt like they were "teaching themselves" (Froman et al., 2020). While some students appreciated the flexibility offered by remote learning, others appreciated the structure of in-person learning. Remote learning requires a higher level of self-discipline, time management, and self-accountability. The almost instantaneous shift to online learning left many students feeling unprepared. Additionally, many faculty felt unprepared as well as this shift did not afford them the opportunity to engage in training for online instruction. Institutions eventually provided training for faculty on how to engage students in online learning and students. Faculty and students also learned how to engage through various platforms.

MENTAL HEALTH

The financial hardships, academic struggles, and unstable home environments are stressors that triggered mental health concerns for college students. Additionally, concerns about the physical implications of COVID-19 and the uncertainty of the impact and end of the pandemic contributed to stress and anxiety associated with the pandemic. Moreover, the suspension of in-person learning and the closing of residence halls contributed to increased levels of loneliness and isolation. First-generation students were more likely to experience mental health concerns during the pandemic, but less likely to seek assistance to address those concerns (Jeong et al., 2021; Soria et al., 2020). To support students' mental health, institutions shifted services online to provide access to students. As more students sought support for mental health concerns, some institutions contracted with outside sources to provide services as well. However, as first-generation students were less likely to seek assistance through traditional avenues, institutions had to find other ways to address these concerns.

Colleges and universities worked diligently to mitigate the impact of the pandemic. While many institutional efforts focused on providing basic needs, they also sought ways increase online engagement to foster a sense of belonging and build trusting relationships with students. The following section will highlight one institution's efforts to support their first-generation college students in virtual spaces throughout the pandemic.

IMPORTANCE OF SHIFTING TO ONLINE PROGRAMMING

During the onset of the COVID-19 pandemic, many students were asked to leave campus and transition to online learning. We also had the task of pivoting quickly to online spaces, such as Zoom and Google Meet, to support students virtually. Challenging times provide opportunities for creative ways to serve our students. First-Generation Student Support was a new department at Virginia Tech when the pandemic began. Our in-person programming had been in operation for one year at that time. Nearly all of First-Generation Student Support's events and programs were changed to virtual programs to serve our students' needs. Additional digital support efforts were also created due to reported feelings of isolation experienced by first-generation students during the onset of the pandemic.

One of First-Generation Student Support's goals was to create a sense of belonging among its first-generation students. Sense of belonging is key to the success and persistence of first-generation students (Strayhorn, 2018). Conversations with students during the onset of the pandemic, especially among first-year, first-generation students, revealed feelings of isolation. They did not feel connected to their peers due to limited opportunities for in-person engagement. In order to foster a sense of belonging, First-Generation Student Support created digital support programming that provided students an opportunity to engage with one another.

DIGITAL SUPPORT PROGRAMMING EFFORTS

When Virginia Tech moved to remote learning in March 2020, First-Generation Student Support transitioned its success programming to virtual platforms. Zoom was primarily utilized to provide academic and social programs, mental health and well-being workshops, support groups, and one-on-one virtual coffee chats with students. Creating these digital support spaces allowed First-Generation Student Support to continue to fully engage students and achieve our learning outcomes. One of the main goals for First-Generation Student Support is to create a social support network for first-generation students. In order to foster student to student interaction and create a sense of belonging, the peer mentoring program hosted monthly events where peer mentors could engage with their peer mentees. The first event that the mentors held was a virtual welcome reception for mentees. Breakout rooms on Zoom were utilized for mentors to talk with the mentees in small groups and begin to share their goals and concerns. The majority of mentees reported feeling more connected to the mentors and scheduled future socially distanced activities and meetings with their mentors.

First-Generation Student Support, along with the peer mentors, also hosted a virtual mini-GobblerFest student organization fair for mentees. Due to the annual Gobblerfest event being moved online in response to the pandemic, mentors reached out to student organizations that mentees showed interest in on the mentee applications. Student organization representatives gave presentations about their respective organizations and offered students to sign up and connect after the fair. Various student organizations, campus departments, and community partners collaborated for the virtual mini-Gobblerfest.

The First-Generation College Celebration Week was reimagined as a week of events that included webinars on student advocacy training for faculty/staff; a virtual dinner and talk with the first-generation student organization; a webinar featuring life at Deloitte with first-generation alumni; a first-generation student exhibit in the Newnan library; a workshop on test prep for finals; a virtual alumni panel on interviewing from an alumni perspective; and a first-generation photo project. The student advocacy training featured the assistant dean of first-generation student success at Virginia Tech discussing how to define the role of faculty and staff in first-generation student success. The student advocacy training was attended by approximately 70 members of Virginia Tech faculty and staff. The virtual dinner was a virtual social mixer that provided first-generation students an opportunity to meet the officers of the first-generation student organization over a meal. Boxed lunches were provided for pick up only at a certain time and location. Students who attended the virtual mixer and workshop had positive feedback to share and enjoyed the opportunity to connect with one another.

Students, faculty, and staff were encouraged to participate in the first-generation photo project. Participants were asked to provide a photo of themselves, along with narratives surrounding their first-generation identities. Project submissions were asked to focus on:

- Intersectionality
- Centrality of race
- Relational identities (roles in family/community, gender roles)
- Rootedness
- Envisioning a future
- Embracing ambiguity
- Competing motivations
- Use lived experiences as knowledge/capital
- Context (questions, climate, campus life)
- Cultivate self-authorship around diversity

In addition to the first-generation photo project, a first-generation student exhibit showcased famous first-generation graduates that many students were unaware of. We shared the photos and history of famous first-gens such as Colin Powell, Michelle Obama, and Oprah Winfrey.

Another concern of students due to the pandemic was the loss of in-person informal advising and conversations. Rapport is built with students during interactions in various spaces on campus, such as the Student Center, dining hall, and student meetings in the office. Prior to the pandemic, it was common for students to stop by for advice and share updates with staff. During the pandemic, "Coffee Talk with Dr. Troy" was created to give first-generation students an opportunity to check in, request assistance, provide updates, or to just talk. Standard hours were set aside each week for students to log into the Zoom link provided and attend the coffee talk. Several first-generation students utilized the coffee talk virtual format. There were also students who preferred to check in weekly. In addition to the coffee talk format, First-Generation Student Support continued the First-Gen Student Support Group, in collaboration with the Counseling Office. The support group provided the opportunity for first-generation students to share their college experiences, find camaraderie, and access to counselors for services if needed.

The pandemic has been a disruption to the world of higher education. However, as we look to serve our students during and post pandemic, we should continue to create virtual spaces to continue support efforts.

MOVING FORWARD

One thing the pandemic did was further expose the disparities between many first-generation students and their continuing education peers. The pandemic also jumpstarted innovation in delivering relevant and intentional virtual programming for first-generation students. As such, institutions should continue to provide flexible engagement opportunities. Although most faculty, staff, and students might consider in-person programming and support services ideal, lingering health and financial challenges, family and work obligations, and even a hesitancy to attend in-person gatherings due to fear of contracting COVID-19 signals the need to continue virtual and hybrid programming. By providing hybrid options, institutions can accommodate students who are able to engage in-person and those who prefer or are limited to virtual options. As we look for ways to continue to support first-generation students using virtual and hybrid spaces, there are several things we need to consider.

> **Identify first-generation students.** Institutions must develop a consistent definition of first-generation college students. As first-generation status is self-reported, it is particularly important to use language that allows students to understand what it means to be a first-generation student at your institution. Asking, "Are you a first-generation college student?" might result in under-reporting if students do not know what "first-generation" means. Additionally, asking students if they are the first in their family to attend college might also result in under-reporting. Students might consider siblings or extended family members when answering this question. It is also important to consider intersecting identities when identifying first-generation students. First-generation students are not a monolithic group and these intersecting identities result in differing needs and experiences.
> **Identify student needs.** After identifying your first-generation students, it is important to learn about their needs to provide relevant and timely

programming. Data on student performance, utilization of resources (mental health services, food pantries, tutoring, etc.), course withdrawal, engagement with learning management systems, as well as other indicators can provide valuable information when planning programming and support. It is also critical to solicit and utilize student input. Administrators, faculty, and staff sometimes assume they know best based on their own experiences and professional knowledge. However, COVID-19 has changed the college landscape, and it is imperative for us to include student voices when trying to figure out what types and levels of support they need. Institutions can survey students and conduct focus groups to identify challenges and barriers to success. Once student needs are determined, ask what digital support programming would address those needs. Students should also be involved in planning and implementing programming. Student insight on the best ways to engage their peers and marketing and advertising activities and events can help institutions maximize the effectiveness of these efforts.

Identify key stakeholders. Before launching digital support programming, practitioners must identify which campus or community partners can contribute to the vision and goals of the program. When identifying your key stakeholders, ask which person(s), departments, or community partners would be impacted most by your work.

Establish campus buy-in. Once the key stakeholders have been determined, reach out to have a conversation about collaboration on a programming component or a particular project. During the initial meeting, share your mission, vision, goals, outcomes, and ideas for digital support programming. Also, discuss how the stakeholder can contribute to the mission, vision, and goals of your programming efforts.

Take an inventory of what is already happening on campus. When planning virtual and digital programming for first-generation students, consider what worked during the pandemic and determine if those activities should be replicated moving forward. Additionally, take an inventory of what other units are doing on campus to support first-generation students and other student populations. Partnering with other units will help to maximize resources, especially when campuses are experiencing strained budgets and staff. Working with other campus units that provide targeted support to other student populations can expand support to first-generations by considering their intersecting identities.

Create opportunities for student engagement. In order to foster student engagement, involvement, and sense of belonging, it is important to create virtual spaces for peer-to-peer student engagement and student to faculty/staff engagement. The pandemic required practitioners to address the feelings of isolation being felt by students. It also required practitioners to think of new ways to bring students together virtually.

- **Promote mental health and wellness.** Research shows that first-generation students report higher levels of depression compared to non-first-generation students (Stebleton et al., 2014). The National Alliance on Mental Illness surveyed 765 college students with mental illness and reported 36% of students cited stigma as the number one barrier to seeking care. Knowing this, institutions should consider establishing virtual support spaces that promote positive mental health versus focusing on mental illness. Students should have a digital support space where they can voice concerns, ask questions, or just talk.
- **Disseminate information through various mediums.** Practitioners often say that students do not check their email, but continue to use it as the primary way to share information. No matter how beneficial or engaging we think virtual programs will be, if students don't know about them, they gain nothing from them. Text messaging is an alternative to email if the appropriate platforms are available. Information about events and resources can be shared through social media. In some instances, events can be livestreamed through social media as well to provide in-person and hybrid options.
- **Use an asset-based approach to develop programming.** Using an asset-based approach to programming helps to create a sense of belonging by demonstrating that the campus community values the strengths, talents, and other characteristics students bring to campus. This is particularly helpful for first-generation college students. Yosso's cultural wealth model (Yosso, 2005) provides a framework practitioners can use to empower students and help them leverage their strengths in the college environment.

CONCLUSION

The COVID-19 pandemic disrupted the college experience for all students, but took a greater toll on first-generation college students. They experienced higher rates of financial, academic, and mental health challenges than their continuing-generation peers. As first-generation students work to steady the course disrupted by the pandemic, institutions need to provide resources and intentional programming and support their recovery and to foster a sense of belonging. Doing so, increases first-generation students' chances to persist, progress, and graduate (Strayhorn, 2018). During the pandemic, practitioners demonstrated the utility of virtual formats to keep students engaged with the campus community. Incorporating virtual platforms and student voice into programming with an asset-based lens will offer students flexibility and encouragement as they continue to adjust to the changing college landscape.

REFERENCES

Barber, P. H., Shapiro, C., Jacobs, M. S., Avilez, L., Brenner, K. I., Cabral, C., Cebreros, M., Consentino, E., Cross, C., Gonzalez, M. L., Lumada, K. T., Menjivar, A. T., Narvaez, J., Olmeda, B., Phelan, R., Purdy, D., Salam, S., Serrano, L., Velasco, M. J., Marin, E. Z., & Levis-Fitzgerald, M. (2021). Disparities in remote learning faced by first-generation and underrepresented minority students during COVID-19: Insights and opportunities from a remote research experience. *Journal of Microbiology & Biology Education*, *22*(2), ev22i1-2457. https://doi.org/10.1128/jmbe.v22i1.2457

Froman, V., Berumen D., Rodrigues, J., & Stute, C. (2020). COVID-19 student survey: Online learning experiences and challenges experienced related to the COVID-19 pandemic. https://www.mtsac.edu/research/images/RIE-Covid-19-Student-Survey.pdf

Goldrick-Rab, S., Coca, V., Kienzl, G., Welton, C. R., Dahl, S., & Magnelia, S., (2020). #RealCollege during the pandemic: New evidence on basic needs insecurity and student well-being. https://hope4college.com/wp-content/uploads/2020/10/Hopecenter_RealCollegeDuringthePandemic_Reupload.pdf.↑

Jeong, H. J., Kim. S., & Lee, J. (2021). Mental health, life satisfaction, supportive parent communication, and help-seeking sources in the wake of COVID-19: First-generation college students (FGCS) *vs.* non-first-generation college students (non-FGCS). *Journal of College Student Psychotherapy* Advance online publication, https://doi.org/10.1080/87568225.2021.1906189

Moore, R., Vitale, D., & Stawinoga, N. (2018). The digital dive and educational equity. ACT Center for Equity and Learning. https://equityinlearning.act.org/wp-content/themes/voltron/img/tech-briefs/the-digital-divide.pdf

Soria, K. M., Horgos, B., Chirikov, I., Jones-White, D. (2020). First-generation students' experiences during the COVID-19 pandemic. Student Experience in the Research University (SERU) Consortium. https://hdl.handle.net/11299/214934

Stebleton, M. J., Soria, K. M., & Huesman, R. L. (2014). First-generation students' sense of belonging, mental health, and use of counseling services at public research universities. *The Journal of College Counseling*, *17*(1), 6–20.

Strayhorn, T. L. (2018). *College students' sense of belonging: A key to educational success for all students*. Routledge.

Yosso, T. J. (2005). Whose culture has capital? A critical race theory discussion of community cultural wealth. *Race Ethnicity and Education*, *8*(1), 69–91, https://doi.org/10.1080/1361332052000341006

About the Editors

Charmaine Troy, PhD is the inaugural First-Generation Program and Operations Manager at Georgia Tech. Prior to joining Georgia Tech, she served as the inaugural Assistant Dean for First-Generation Student Success at Virginia Tech. She has presented at various state and national conferences on first-generation student success practices and how to develop and implement first-generation student programming. Dr Troy earned a BA in journalism and mass communication from the University of North Carolina at Chapel Hill, a master's in public administration (MPA) from North Carolina Central University, and a PhD in higher education from Morgan State University.

Karen Jackson has worked in K-16 education over 25 years and is currently an assistant professor of education and associate dean of advising programs at Georgia Gwinnett College. She leads an award-winning team that provides academic advising, coaching, and targeted programming for a diverse group of students. She has an EdD in Education Policy from George Washington University, a MEd in Higher Education from the College of William and Mary, and a BS in Public Administration from James Madison University.

Ben Pearce has worked on the development and implementation of several first-generation student programs at Georgia Gwinnett College as well as for the TRiO program at Georgia State University – Perimeter College. Ben currently works at Emory University as a Program Coordinator for the Department of Economics. He has an MA from Kennesaw State University and BA from Mercer University.

ABOUT THE EDITORS

Diana Rowe is a Senior Student Success Advisor with over 19 years of experience in higher education. Ms. Rowe is a first-generation college graduate that has worked in the areas of admissions and recruitment, advising, and student success, leads programming for the Grizzly First Scholars first-generation learning community at Georgia Gwinnett College, and also coordinates programming for first-generation students. She has a BA in Sociology from Florida Atlantic University and an MS in Higher Education Administration from Florida International University.

About the Contributors

Michelle L. Ashcraft serves as Director of Purdue Promise and ScholarCorps Site Supervisor at Purdue University in Student Success Programs. She is a first-generation college graduate, and has worked in higher education for 13 years in the areas of new student orientation, first-year experience, academic coaching, and holistic support for low-income and first-generation students, including TRIO and promise programs.

Tamara Bauer is a program director and instructor at the Staley School of Leadership Studies at Kansas State University. She teaches all of the core classes for the leadership studies minor including a first-year introductory leadership class that enrolls over 600 students each fall and utilizes peer leaders to facilitate small groups. She has taught the first-year connection course for first-generation students, and also co-coordinates Wildcat Dialogues, an intercultural learning event for all first-time students focused on creating communities of belonging.

Trista Beard is the Director of the University of Southern California's Norman Topping Student Aid Fund, the nation's first student-initiated, student-funded, student-governed scholarship and retention program. Dr Beard completed her EdD at USC, and her work focuses on equitable access and outcomes for first-gen and low-income students.

Angelica Caudillo, MS, Program Manager, Bakersfield College. Angelica is a former EOP counselor at the University of California, Santa Barbara, where, for over five years, she used a holistic model for counseling to support the persistence, retention, and success of all students, including transfer and first-generation college students. As an EOP Transfer Counselor, she focused on transfer student services and programming, collaborating with a multitude of campus partners and designed and revamped signature programs as well as implemented the first week-long transfer summer transitional residential program.

ABOUT THE CONTRIBUTORS

Kevin Cook is a first-generation student who is Associate Director for Housing and Dining Services and Graduate Faculty Associate in Special Education, Counseling, and Student Affairs at Kansas State University. Kevin oversees all aspects of academic support, leadership development, diversity, enrollment management, and marketing functions for Housing and Dining. This includes being the main liaison with the first-year experience program and living learning communities.

Matt Daily currently in his seventh year at the University of Portland, where he directs all first-generation support efforts on campus. He has been involved in both higher education and K-12 for the duration of his 24-year career in education as a teacher, instructor, academic advisor, coach, and academic program administrator. He frequently writes, researches, and serves as a group speaker/facilitator/program reviewer regarding the first-generation college experience.

Yasmine Dominguez-Whitehead, PhD, Transitions Director, University of California, Santa Barbara. Yasmine's research interests and work are concerned with equity, social justice, and inclusion in higher education. She has published her work widely in the following international peer-reviewed journals: *Studies in Higher Education*, *Journal of College Student Development*, *Assessment and Evaluation in Higher Education*, and *Cambridge Journal of Education*. As the daughter of immigrants and a first-generation college graduate who grew up in a working class neighborhood, she is passionate about supporting first-generation college students and promoting the success of students, particularly in their first year of college.

Thomas Dickson is the Assistant Vice Provost for Undergraduate Education at the University of California, Riverside where he oversees Student Engagement programs and the campus First-Gen Initiative. Dr Dickson, a first-generation and low-income student himself, has a passion for unveiling hidden curriculum, improving resource accessibility, and student career readiness programming. Dr Dickson holds a Bachelor of Arts in Psychology from Arizona State University, a Masters of Education in Counseling and Higher Education from Northern Arizona University, and a Doctorate in Higher and Postsecondary Education from Arizona State University.

Gregory Eiselein is Professor of English and University Distinguished Teaching Scholar at Kansas State University, where he also serves as the Director of the first-year experience program, K-State First. The author or editor of seven books, his research focuses on nineteenth-century American literature and on first-year college student learning.

Trebby L. Ellington is a fourth-year Hall Director at the University of Michigan where she is responsible for facilitating the living-learning experience with

ABOUT THE CONTRIBUTORS

residents by utilizing a strategic community development model to assess student experiences. She does non-clinical case management, behavioral intervention, bias and crisis response, including developing meaningful relationships with campus and academic partners like the 1st Gen Theme Community and Health Sciences Scholars Program. Trebby received her Master of Education in Higher Education from Loyola University Chicago and Bachelor of Arts in Criminal Justice from Indiana University Bloomington.

Martha Enciso serves as the Associate Vice President for Student Affairs at California State University, Fullerton (CSUF) where she oversees the area of Identity and Belonging, which encompasses Diversity Initiatives and Resource Centers, Retention Initiatives and Special Population and teaches in the Higher Education program at CSUF. Dr Enciso has experience working in academic and student affairs and focuses on creating intentional cross divisional partnerships to address equity issues on campus. Dr Enciso received her EdD in Educational Leadership, Master of Education in Postsecondary Administration and Student Affairs, and a Bachelor of Arts degree in Sociology all at the University of Southern California.

Carina Gonzalez is a first-generation college graduate who earned her Bachelor of Science from the University of La Verne and her Master of Education from the University of Southern California (USC). She currently works at USC with the resilient and talented students of the Norman Topping Student Aid Fund. Carina is passionate about helping students achieve their academic and career goals.

Tiffany N. Hughes is a doctoral student in the Department of Educational Leadership and Policy at The University of Texas at Austin. Before becoming a Longhorn, she earned an MEd in Counselor Education with an emphasis in Student Affairs from Clemson University and a BA in English from Howard University. Her research interests focus on elevating the narratives of students on the margins and examining and implementing practices that cultivate diverse, equitable, and inclusive higher education environments for underrepresented and minoritized populations.

Erin Kline has a Masters in Sociology and Social Movements and a PhD in Sociology, specializing in race, gender, and class. She has worked in higher education for over ten years both in the classroom and in student support services. Currently, Dr. Kline is the Associate Director of Diversity and Inclusion at Southwest Minnesota State University.

Jefferson Lee IV has a Masters in Counseling and Human Resource Development with an emphasis on student affairs. He also holds a Masters in Business Administration with a focus on diversity. He has worked in higher

ABOUT THE CONTRIBUTORS

education for over 22 years as the Director of Diversity and Inclusion, Access Opportunity Success and the Mustang Pathway Program, and operated as the Campus Diversity Officer for seven of those years.

Yasamin "Yasi" Mahallaty (she/her/hers) is the Expansion Manager at CareerSpring, a career resource for first-generation and low-income students. The proud daughter of Iranian immigrants, Yasi holds a Bachelor's Degree from the University of San Diego, a Master of Science in Education from Fordham University's Graduate School of Education, and an MA in Educational Transformation, Advocacy, and Policy from Georgetown University.

Kadaisha Miller is a senior at the University of South Carolina Upstate where she is majoring in Psychology and minoring in Organizational Communications. She currently serves as the Student Government Association Senator for the Department of Psychology. Kadaisha works as the Human Resources intern for Draexlmaier Group where she contributes to improving processes, planning events, and recruiting for the student programs.

Elizabeth Montgomery is the Associate Director of Student and College Engagement at the University of California, Riverside's Career Center. Elizabeth is a higher education professional counselor who specializes in helping college students and alumni engage in self-assessment, career exploration, experiential activities, and internship and job search skill development. Elizabeth has a Bachelor of Arts in Psychology from The University of Texas at Austin, a Master of Arts in Professional Counseling from Texas State University San Marcos, and a Teacher Certification from Huston-Tillotson University.

Kiley Moody serves as Managing Director of Scholar Services at Kansas State University, where she works directly with first-generation students. Kiley works with or manages a variety of scholarships and programs focusing on access to higher education.

Rebeca Paz serves as assistant director for the Office of First-generation Students at Kansas State University. Throughout her extensive career, she has served in several capacities working with retention programs and specifically, first-generation and underrepresented students.

Malaphone Phommasa, PhD, Assistant Dean of Academic Success Initiatives, University of California, Santa Barbara. Malaphone's role is dedicated to supporting the success of UCSB's transfer student and first-generation college student populations. She was the founding director of UCSB's Transfer Student Center, along with multiple signature events for the transfer student population. As a proud daughter of Lao refugees and being a first-generation college graduate, Malaphone's research interests center on supporting the persistence and retention of minoritized and marginalized student populations.

Albert Ramirez (he/him/his) is the Associate Director of the Georgetown Scholars Program (GSP) at Georgetown University. Prior to his work supporting first-generation and low-income college students, Albert held program and policy roles at organizations focused on leadership development, community organizing, and food and economic justice. Albert is the proud son of Filipino immigrants, and holds dual majors in Economics and Environmental Studies from St. Louis University.

Charlie Rodnuson is a Practice Coach at San Diego State University and a Marriage and Family Therapy Associate. Charlie incorporates therapeutic approaches of mindfulness and person-centered psychology into his work to support students in realizing and accomplishing their goals of pursuing a higher education and a fulfilling career. Charlie has a Bachelor of Arts in Psychology and Social Behavior from University of California, Irvine and a Masters of Counseling Psychology in Marriage and Family Therapy from Argosy University.

Lisa Lambert Snodgrass is an Assistant Professor of Higher Education in Educational Leadership and Policy Studies in the Department of Educational Studies at Purdue University. Lisa's 20+ years in education have been diverse, including serving as a high school English teacher and a middle school principal before moving to higher education administration where she worked as Director of Career Development for nine years. As a faculty member and scholar, Dr. Lambert Snodgrass's research interests center on the cultural dimensions of student, faculty, and staff experiences in K-20 settings.

Kimberly Walker, PhD serves as the Associate Vice President of Academic Affairs at the SC Technical College System Office and is an institutional effectiveness expert with over a decade of experience in higher education and governmental agencies.

Kari Weber, MS, Transfer Student Center Director, University of California, Santa Barbara. Kari has served as the UCSB Transfer Student Center Director since 2020 and began as the Student Activities Coordinator in 2017. Her work aims to help transfer and first-generation transfer students feel connected and at home within a large university. She strives to create community and provide academic and social resources – expanding opportunities for transfer and first-generation transfer students at UCSB.

Index

1st Gen theme community 129–131; application process 133; assessment plan 136–137; check-in meetings 131; conceptual framework 131–133; difference-education interventions 132; experience scaffold 135–136, 138–139; funding 134; goals 131; lessons learned 138–139; *Making the Most of Michigan* course 131; marketing 133; outcomes 137–138; recommendations for implementation 139–141; recruitment 133; resident advisor 130, 131, 134, 135; sense of belonging and 137; stakeholders 130; student selection 133–134; website 133

21st Century Scholars (TFCS) 167–168

"25 Days of Christmas" campaign 29

academic and social support 5–6; mentorship 6; Validation Theory 5–6; *see also* mentors/mentorship; virtual support programming

ACCUPLACER tests 48, 50, 51

admissions, referrals and 47, 48

Alumni Mentor Program: assessment 106; goals 104; program implementation and stakeholders 104–105; program outcomes 106

Arslan, G. 84, 89

Asian American and Native American Pacific Islander-Serving Institution (AANAPISI) 114

aspirational capital 7, 81, 90

assessment 67, 159, 190; 1st Gen theme community 136–137; ACCUPLACER tests 48, 50, 51; Alumni Mentor Program 105, 106; Faculty Mentoring Program 117, 122; Horizons program 177–178; K-State First 154–156; Mustang Pathway Program (MPP) 50, 51; Obtain Resources, Become Informed, Target Success (ORBITS) 192; Peer Mentor Program 101; Purdue Promise 177–178; Regional Network Program 107–108; Summer Launch program 35–37, 41; Table Talk 118; Topping Scholars Program 82, 89, 90; TRIO program (USC Upstate) 18–19; Weber Honors College 212

asset-based practice 152–153, 224

Bears and Encouraging and Mentoring (BEAM) peer mentoring program 58–60

belonging *see* sense of belonging

Black, Indigenous, People of Color (BIPOC) 44

buy-in 22, 223; intrusive advising and 23–24

234

INDEX

capital 90; aspirational 7; cultural 44, 81, 132–133, 148, 190; familial 7; linguistic 7; navigational 7, 80, 188; resistance 7; social 3–4, 7, 85, 188

career development 4, 5, 168, 170, 186–190, 193–195; Alumni Mentor Program and 106

CAT Communities 146–147, 155–156; co-curricular events 153; first-generation themed 147; peer observation 157; student learning outcome (SLO) assessment 156–157; tracking data 157–158; *see also* living learning communities (LLCs)

Chartwells 48

check-in meetings, 1st Gen theme community 131

CliftonStrengths tool 147, 153

cognitive behavioral therapy (CBT) 75, 76

collaboration 28, 31, 44, 49, 51, 54, 64, 65, 152, 159; Purdue Promise/ Horizons 172; stakeholders and 148–149; study abroad programs and 175; third-party vendor 172–173; Topping Scholars Program and 86

collective care 83

College and Career Readiness Standards for Adult Education (CCRS) 50, 52

communication, intrusive advising and 22, 23

community 91, 92; awareness 81; -building 82–84, 93; Topping Scholars Program and 78

Community Cultural Wealth 7, 45, 76, 80, 132, 188

Connections Across Topics (CAT) 146

Continuous Improvement Blueprint 19

counseling 13, 14, 47, 114; Mustang Pathway Program (MPP) 49; Topping Scholars Program 91; *see also* intrusive advising

Covid-19 pandemic 16, 66, 109, 188–189, 215; academic impact for first-generation students 218–219; advising and 221–222; digital support programming efforts 220–222; Faculty Mentoring Program and 121; federal funding and 217; financial impact for first-generation students 217–218; first-generation college students and 217; living learning communities (LLCs) and 159; Living-Learning Programs (LLP) and 140–141; mental health impact on first-generation students 219; online programming and 219–220; Student Experience in the Research University (SERU) study 217, 218; study abroad and 180–181; Topping Scholars Program and 86–89; virtual support programming 220–224

critical race theory 132

cultural capital 44, 81, 132–133, 148, 188, 190

cultural mismatch theory 6

curricula 4; AAC&U Knowledge and Competence Rubric 177

difference-education interventions 44–45, 49, 132

Dining with Faculty, assessment and outcomes 118–120

discrimination 2–3

diversity 43, 93, 132, 214

Duru, E. 84, 89

Earl, W., "Intrusive Advising for Freshmen" 14

early intervention 21; intrusive advising and 22–23

empowerment 5, 78, 91

engagement 4, 30, 35–37, 99, 146, 223; High Impact Practices (HIPS) 64; Summer Launch program and 38–39

Engle, L. C. 167

equity 43, 77, 93, 132, 214; by design 45, 50

evidence-based practices 45

experience scaffold, 1st Gen theme community 135–136, 138–139

235

INDEX

faculty 119-120, 123; academic and social support 5-6; Georgetown Scholars Program (GSP) 99; living learning communities (LLCs) 150; Mustang Pathway Program (MPP) 49-50; professional development opportunities 161; relationships and 119; -student luncheon 83; Summer Launch program and 38; Table Talk and 118; TRIO program (USC Upstate) and 18; Weber Honors College 210

Faculty Mentoring Program 113, 123; assessment 117, 122; Covid-19 and 121; Dining with Faculty 115; feedback 121; funding 116, 122; lessons learned 121-122; marketing and student recruitment 116-117; orientation 116-117; outcomes 117; program challenges and improvements 120-121; program design and structure 115; purpose of 115; relationships and 123; stakeholders 117; Table Talk 115; *see also* Dining with Faculty; Table Talk

familial capital 7

Federal Trio SSS grant program 14-15; Annual Performance Report (APR) 19, 20; *see also* TRIO program (USC Upstate)

feedback 34, 50, 51, 61, 159; 1st Gen theme community 137; Faculty Mentoring Program 121; K-State First 155-156; Mustang Pathway Program (MPP) 52, 53; Peer Mentor Program 101; Summer Launch program 32, 38

financial support 5; living learning communities (LLCs) and 152; *see also* Federal Trio SSS grant program; funding; grants; scholarships

"Finding Your Fit at Michigan: Theme Communities & MLCs" 133

First-Generation (FGEN) program 28; foundations 29-30; goals 30; "How to Survive and Thrive your Freshman Year" 32; mission 29; partners 31; Summer Launch 30-41; *see also* Summer Launch

first-generation college students 15, 24-25, 28, 33, 36, 43-44, 50, 57, 73, 75, 76, 79, 84, 85, 89, 90, 92-94, 98, 113, 114, 123, 140, 150, 184-185, 213, 221; 21st Century Scholars (TFCS) and 167-168; academic and social support 5-6; career development 5; community awareness and 81; Covid-19 pandemic and 217; difference-education interventions 44-45; financial support 5; honors programs and 203-204; identifying 222; identity 148, 153; imposter syndrome 75, 80, 92, 145; income and 3; institutional support 4-5; intersectionality and 2-4, 132; Kansas State University (K-State) and 147-148; marginalization 2-3, 21, 113, 114, 132; needs 222-223; peer-to-peer exchanges 39; resilience and 113; self-identification 160; sense of belonging and 4-5, 145, 148; service learning and 63-64; strengths and challenges of 7; study abroad and 167, 170-172; visibility 161; Weber Honors College and 207; well-being and 82-83

funding: 1st Gen theme community 134; Covid-19 and 217; Faculty Mentoring Program 116, 122; Horizons program 173-174; living learning communities (LLCs) 152; Mustang Pathway Program (MPP) 47-48; Necessity Fund 99; Obtain Resources, Become Informed, Target Success (ORBITS) 191; Purdue Promise 171-174; Topping Scholars Program 74, 78, 79; TRIO program (USC Upstate) 18; Weber Honors College 204

INDEX

Garriott, P. O. 139
Generation Study Abroad 167
Georgetown Scholars Program (GSP) 98–99; Alumni Mentor Program 104; lessons learned 108–109; membership 99; Necessity Fund 99; Peer Mentor Program 100–101; Regional Network Program 106; relationships and 99, 100; staff 99, 108; whole institution approach 99, 109; *see also* Alumni Mentor Program; Peer Mentor Program
Georgetown University 98
Georgia Gwinnett College 57, 58, 61, 67; Honors Program 61; Office of Student Involvement 65; peer mentoring 60; programming 60; *see also* Grizzly First Scholars program
goals: 1st Gen theme community 131; Alumni Mentor Program 104; Obtain Resources, Become Informed, Target Success (ORBITS) 186–187; UP's First-Generation (FGEN) program 30; USC Upstate TRIO SSS program 14–15
graduate students, Topping Scholars Program and 91
grants 5, 24, 47, 50, 98, 134, 171, 217; "mini-" 25; Necessity Fund 99; Pell 13, 168; Topping Scholars Program and 77–79; *see also* Federal Trio SSS grant program; funding
Grizzly First Scholars program 58; curricular advising 59; goals and objectives 58–59; Learning Community Day 66; lessons learned 67–68; linked courses 59; mentor recruitment 60–62; outcomes 66–67; peer mentor training 62–63; programming 58–59, 67–68; relationships and 64–65, 68; service learning 59, 63–64; Service-Learning Symposium 66; tutoring 59; workshops 59

hidden curriculum 6, 29, 30, 33, 40, 45, 80, 99, 117
high schools, TRIO program (USC Upstate) and 17
higher education, equity gap 6
high-impact practices (HIPs) 64, 211, 215
Hispanic-Serving Institution (HSI) 114
honors programs 203–204
Horizons program 168–170, 173; application process 176; assessment plan 177–178; course approval 176–177; course components and requirements 179; information sessions 176; Intercultural Development Inventory (IDI) Qualified Administrators (QAs) 172; journal assignments 179; lessons learned 180–181; outcomes 179–180; pre- and post-course assessment 178; program planning 174; reflective writing assignments 179; stakeholders 170–171; third-party vendor partners 172–173, 175
Hurtado, S. 113
hybrid programming 222
identity 78, 146; community 93; diversity and 2; ethnic 4; first-generation student 1–2, 145, 148, 153, 160; intersecting 2–4; leadership 147; Topping Family 84, 92

imposter syndrome 75, 80, 92, 145
inclusiveness 4, 43, 93, 132, 214
income, first-generation college students and 3
Institute of International Education (IEE), *Generation Study Abroad* 167
institutional racism 43
institutional support: career development 5; financial support 5; post-graduation services 5; sense of belonging and 4
intentional engagement opportunities 1
Intercultural Development Inventory (IDI) 179; group profile reports

237

INDEX

180; Qualified Administrators (QAs) 172, 178
internet access, TRIO program (USC Upstate) and 16
intersectionality 2, 116; 1st Gen theme community and 132; sense of belonging and 3–4; social capital and 4
intrusive advising 14–16, 19, 21; campus buy-in 22–24; careful communication 22, 23; early intervention 21–23; recommendations 24–25; relationships and 23; robust technology and 22

Jack, A. A., *The privileged poor: How elite colleges are failing disadvantaged students* 140
Junior Achievement 65

Kansas State University (K-State) 145–146; Connections Across Topics (CAT) 146; first-generation themed CAT communities 147; mission 145; Office of First-Generation Students 150–151; Strategic Enrollment Management plan 145–146; understanding and supporting first-generation students 147–148
K-State First 146; academic advisors 151; assessment 154–155; asset-based practice 152–153; associated academic programs 150; CAT Communities 146–147; co-curricular events 153; course evaluation 155–156; designing the experience 152–154; first-generation themed CAT communities 147–149; first-year experience office 149; implementation through collaboration 148–149; Learning Assistant 146; learning outcomes 146; lessons learned 159–160; Office of First-Generation Students and 150–151; on-campus housing 149; peer observation 157; professional development opportunities 154;

resident learning assistant (RLA) 151, 154, 155; retention rates 158; stakeholders 148–149, 151, 162; student feedback 155–156; student learning outcome (SLO) assessment 156–157; tracking data 157–158; *see also* living learning communities (LLCs)
Kuh, G. 30

leadership 41, 46, 60–62, 67, 80, 93, 100, 103, 137, 140, 147, 150, 170, 177, 204
Learning Assistant 146
legislators, TRIO program (USC Upstate) and 18
linguistic capital 7
literacy 14
L.I.V.E. Advising 75, 76
lived experiences 2
living learning communities (LLCs) 145, 146; academic advisors 151; associated academic programs 150; collaboration and 159; Covid-19 and 159; faculty 150; first-generation themed 147–149; lessons learned 159–160; necessary resources 152; Office of First-Generation Students and 150–151; peer observation 157; recruitment 160–161; resident learning assistant (RLA) 151; retention and 150; scholarships 161; stakeholders 162; tracking data 157–158; *see also* CAT Communities; K-State First
Living-Learning Programs (LLP) 129, 136, 138, 140; *see also* 1st Gen theme community

marginalization of first-generation college students 2–3, 21, 113, 114, 132
marketing: 1st Gen theme community 133; Faculty Mentoring Program 116–117; Mustang Pathway Program

(MPP) 47–48; Topping Scholars Program 85–86
mental health 16, 54; Covid-19 pandemic and 219; mentorship and 109; virtual support spaces 224
mentors/mentorship 6, 30, 44, 46, 54, 65, 78, 81, 108–109, 114, 120, 188, 189; Alumni Mentor Program 104–107; Bears and Encouraging and Mentoring (BEAM) peer mentoring program 58–60, 67; difference-education interventions 49; K-State First 146; Living-Learning Program (LLP) 140; peer 45, 49, 60, 220; Peer Mentor Program 103; recruitment 60–62; selection process 61; Topping Scholars Program 83, 91; *see also* Peer Mentor Program
Michigan Learning Communities (MLCs) 129, 133
"mini-grants" 25
"mock class" 34, 37
Mustang Pathway Program (MPP) 43–46; assessment 50, 51; counseling 49; difference-education interventions 49; equity by design 45, 50; faculty selection 49–50; funding and marketing strategies 47–48; Global Experience course 49; implementation 48–50; Launch Sessions 48–49; lessons learned 53–54; move-in day 48; online informational sessions 47; outcomes 51, 52; Pathways Scholars 46; peer mentors 45, 49; programming 50; recruitment 46–47; relationships and 46, 47, 49–50, 54; stakeholders 50; student evaluation of the program 52, 53
Mwawai, M. 29

National Association of Colleges and Employers (NACE) Career Readiness Competencies 187, 192–194
National Center for First-Generation Student Success 28

navigational capital 7, 80, 90, 188
Necessity Fund 99
network(s/ing) 16, 76, 85, 106, 108, 139, 188; peer 83; social capital 137; social support 220–221; workshops 81; *see also* social capital

Obtain Resources, Become Informed, Target Success (ORBITS) 185; application process 189; assessment plan 192; career assessments 191; career decision-making process 186; course content 190; design 188–189; First Destination Survey 193–194; funding 191; goals 186–187; learning outcomes 187–188; lessons learned 194–195; mentors 189; National Association of Colleges and Employers (NACE) Career Readiness Competencies 187; program costs 191; recruitment 189; sample timeline and task list 196–198; stakeholders 191; student selection 189; student success outcomes 192–193; syllabus sample 198–202
on-campus housing, K-State First 149
ONDAS Student Center 114, 116, 120, 122
online learning *see* remote learning
oppression 2–3
orientation: Faculty Mentoring Program 117; Mustang Pathway Program (MPP) 48
outcomes: 1st Gen theme community 137–138; Alumni Mentor Program 106; Dining with Faculty 118–120; Faculty Mentoring Program 117; Grizzly First Scholars program 66–67; Horizons program 179–180; K-State First 156–157; Mustang Pathway Program (MPP) 51, 52; Obtain Resources, Become Informed, Target Success (ORBITS) 187–188, 192–193; Peer Mentor Program 103; Purdue

INDEX

Promise 179–180; Summer Launch program 36–37; Table Talk 118–120; Topping Scholars Program 89, 90; TRIO program (USC Upstate) 19–20; Weber Honors College 213–214
Outdoor Pursuits 35, 39

partnerships: Grizzly First Scholars program 65–66; Topping Scholars Program 85–86; UP'S First-Generation program 31
Pathways Scholars 46
pedagogy 4, 6, 43, 157; Global Experience course 49
Peer Mentor Program: assessment 101; implementation and stakeholders 100–101; outcomes 103
peer mentoring 45, 49, 60, 220; BEAM (Bears and Encouraging and Mentoring) program 58–59; training 62–63
peer-to-peer exchanges 39, 153
Pell Grant 13
persistence 20, 58, 67, 82, 84, 92, 113, 131, 145, 148, 153, 157, 159–162; *see also* resilience
Pike, G. 30
post-graduation services 5
power 2–3
programming 45, 46; Grizzly First Scholars program 58–60, 67–68; Mustang Pathway Program (MPP) 50
Purdue Moves scholarship 169–170, 173
Purdue Promise 167–168, 170; application process 176; assessment plan 177–178; course approval 176–177; course components and requirements 179; funding 171–172; information sessions 176; Intercultural Development Inventory (IDI) Qualified Administrators (QAs) 172; journal assignments 179; lessons learned 180–181; outcomes 179–180; pre- and post-course assessment 178;
program planning 174; reflective writing assignments 179; stakeholders 170–171; subsidies 173; third-party vendor partners 172–173, 175
Purdue Study Abroad 173–174

Qualtrics 178

racism 3, 4, 132; institutional 43; structural 4
recruitment: 1st Gen theme community 133; Faculty Mentoring Program 116–117; living learning communities (LLCs) 160–161; mentor 60–62; Mustang Pathway Program (MPP) 46–47; Obtain Resources, Become Informed, Target Success (ORBITS) 189; Weber Honors College 208–209
Regional Network Program 106; assessment 107–108; program implementation and stakeholders 107
relationships 14, 16, 17, 29, 38, 80, 91, 172; academic advisor 151; with faculty 119; Faculty Mentoring Program and 123; Georgetown Scholars Program (GSP) and 99, 100; Grizzly First Scholars program and 64–65, 68; intrusive advising and 23; Mustang Pathway Program (MPP) and 46, 47, 49–50, 54; peer-to-peer exchanges 39; Summer Launch program and 40
remediation 4
remote learning 77; Covid-19 pandemic and 86–89, 121, 219, 220; Faculty Mentoring Program 121
Rendón, L., validation theory 5–6, 75
resident advisor, 1st Gen theme community 130, 131, 134, 135
resident learning assistant (RLA) 151, 152, 154, 155
resilience 45, 113, 152
resistance capital 7, 81, 90

INDEX

retention 45, 64, 86, 137, 145, 149; K-State First 158; living learning communities (LLCs) and 150; TRIO Program and 51; Weber Honors College and 213

Rosenberg, J., "Mastering the Hidden Curriculum" 99

Rowh, M. 21

San Diego State University (SDSU) 203, 208, 215; First-Generation Student Success Initiative 215; Transfer Student Success Office 208 209, 214; transfer students 204; Weber Honors College 204; *see also* Weber Honors College

Sauvie Island 34, 35, 39

scholarships: Purdue Moves 169 170, 173; Purdue Promise 167 168; Topping Scholars Program 73; *see also* grants

school belongingness scale 84, 89

sense of belonging 3, 30, 36, 37, 44, 73, 91, 118, 146, 152, 220; 1st Gen theme community 137; first-generation college students and 145, 148; intersectionality and 3 4; Summer Launch program and 33; Topping Scholars Program and 83 84, 87

service learning 59, 63 66

Six Dimensions of Wellness 82 83

SMSU Foundation 50

social capital 3 4, 7, 81, 85, 90, 188

Soria, K. M. 3

Southwest Minnesota State University (SMSU) 43, 44, 46; *see also* Mustang Pathway Program (MPP)

stakeholders: 1st Gen theme community 130; Alumni Mentor Program 104 105; Faculty Mentoring Program 117; Georgetown Scholars Program (GSP) 100 101; Horizons program 170 171; K-State First 148 149, 162; Mustang Pathway Program (MPP) 50; Obtain Resources, Become Informed, Target Success (ORBITS) 191; Purdue Promise 170 171; Regional Network Program 107; Topping Scholars Program 74 75; Weber Honors College 211

standardized testing 4

Starfish 22, 24

Stebleton, M. J. 3

Stephens, N. M. 44

stipends 5

structural racism 4

Student Experience in the Research University (SERU) study 217

student loans 14

study abroad 79; assessment tools 178; building the itinerary and contract 175; Covid-19 pandemic and 180 181; financial aid and billing 175 176; first-generation students and 167; Horizons program 170 172; making travel arrangements 175; Purdue Moves scholarship 169 170, 173; Purdue Promise 170 172; selecting a country and provider 174 175; Weber Honors College requirement 210 211; *see also* Horizons program; Purdue Promise

summative assessment, Peer Mentor Program 101

Summer Launch 31; adjustments in structure 32; assessment 35 37, 41; course corrections 33; engagement and 38 39; faculty and 38; feedback 32, 38; "mock class" 34, 37; outcomes 36 37; Outdoor Pursuits and 35, 39; relationships and 38, 40; sense of belonging and 33; stakeholders 38; Student Ambassador position 33, 37 40; unexpected outcomes 37 38

Table Talk: assessment 118; outcomes 119 120

Talent Search 13

241

INDEX

technology, intrusive advising and 21, 22

theme communities 129–133; *see also* 1st Gen theme community

Topping Scholars Program 73, 75, 81; advisors 77, 78, 83; assessment 82, 89, 90; belonging and 83–84, 87, 92; campus-wide partnerships 85–86; challenges 91–92; collective care 83, 86; community-building 78, 83–84; counseling 91; Covid-19 pandemic and 86–89; culture of care 86, 93; empowerment and 78; Faculty Lunch & Learn Series 83–84; faculty-student luncheon 83; funding 74, 78, 79; governing board 74–75; graduate students 91; grants 77–79; implementation 92; imposter syndrome and 80, 92; interventions 80–81, 91; lessons learned 92–93; L.I.V.E. Advising 75, 76; mandatory programs 80, 83; measuring student success 76; mentoring 78, 83, 91; mission 73–74, 76–77; outcomes 89, 90; Six Dimensions of Wellness framework 82–83; social media and 85–86; staff 81; stakeholders 74–75; strategic programming 79–80; study lounge 77, 78; validation theory and 75; well-being as a core value 82–83

training 161, 221; Intercultural Development Inventory (IDI) Qualified Administrators (QAs) 172; peer mentor 62–63

Transfer Receptive Culture (TRC) 205–206

Transfer Student Center 114, 116, 120, 122

transfer students 115, 213, 215; application process for Weber Honors College 208; at San Diego State University (SDSU) 204; WHC enrollment 208–209

trauma 54

TRIO program (USC Upstate) 13, 14; academic counseling 15–16; advising process 14; assessment plan 18–19; counseling 14; early intervention 22; faculty and 18; first-year seminar course 15; funding 18; goals 14–15; high schools and 17; internet access and 16; intrusive advising 15, 16, 21; legislators 18; mandatory advising sessions 16; mental health and 16; mid-semester check-in 16; mission 14–15; on-campus orientation 15; outcomes 19–20; relationships and 23; stakeholders 17–18; university administrators and 17; university support 25; *see also* intrusive advising

tutoring 13; Grizzly First Scholars program 59

University of California, Riverside (UCR) 185, 186; *see also* Obtain Resources, Become Informed, Target Success (ORBITS)

University of California, Santa Barbara (UCSB) 114; ONDAS Student Center 114, 116, 120, 122; Transfer Student Center 114, 116, 120, 122; *see also* Faculty Mentoring Program

University of Michigan (UM) 129; Living-Learning Programs (LLPs) 129; theme communities 130; *see also* 1st Gen theme community

University of Portland: "25 Days of Christmas" campaign 29; First-Generation (FGEN) program 28; hidden curriculum 30, 40; Outdoor Pursuits 35, 39; Summer Launch Pre-Orientation initiative 28; *see also* First-Generation (FGEN) program

University of South Carolina Upstate (USC Upstate) 13; Continuous Improvement Blueprint 19; Office of Institutional Effectiveness 19; Starfish 22, 24

University of Southern California (USC) 73
Upward Bound 13, 17
US Education Opportunity Act of 1964 15
USC Norman Topping Student Aid Fund 73, 74, 84

validation theory 5–6, 75
Virginia Tech 220, 221
virtual support programming 220–221; asset-based approach 224; campus buy-in 223; engagement and 223; identify key stakeholders 223; identifying student needs 222–223; mental health and 224
volunteering 81, 109

Weber Honors College 204; academic advising 210; admission process 207–208; assessment plan 212; conceptual framework 205–206; exit interview 212–213; faculty 210; funding 204; graduation survey 212; high-impact practice (HIP) 211; honors team 204–205; housing 205; implementation 207; intentional recruitment plan 208–209; Introduction to Honors course 209–210, 213–214; learning outcomes 206–207; lessons learned 214; mission 206; outcomes 213–214; stakeholders 211; study abroad requirement 210–211; transfer students 208, 213–215; virtual options 215; withdrawal process 212
well-being 73, 74, 78, 82–83
whole institution approach 99, 109
workshops: Grizzly First Scholars program 59; networking 81
WorldStrides ISA 172–173

Yosso, T. J. 7, 76, 80, 188

Zoom 47, 87, 88, 107, 159, 189, 220, 222

Made in the USA
Middletown, DE
22 September 2022

10987624R00144